FISH

Grilled & Smoked

150 Recipes for Cooking Rich, Flavorful Fish on the Backyard Grill, Streamside, or in a Home Smoker

JOHN MANIKOWSKI

Illustrations by John Manikowski

Storey Publishing

*The mission of Storey Publishing is to serve our customers
by publishing practical information that encourages
personal independence in harmony with the environment.*

Edited by Dianne M. Cutillo and Andrea Dodge
Art direction by Kent Lew
Cover and text design by Kent Lew
Cover photograph by © Kevin Kennefick
Text production by Jennifer Jepson Smith
Artwork © John Manikowski
How-to illustrations by Melanie Powell
Indexed by Susan Olason, Indexes &
  Knowledge Maps

Copyright © 2004 by John Manikowski

Printed in the United States by Von Hoffmann
10 9 8 7 6 5 4 3 2 1

Library of Congress Cataloging-in-Publication Data
Manikowski, John.
    Fish grilled and smoked / John Manikowski.
        p. cm.
    Includes index.
        ISBN 1-58017-502-3 (alk. paper)
    1. Cookery (Fish) 2. Barbecue cookery. 3. Smoked fish. I. Title.
    TX747.M254 2004
    641.6'92—dc22
                                    2004001516

Contents

Dedication

This book is for Carole Clark,
a powerfully devoted friend who made a supremely
difficult decision on my behalf, one that ultimately enabled me
to return not just to life, but to a renewed life of
enrichment and creativity.
Thank you forever, Carole.

Introduction

IF YOU ARE READING THIS, you likely eat fish. I love eating fish grilled, smoked, prepared in any way — even raw. The fresher the better, of course.

The Romans shared this love of fresh fish in the first century A.D. So much so that serving fish as fresh as possible was a mark of generosity to a senator's guests, considering that a live fish cost an enormous amount of money; delivery of live fish from a distance posed a problem of logistics and transportation back then. According to Maguelonne Toussaint-Samat's book *History of Food* (Blackwell Publishers, 1992), an endearing host was one who served a live fish in a crystal vessel that was heated directly at the dinner table, the

heat gradually increased so that the fish cooked slowly in full view of guests. That practice produced fresh cooked fish, no doubt, and is not all that different from the practice of contemporary Japanese restaurants that allow diners to point at a fish in a tank, the one they would prefer for dinner. The presentation is all that differs.

Another piscatorial tale of interest informs us about an unfortunate French servant in 1671 who committed suicide because the live fish he ordered, though driven at breakneck speed by horse-drawn cart and water barrel to the table of Prince de Conde, did not arrive on time, alas. His dedication is certainly to be applauded.

There are 20,000 or more species of fish in the oceans, lakes, and streams of the world, and when I look at the iced banks of fillets in my fish market, I wonder about the unaccounted-for 19,960

species I don't see. Am I satisfied with the old standbys of salmon, cod, shrimp, tuna, and trout?

Unfortunately, many more species than you might believe are on the decline because of humankind's appetite for the piscine. We love to eat what we want when we want it and are, for the most part, able to do so. We must take action to prevent further loss of these species if we want to continue enjoying our outdoor barbecues so freely. Please be aware that some species of shark, marlin, and swordfish, among several others, need help or they could disappear. It is for this reason that I do not include recipes for them. Ten years ago I stopped buying shark for our restaurant Charleston in Hudson, New York, and now I hope more people worldwide will help in the attempts to reestablish some dwindling populations of fish. Effective conservation and sustainable management of both ocean and freshwater fisheries are needed at national and international levels so that living aquatic resources can continue to meet global needs. That said, I cook fish often, I fish often — mostly catch and release, though — and I will never discourage anyone from enjoying a meal of whatever he or she wishes to eat, whether it be vegetarian, red meat, poultry, or fish.

Fish is good for you: The American Heart Association recommends that people eat at least two servings of fish per week. Both the *Journal of the American Medical Association* and the *New England Journal of Medicine* reported in 2002 that several weekly servings of fish — a prime source of omega-3 fatty acids — seem to help protect both men and women from heart disease. Green, leafy vegetables, nuts, canola and soybean oil, and tofu are also sources of omega-3 fatty acids.

Eicosapentaenoic acid and docosahexaenoic acid (DHA), two omega-3 fatty acids commonly referred to as "good fats," are natural oils found in fish. It turns out that these oils are beneficial to the platelets in blood, making them less sticky, which is helpful in the prevention of heart attack and stroke. DHA can stabilize irregular heart rhythms and help with brain cell functions. A study at Purdue University showed that boys with attention deficit disorder problems had less omega-3 fat in their brain cells. Increasing omega-3 fat worked for some of the test patients.

Japanese women have only one third the breast cancer rate American women have. It is believed that the typical Japanese diet, which is rich in fish and soy, may account for this difference. The average life expectancy of Japanese and other Asian peoples — whose diets center on fish and soy — is 79 years.

Research suggests that one serving per week of cold-water fish exceptionally high in omega-3 fats may reduce the risk of heart attack by 50 percent in people with already weakened hearts. A study performed by public health experts at the University of Cambridge in England in 2002 suggests regular consumption of fish such as salmon, tuna, mackerel, and herring might reduce the risk of asthma symptoms by roughly half.

Americans eat 17 times as much omega-6 fatty acid as they do omega-3 fatty acid, which is not healthy. Omega-6 fatty acids come in the form of vegetable oils, eggs, and fish. We should consume five times as much omega-3 as omega-6. Cold-water fish, including freshwater fish such as lake trout, chub, lake herring, and whitefish, are especially high in omega-3 fatty acids.

One 3½-ounce serving from fish high in omega-3 fats such as fresh anchovies, sardines, salmon, halibut, herring, and albacore yields more than 1,000 milligrams of omega-3 fat. Americans consume a maximum of only 1,400 milligrams of omega-3 fat per *week*.

According to the United States Food and Drug Administration, fish with high levels of mercury should be eaten with caution. The fish with the highest levels of methylmercury are king mackerel, shark, swordfish, and tilefish (golden bass or golden snapper). Women of childbearing age and children should not eat these fish at all and should limit their fish consumption to no more than 12 ounces a week. By consuming a wide variety of freshwater and saltwater fish species as part of a balanced diet, anyone should be able to reap the health benefits of omega-3 fatty acids.

Last, most fish are also naturally high in many essential vitamins, such as A, C, and D, and some varieties are particularly high in antioxidant E; zinc, iron, and calcium also come with the naturally healthful package.

So eat fish.

Selecting Fish

In February 1999, the Food and Drug Administration revised its guidelines for seeking and keeping fresh fish. Here are a few of those guidelines:

■ Your fishmonger's iced shelves should hold fish that have clear eyes that bulge a little. Only walleye have naturally cloudy eyes.

■ The flesh should be firm and shiny. Dull flesh may mean old flesh. Gills, if any, should be bright red and not slimy.

■ Never buy unrefrigerated fish or fish that has not been kept on ice. Sitting on a bare wooden display at a weekend fresh market for more than 3 hours

without ice can accelerate the growth of *C. botulinum* bacteria.

■ If the flesh does not spring back when pressed with your finger, it is not as fresh as it should be.

■ Fresh fish does not smell fishy or like ammonia. Fresh fish does not stink. If it does, don't buy it.

■ Refrigerate fish immediately upon arriving home and store in the coldest part of the refrigerator or on ice. Anglers coming home from the stream should consider bringing along a cooler of ice to cool down the catch, especially during warmer months.

■ Don't buy partially opened packages of frozen seafood or ones with freezer burn.

■ If shellfish, such as mussels, clams, lobsters, and oysters, die during transportation, or if the shells are cracked and open, discard them. You'll know when shellfish are alive; they will close up when the shell is tapped.

Preparing Fish

First, a good knife is important to own; it will become an often cherished tool. I have too many store-bought and several beautiful handmade knives, some now collectible (from master knife maker Bud Nealy of Stroudsburg, Pennsylvania), and I enjoy nothing better than using them, in the field and in the kitchen.

An ideal knife for filleting fish will be long and thin. Always — always — start with a sharp knife. A dull knife makes sloppy, uneven cuts; sometimes this may include your own fingers. Take the time to sharpen any knife: It is worth the effort and prevents accidents. A knife can become dull after cleaning just two or three large fish, so keep a sharpener handy, too.

Have nearby a bucket of water (or hose), newspapers, plastic garbage bags, paper towels, and, if possible, a fillet glove. A fillet glove is made from nearly impenetrable material (preventing cuts) and allows for a firm grip on a slippery surface, so it might be a good item to own if you clean fish often. Take a look at *Figure 1.1* for a review of basic piscine anatomy.

To begin, thoroughly wash the fish to remove grime and slime. Let it dry for a few minutes. (Wet fish slip away from your grasp all too easily.) Lay the fish on a hard surface and on a thick layer of newspapers so when you are finished, you can simply roll the mess into the newspapers and discard.

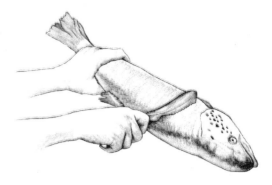

Figure 1.2 **Scaling**

If you intend to skin your fish, there is no need to scale it. Trout need to be neither scaled nor skinned; the grilled skin is delicious.

To scale a fish, wash and let it dry a bit first, as I mentioned earlier, but I've found fish that can be dried out, after being out of the water for longer than an hour. Mist the fish lightly, or scaling can be a chore. Hold down the tail with your fingers or even a spring clamp (for unusually large fish). With a fish scaler or a sturdy kitchen knife, scrape the scales from tail to head against the "grain" *(Fig. 1.2)*, including around the pectoral

Figure 1.1 **Fish anatomy**

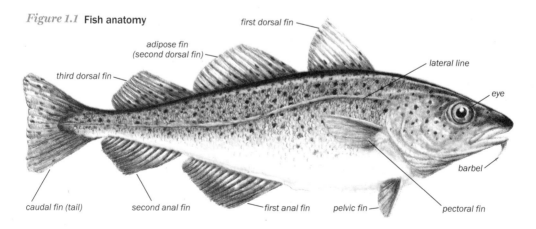

Figure 1.3 Removing the head

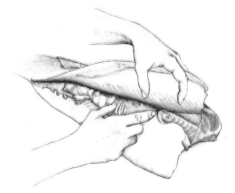

Figure 1.4 Removing the innards

fin and up to the gills. I find scaling freshly caught fish easier if I don't gut the fish first; however, the FDA recommends doing so as soon as possible after a catch, bluefish especially. Most store-bought fish in the United States will have been gutted ahead of time.

To keep fish whole, cut off the head by slicing down behind the gills at an angle and discard *(Fig. 1.3)*. For very large fish you may need a hefty knife, such as a sharp 12-inch chef's knife or a cleaver. Slice horizontally along the belly and remove the innards *(Fig. 1.4)*. Clip or cut off the fins and be careful: Some fish, catfish and bluegills especially, have spiny, sharp fins that hurt and can itch relentlessly. Remove the kidney line (the black line adhering to the underside of the spine) using a teaspoon or the back of your thumbnail *(Fig. 1.5)*. Wash carefully.

To fillet, make a slice along the back, top side of the spine, holding the knife at a downward angle *(Fig. 1.6)*. Below the head and pectoral fin, hold the knife perpendicular to the length of the body and slice down to the spine, but not

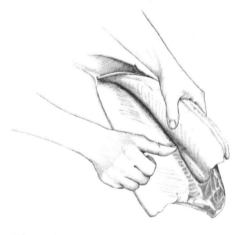

Figure 1.5 Removing the kidney line

Figure 1.6 Cutting fillets, slicing along the back

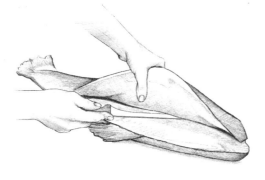

Figure 1.7 Cutting fillets; continuing the slice

Figure 1.8 Cutting fillets; finishing the slice

through it, while holding the head tightly. Be careful not to puncture the abdomen because the innards' acids could affect the taste. Slice along the backside, with the knife flat on its side and pointing down so the tip slides over the bones.

Continue slicing *(Fig. 1.7)* back to just between the dorsal and adipose fins (about two thirds of the way down), then slide the knife through without cutting into the ribcage; continue slicing to the tail *(Fig. 1.8)*. Remove the knife, turn over the fish, and repeat the steps.

If you prefer to skin your fillets, place the skin-side down and hold the tail end of the fillet with your fingers or a clamp. Holding the blade nearly flat, begin slicing near your fingers, carefully and *away* from your hand *(Fig. 1.9)*. Slide the knife through the length of the fillet and finish cutting off the skin.

To cut a fish into steaks, lay it on its side or belly. Gut it, scale it, cut off the head, and cut steaks between 1 and 2 inches thick *(Fig. 1.10)*, depending on the size of the fish and your preference for grilling.

Always wash steaks or fillets in cold water and refrigerate as soon as possible.

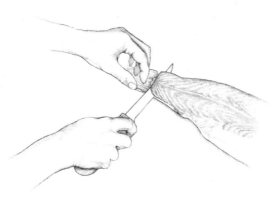

Figure 1.9 Skinning fillets

Figure 1.10 Cutting steaks

Figure 1.11 **Killing a lobster**

Kill live lobsters by inserting a sharp knife into the "cross" at the base of the head, the first joint where the head and body are joined together. This will detach the spinal cord, killing the lobster quickly *(Fig. 1.11)*.

Cooking Fish Safely

Directions for indirect smoking and hot smoking will be addressed in these pages. You'll find any additional instructions in the individual recipes.

Bacterial growth occurs between 40°F and 140°F. Most bacteria are killed at around 160°F, so maintain the heat level of a grill or smoker between 160°F and 185°F, or higher. Cold smoking, which cannot be easily accomplished on a grill, is more often performed in larger smokers or in a smokehouse.

Hot smoking (also called barbecuing) is achieved by maintaining the grill temperature at 200°F to 225°F. Grilling over 300°F is more in the realm of roasting, even though it creates a smoky environment for the food.

Smoke grilling is a term I've coined for this book to indicate smoking foods on a grill. It is accomplished by cooking foods while at the same time encapsulating those foods within a dense smoke by closing the lid of the grill. Smoke grilling is achieved in one of two ways.

The first is *indirect smoke grilling,* which is grilling food on the "cool" side of the grill, with charcoal or gas as the remote heat source emanating from the opposite side of a grill. Food cooks more slowly in this manner, and absorbs more smoke. Depending upon the amount, it may take an hour to 90 minutes to completely cook and smoke food by this method. The second method is by *direct smoke grilling,* which is grilling the food directly over the smoke pan on the "hot" side of the grill. Foods cooked on the hot side will cook faster because they are closer to the heat source. Either way, a smoke pan, holding clean, unadulterated organic combustibles for flavoring purposes, is used. The smoke pan tightly encloses the combustibles, smoldering rather than completely igniting them, and drawing out smoke, not heat. Smoke-grilled fish will be more perishable than fish smoked in a smokehouse, where the time in the smoke-filled environment is extended by many more hours, helping preserve it longer.

Another style of smoke grilling is an abbreviated form of hot smoking, a version that imparts a hint of smoke into grilled food. If you choose this technique, place the fish directly over the smoke pan. The smoke pan will deflect heat around itself, allowing the fish to cook as it is being bathed in smoke. This may require a few more minutes of grilling because the fish is not directly over the heat source.

Most modern grills have no difficulty getting up to 400°F or even higher when equipped with four to six gas burners or when the charcoal is mounded high. Every grill is different, so test your own grill with a thermometer, and experiment. It helps to keep notes.

If you use a brine or marinade (I use the words interchangeably), marinate fish in a covered container in the refrigerator. Marinades and brines are applied either by immersing fish in a solution of salt, sugar, wine, and herbs and spices or by injecting that solution into the fish with a syringe. Do not reuse brine that has been expelled from raw fish. In some recipes, you may be asked to boil a brine, which will kill any bacteria.

When transferring raw or cooked fish from one place to another, keep it cool and don't expose it to direct sun, which will quickly spoil fish and encourage bacterial growth. While traveling, use ice, reusable ice packets, and coolers for added safety. Fish will deteriorate more quickly than will most other foods.

Scromboid poisoning, or histamine poisoning, results from improper handling of certain kinds of fish (usually exposure to extreme temperature or poor handling soon after being caught), and can cause nausea, burning of the mouth, vomiting, and diarrhea. Refrigerate fish immediately in the coldest part of the refrigerator or keep on ice. Here are a few FDA recommendations for cooking and consuming fish safely.

▪ Cook all fish to an internal temperature of 145°F for at least 15 seconds. If you don't have a thermometer, try this: Slip a knife into the flesh and pull it aside. The edges should be opaque and the center slightly translucent, with flakes beginning to separate. After cooking, always let fish stand for 3 to 4 minutes.

▪ Color: Lobsters are red when cooked; scallops become milky and opaque, as well as firm to the touch.

▪ When shellfish are thoroughly cooked, they will open. Discard any that do not.

▪ Keep fish hot, at least 140°F to serve. Do not leave cooked fish unrefrigerated for more than 2 hours.

▪ People with liver disorders or weakened immune systems should thoroughly cook seafood before eating it.

PART ONE

On the Grill

Chapter 1

Grills and Grilling

THE FIRST GRILL I owned, until it rusted into oblivion, was a five-dollar patio-sized hibachi, a cast-iron grill from which I certainly got my money's worth. I used it on the balcony/fire escape of a third-floor walk-up apartment in Boston.

Later, I graduated to a larger charcoal kettle grill, big enough for *two* chickens or a whole fish, a giant step up. I remember grilling just about anything and everything. I also recall days grilling on an outdoor grill I had made for Konkapot Restaurant in Mill River, Massachusetts, in the first years of my venture into the food business. We grilled outdoors, winter included, with snow nearly putting out the fire during some particularly nasty New England weather. (A perplexed customer once asked, as I delivered a grilled entrée to him in the toasty dining room, why I had snow on my shoulders.)

Grilling for me was an important method of cooking. It still is. I suppose grilling is embraced by many because of the age-old appeal of fire-flavored foods, reminiscent of the outdoors.

This book is intended, in part, for those who not only enjoy the taste of grilled fish, but would like to experiment with the flavors of smoked fish as well. For the outdoor cook who does not want to bother building anything and who would rather get started immediately, this book is written for instant use. If you already have a grill, which many if not most people do these days, you'll need little else to begin. The few additional things you will need I tackle in Tools of the Trade, pages 14–17. If you are looking to buy something new in the way of outdoor grills, read on.

A Guide to Grills

My intention here is to not endorse specific products, even though I may lean toward a few that I have found more accessible than others. I may also recommend a unique design feature or two.

All in all, there are many products intended for grilling and smoking in this technologically advanced age. I will do my best to offer enough material to give you, the grill master, some expertise (garnered from more than 35 years of varied successes — and failures) with which to experiment. You will then make the final decisions about whether to grill, smoke, or contrive another combination that works best for your outdoor cooking needs.

As you may already know, every grill master feels as if he or she has perfected the *best* recipe for walleye, the subtlest way to smoke tuna, the *only* method for smoke grilling bluefish. Hopefully this book will inspire you to try something new, something challenging, a combination you never thought of before. If nothing else, mix and match new ideas with old recipes: Experiment, contrive. I find that in discussing techniques of cooking, grilling, and smoking foods with other fire builders, I always learn something. After decades of playing with fire, I not only appreciate new input, but I welcome it as well. As should you.

On to those new fandangled grills.

The good news is that hibachis are still available. They cost slightly more than the five dollars I paid for my first one, but are still affordable. Prices for grills run as high as — ready for this? — yes, ten thousand dollars. Such is the cost of the ultimate "machine" that does everything but wash the dishes and put the kids to bed. Do you need this?

Consumer Reports, online or in hard copy, is a good reference for those seeking advice on purchasing anything from automobiles to food processors to grills. The independently supported reports are written by assumedly unbiased experts. Check out its online product recommendations as a starting place.

Word from a neighbor across the fence is another source, even though it will be based on one person's opinion. But who best to ask advice from than someone who has tried a product? Don't get sucked into the one-up syndrome, however: Possibly the inexpensive model in black is all you will need for your purposes, rather than the one in stainless steel just because it *looks* spiffy.

Most gas grills sold in America sell for under three hundred dollars and six out of ten grills sold are gas fueled. I looked at a high-end stainless-steel gas grill with six burners, two side-warming burners (on which one could cook a complete meal), and a slide-out drawer in which to lay corn or wood chips for smoking. If you are ready to spend four thousand dollars, it is a good price. It does lie somewhere in the middle range of outdoor grill prices these days. You can also buy a good-quality outdoor grill for one thousand dollars, but you don't need to.

While researching grills, smokers, and other equipment for this book, it became increasingly evident to me that the perfect grill may not exist, at least for my purposes. I wanted one that would both cook and smoke with either gas or charcoal for a variety of purposes. I found a smoker that included a side chamber for the wood logs from which the smoke is piped into a primary chamber, essentially a miniaturized version of a similar concept of mine, detailed in chapter 11. But it was only a smoker, no grilling possibilities. Sizing it up for a few minutes, I visualized what I would do with it if I were to take it home. I might have been tempted, but I didn't want to rebuild the product; I didn't have the time or desire. As most people do today, I wanted it done for me.

Gas grills are convenient, no doubt. No fuss, instant fire. Look for a grill with heavy grates that are removable for cleaning. It should have porcelain-coated heavy steel grill bars (or grates) set close together for the most durability. Thin, flimsy aluminum will eventually deteriorate and need replacing. More important, aluminum neither distributes nor holds heat well enough for intense grilling purposes — at least, not well enough to sear foods.

In order to smoke-grill, a gas grill with at least two burners is necessary. Four is good, six or eight even better, but then we're getting on up into pricey stuff. For most outdoor entertaining, four burners should suffice. Look for a grill with the most square inches of grilling space you can afford. Four hundred to 600 square inches should be enough for most needs, perhaps more if you do a lot of group entertaining.

The better gas grill, I feel, is one with grates (on which food is placed) that are divided in half — that is, one movable grate on each side, each spread over two (or more) burners. This kind of grill is designed for easy cleaning and operation. Look also for a pull-out bottom tray that can be easily cleaned.

Each of the gas burners should have its own control switch so only one or two burners can be lit if you need to maintain low heat, such as for indirect smoke grilling (see page 13 for a description of indirect smoke grilling).

Of course, if you want, all four burners can be lit for grilling at 600 degrees or more, depending upon the model. Two burners alone rarely achieve that temperature.

One drawback I've found with gas grills is that the heat is often not as hot as with charcoal. If you fall into the professional category, you may want a more expensive model for its British thermal unit (BTU) output. For the most part, though, the more bells and whistles you add, the higher the price tag.

So, with most grilled or smoke-grilled recipes in this book, adjust the timing according to whether you prefer using gas or charcoal. Charcoal fires burn hotter and faster than gas fires, even gas grills with lava rocks.

A grill design I'd like to see improved upon is this: More grills — gas and charcoal — should allow you to raise or lower either the heat source or the grates themselves in order to more effectively control the cooking. A small cast-iron hibachi design does have this feature, but not many others do.

An old kettle-shaped standby since 1954, one of Weber's models has a particularly clever new feature: It ignites the charcoal with a small gas burner underneath the wire baskets that contain the charcoal. This innovative idea helps keep awful-tasting lighter fluid away from our grilled foods.

Corn- or pellet-fired grills crept onto the market not long ago. A small electric auger on these uniquely designed grills feeds dried corn kernels or tiny compressed wood pellets, dropping a calculated few at a time into the firing chamber. One model uses ceramic "rocks" that lie across the entire heating surface, which is just under the grates; the rocks conduct heat and are beneficial in holding the heat for long periods with the lid shut. The cost of firing one of these grills is noticeably low. Wood pellets come in different woods for various flavorings. These grills are easily adapted for both types of smoke grilling.

How about a grill that pops up with the touch of a foot pedal from a portable unit, exposing an ice chest below? Take it to the beach for those summer days when you want it all, hot and cold, neatly tucked into the trunk of your automobile. Hmm.

Indirect smoke grilling — a focus of this book — is easily accomplished on charcoal grills. Heap burning charcoal on one side of the heating area, with a smoke pan of corn kernels or wood directly on top of the charcoal and the fish or other foods lying on the opposite, "cool" side of the grate. With the dome-shaped lid in place, the container serves as a simple, efficient smoker.

Don't forget to look for a grill that has parts that can be removed for cleanup. At one time I owned a grill that had no access to the bottom pan where all the drippings and juices ended up. Ultimately it became a messy, disposable grill, frustrating and not very economical in the long run.

So you choose, gas or charcoal. Either way, you'll be happy dining with that *plein air* taste associated with outdoor cooking.

Preheating Instructions

For the purposes of clarification in this book, I will begin most grilled or smoke grilled recipes with: 1) Preheat a grill, or 2) Prepare a grill for smoke grilling.

Preheat a grill. Ignite the heat source, either gas or charcoal, in preparation for grilling food. In the case of a gas grill, this involves opening a valve and igniting the gas. Simple enough. Five to 10 minutes should suffice; the grate should sizzle when a drop of water is splashed on it. Remember, you want the fish, vegetables, or whatever foods you cook to sear quickly on the outside, sealing in the natural flavors and juices. If your grill is not hot enough, food will stick to it, often ruining your efforts. To preheat a charcoal grill, ignite the charcoal with newspaper or kindling and let the charcoal burn until most pieces are gray.

Remember: *Always* brush or spray cooking oil on the grate, and on the bottom of the food if possible, beforehand to prevent sticking. It is disheartening to watch your labors disappear before your eyes, and your guests' eyes, as a delicate fillet crumbles apart, sticking to a metal grate.

Prepare a grill for smoke grilling. Preheat the grill as instructed above. Fill the smoke pan with dried corn kernels or wood chips and cover. When the charcoal is gray or the burners sizzle when a drop of water is splashed on them, place the smoke pan directly on top of the heat source. If indirect smoke grilling is called for, move the hot charcoal to one side of the grill before placing the smoke pan on top. If using a gas grill, just leave off the burners on one side when you ignite. Wait until the corn or wood begins to smoke, about 10 minutes. Again, don't forget the cooking oil.

Tools of the Trade

When preparing to smoke-grill, I like to plan which tools and utensils I might need, gather them together, and place them where they can be located quickly. It's really frustrating to have to search for a tool or gadget while preparing food, so think ahead about each of the various steps involved. Organize yourself and all the tools for the task and your work will

unfold with calm and ease rather than tension.

The Smoke Pan

This pan, or tray, is, ideally, a cast-iron container in which corn kernels or wood chunks or chips are placed and then set directly on a fire in a grill. Once the corn or wood ignites, a cover keeps out most of the oxygen, smoldering the pan's contents and creating a smoky environment in which to cook and flavor food. The pan should be enameled, if possible, and come equipped with a slotted cover (though the slots or holes may be on the sides of the pan itself, as with mine) and handles on the sides. It should be large enough to hold 3 to 4 cups of corn kernels and some wood chunks or chips. The size of my smoke pan (see below) is a common size that will fit most grills. The cast-iron smoke pan I prefer and use exclusively on my grill is one I found quite by accident in a camping store. This grill pan is produced by Coleman, a manufacturer of outdoor camping equipment. It is a solidly fabricated, enamel-coated cast-iron pan with a heavy lid and venting holes along the sides. Intended for open fires, this is a small hunk of durability. It measures 3 inches by 10 inches by 10 inches, nearly an ideal size for most any home patio grill.

Other cast-iron pans may be found in hardware stores, large discount home-building chains, and mail-order catalogs. I saw a small one at a gardening supply store for about three dollars. It was too small for my needs, but seemed well suited for the smallest grill or table-top hibachi.

In a pinch, disposable aluminum baking pans, found in the baking section of a supermarket, will do. Sizes range from very small (best for corn kernels and sawdust) to large (good for wood chunks and chips). If you can't find the right size, buy two small ones. These pans are disposable, lightweight, and convenient. Cover with aluminum foil punctured with holes.

If an aluminum pan is not available, cut and lay out two 18-inch squares of *heavy-duty* aluminum foil, one on top of the other, and place two or three wood chunks or smaller wood chips and/or 2 to 3 cups of dried corn kernels in the center. Cover with another sheet of foil and pinch together the edges of the lid and bottom to form a sealed "smoke pan." Poke six to eight holes in the top and lay the makeshift pan directly on top of a bed of hot gray charcoal or straddle across two metal burners on one side of a gas grill. Wait until the corn and/or wood chips begin to smoke, about 10 minutes.

Fireproof Container

You'll need some sort of fireproof container to dump spent coals into. Keep a metal bucket near the grill or, as I did in a hurry one day, grab an aluminum roller paint tray and line it with foil. It's just the right size to accommodate the burnt "wafer" residue from dried corn. For obvious reasons, do not use a plastic tray or bucket.

Wire-Mesh Basket

This is a handy tool to own; it's ideal for grilled and smoked foods in general, not just fish. The device is a wire-mesh container with a handle and wire-mesh lid, hinged and able to be locked in place to hold its contents securely. It can be flipped over to cook food on both sides.

The one I use measures 12½ inches by 13½ inches with a 12-inch handle. While pricing and comparing products from various manufacturers, I found this particular one a bit more expensive than some at about $25, but having purchased a flimsy, poorly constructed one at a lower price that I later was forced to discard, I would consider this a good value. It will serve you longer.

Essentially, place a fillet, a whole fish, or a fish Wellington (see pages 144–146) into the basket and clamp it down to lock into place. Do not use any food smaller than the opening of the mesh openings or, obviously, it will fall through. Thus, onions, garlic, and small-cut vegetables are out. Solid mass is what this device was intended for. Whatever you plan to clamp into a fish basket, brush or spray the insides of the mesh with oil before placing food inside.

Elongated fish-shaped wire-mesh baskets make grilling or smoking whole fish even simpler. Look for these where other cooking equipment is sold.

Perforated Grilling Pans

One day I was in a mall waiting for a friend and I dropped into a sporting goods store. I spotted something in the outdoor cookware section, a 12-inch round Teflon-coated pan with a handle. The pan has 2-inch-high sides and the bottom has been drilled with holes, which allows heat to penetrate the pan from the bottom.

An additional appeal to my newest purchase (for eight dollars) is its handle, which folds across the top for portability and storage.

I use the pan often. It's great for sautéing vegetables and grilling fish and pizza.

Grill Wok

A grill wok is a perforated pan with a flat bottom, but with sides angled high, like a Chinese wok. It works well for stir-frying vegetables. No need for oil or butter, for those who prefer little or none. A 12-inch grill wok will fit most grills, though they are available in larger sizes.

Spatulas

Buy two metal, not rubber, spatulas as wide as you can find. Outdoor cooking manufacturers make metal spatulas, around 7 inches wide. Using two to lift an entire side of smoked salmon or shad off the grill makes grilling and smoking considerably easier. Turning without enough support can ruin delicate fish quickly, causing them to flake into pieces.

Tongs

After enough years in front of a professional stove and grill, tongs have become an extension of my arm. I couldn't manage without them. I like simple tongs with a spring action. They are made in several lengths, but for most things I prefer the 12-inch size. Look for inexpensive tongs and other equipment in a restaurant supply company.

Towels, Mitts, and Aprons

These are essential for avoiding blisters. Most parts of a grill are hot, including the cover handle, grates, and all exposed metal. Assume whatever you grab will be hot.

When working around a steel smoker, where virtually all parts are metal, use mitts or towels at all times. Hot racks require that the cook use protection when they are removed, as does a smoke pan cover without wooden handles.

In addition to the towels and mitts I use to protect against heat, I feel naked without at least one towel tucked under my belt for wiping hands. Aprons? Well, sure, they keep your clothes from getting spattered with oil and food.

Skewers

Metal skewers conduct heat, cooking the food they are skewering faster. Recall the cooking hint about sticking a nail into a potato that is to be baked? It shortens the cooking time.

If you use wooden skewers, 11½ inches long by ¼ inch thick seems to be the average size, though they are made in longer lengths that are good for skewering big shrimp or small whole fish. I've found that skewers of about ⅜ inch thick hold up better for long grilling time. Don't forget to soak wooden skewers in water for about 30 minutes prior to use to prevent burning.

Cooking Sprays

Cooking spray was a great invention. It is a sodium-free, cholesterol-free, and calorie-free oil that is sprayed onto a surface to prevent sticking. Why didn't someone come up with this idea sooner? Spray all grates, the inside of pans, wire-mesh baskets, *and* the underside of fillets and whole fish, if you can, to prevent sticking. It works. Get in the habit of using cooking spray and you'll agree it makes cooking and cleanup so much easier. Grates scrape beautifully clean if sprayed beforehand. Pizza releases more easily from a pan, even a Teflon pan, after a coating of cooking spray.

Wire Brushes

You've got to have one. About 12 inches long, it will reach the deepest part of any grill. Cleanup is easiest when it's done immediately after cooking rather than after the grill has cooled down and bits of food stick unmercifully to the grates. Remember to clean the brush, too. Scrubbing a grate with a bacteria-filled brush isn't a healthy practice. Keep all utensils and equipment clean at all times.

Chimney Starters

A "chimney starter" for starting a wood fire is an environmentally friendly contraption that uses newspaper to start the fire in a grill. But do not use the colored-ink sections; colored ink, unlike black ink, emits toxic fumes when it is burned. The concept is simple: a chute, or tower, that is open at the top and has a platform on the bottom that separates a layer of charcoal from crumbled newspaper. The paper is lit with a match from beneath. After 15 to 20 minutes, the charcoal is ready to be added to the grill. Spread the coals with each piece touching another. Isolated, the coals tend to slowly die out, so keep them close together. Once the bed has burned down to an even shade of gray, the coals are ready for the smoking process. Also, by this time the grate will be sufficiently hot and ready to accept the fish.

Water

Spray bottles used for misting plants come in handy to douse unwanted flames. Always keep one nearby.

Optional equipment, much like that for an automobile, can sometimes drive you to extremes. Each new gadget on the market seems attractive — you've got to have it! Resist the impulse and settle for the above list; it will get you started. Later, when you have spent some time at the grill, you will know whether you need more gadgets, and you can take it (slowly) from there.

The Soft Smoke

I HAVE DISCOVERED what I believe to be an exciting new/old smoking vehicle. A fuel for smoking fish, a fuel easily found in any farm supply store, hardware store, and even supermarket; it's inexpensive, too. Corn. Dried whole corn kernels.

Loosely packed corn kernels burn down and blacken evenly, creating an aroma reminiscent of tall cornstalks rustling as one hunts pheasant on a cool autumn day. An almost floral scent smolders, a hint of popcorn wafting an organic, sweet vegetable smoke into the air. As with wood, it is earthy, but corn smoke is less rugged. It is the "soft" smoke.

Countering the harshness of mesquite and hickory wood for smoking (except for hams, bacon, and the like), corn smoke is its opposite, soothing to the palate, its perfume more . . . serene. Related, if you will, to the aroma of a fine, aged burgundy. Fish encapsulated by a corn smoke is gently caressed, naturally sweet.

Encapsulating fish with what I call a soft smoke environment may be simply rediscovering something old — certainly corn has a history as long as humankind itself, and I have used corncobs in my smokehouse for years — but bear with me; I think you'll be pleased with the results if you venture forth into the world of corn smoke.

Corn-Fired Stoves

Just a couple of years ago, I noticed dried corn being used as a source of heat in corn-fired stoves, a relatively new concept in heating units. I've known about pellet-fired stoves for several years (living in a harsh winter environment, where we use wood-burning stoves) but I had never heard of corn-fired stoves. It sounded intriguing. I sought out corn-fired stoves to examine (few and far between they were, being so new) but then unexpectedly found dried corn in a farm supply store, the same kind from which you buy garden seeds, spring sets, and bird feed. Sleuthing away with my culinary curiosity, I felt I might be on to something.

The owner of the farm supply store proudly fired up both his new stove, used to heat the storefront, and a cooking grill. The top of the grill, just under the grate, is covered with many small, unglazed porcelain, plaquelike squares pierced full of holes. The purpose is not unlike that of lava rocks: to capture, hold, and throw out accumulated heat.

The porcelain plaques, however, are situated between the burning corn and the food. I wondered if the food benefited from the smoldering corn; the store owner informed me that it did not. My immediate thought was: Why not? The corn gave off a distinctly perfumed aroma while it burned, not sickly perfume sweet, but organic, more fieldlike, as in the downwind breeze off a late summer cornfield, or like popcorn popping. I thought, "Why not make use of that byproduct?" It sure smelled good. Why not use the dried corn as a *flavoring* vehicle, not just for heat?

Creating a Soft Smoke

I saw the reason why a corn-fired grill flavors food minimally, if at all. It is fired too hot; it is fired to produce heat. It does not smolder and give off smoke. I would change that system in time.

So, setting out to experiment and test recipes, I first mixed together two-thirds whole dried corn kernels with one-third dried cracked corn, my thinking based upon years of burning hardwood chips. Often, I'll mix small chips, shavings, or sawdust with larger chunks of wood. The mix serves to first ignite the smaller chips and later the larger ones, in essence melding the burning process from one size to another in a smooth transition. Otherwise, large chunks of wood take a longer time to ignite. The size ratio is, of course, considerably different — large wood chunks are bigger than dried corn kernels — yet the concept still applies. I continued my experimenting, mixing, and smoldering; I wanted to devise a way for a grill to be used as a smoker.

I filled a pan with dried corn kernels, covered it, ignited it, and laid a fillet on the grill. I shut the lid but couldn't contain my eagerness and opened it too many times, until the need to slap my own hand took over and I behaved long enough to eventually smoke-grill the first fillet, which was, incidentally, a rainbow trout.

The most impressive aspect of that first time smoking with a corn smoke was the aroma. Wonderfully delicious it was, as I described earlier. Tasting, smacking my lips, and embracing the results of my newfound process, I deemed it a success; indeed, it *smokes*.

Read on and you, too, can create a delicate, smoky taste using dried corn kernels. The best part? It's easily accomplished on any outdoor grill.

Often, even while using the soft smoke technique, I'll lay on a stick or two of pruned grapevines that I've cut to fit the smoke pan or a chunk or two of apple, maple, or sassafras wood, whichever I have on hand. Once the corn has finished smoldering, the wood continues to burn, thus increasing the length of time for smoking. Usually, however, I prefer just the use of corn kernels. I'll offer instructions for both a pure corn smoke and a mix because the taste *is* different, and some people like the added woodsy flavor of a mix to their foods. I suggest you first try a recipe using corn alone and then compare by adding a few pieces of wood to the mix with another recipe — or better yet, the same recipe — and discover how they vary. What do you have to lose? About 35 cents, the cost of 1 pound of dried whole corn. (Cheaper even in 50-pound bags in my area — 12 cents a pound!)

How to Do It Yourself

Now for the how-to business. Whole corn will combust occasionally throughout the smoke-grilling process, especially if you don't use a cover on the smoke pan. A cover, however, is a must to choke off oxygen, so don't go without one. Even with a cover, you need to be vigilant, handy with a misting bottle or a cup of water to sprinkle over the flames. Combustion will occur whether you are using corn kernels or wood chips. So don't go off to split some wood or pick up the telephone to call Aunt Millie; the grill needs your full attention.

To the grill. I'm generalizing now perhaps, in describing a typical grill that many outdoor cooking enthusiasts own, but let's assume your gas grill — more about charcoal later — is on a portable frame with wheels, is waist high, and has at least two burners down in the innards of the unit, possibly four, six, or even eight burners if you've spent more money for a substantial product.

This grill will have one or two ascending warming shelves above the grilling area. The porcelain or enameled grates that support the food are in two sections and able to slide back and forth and be removed for ease of cleaning. Many grills are adaptable in one way or another. With a little ingenuity and improvisation, anyone can convert a grill for smoke grilling within minutes.

The internal size of the grill on which I primarily used to test recipes can accommodate a smoke pan (a cast-iron box in which to hold corn kernels) equipped with a vented cover. Your specific size requirements may vary, but a good smoke pan should span two cast-iron burners. I've found this to be enough for one smoking session, 45 minutes to an hour, enough time to cook and flavor fish. With additional wood, or more corn, you can easily extend the time needed to complete a smoking but you'll have to first remove the charred bits and discard them. Read more about smoke pans on page 14.

In a pinch, you may simply fashion your own makeshift smoke pan out of heavy-duty aluminum foil. Some grills' high BTUs, however, are powerful enough to melt the aluminum. This happened to me the first time I tried it on a new grill. Use two layers of heavy-duty aluminum foil and don't place the aluminum directly on the burner where the heat is the most intense. With the help of small stones or half a brick, create an air space between the aluminum "pan" and the burner by raising the pan off the flame. This small bit of extra effort will serve you well for many smokings.

Charcoal. Charcoal? Of course. The same standards apply whether you use gas or charcoal for the heat source. It doesn't matter; you merely want to combust the corn and/or wood. You are not using the corn or wood for heat; gas or charcoal will be doing that.

First, you must ignite the charcoal to get it burning and hot. Never use charcoal lighter fluid! It will taint your food to the point where a distinct petroleum flavor will dominate, something you definitely do not want. Some manufacturers claim that their product does not affect the flavor of the food, but why even worry about it when small sticks or newspaper are readily available and often more efficient?

Electric coils are handy when you grill near the house or close to an outlet. Lay the coils on a baking or other type of flat fireproof pan. Mound charcoal on top and plug in. The coals will ignite in about 20 minutes; you can then transfer directly to the grill.

Chimney starters are a smart concept. Old newspaper is lit inside and at the bottom of an aluminum "tower," above which is held charcoal chunks. As the newspaper burns, the charcoal ignites, ready in about 15 minutes.

Even with a small bowl-shaped tabletop grill with a lid, you can create a smoky environment, just on a smaller scale. Make an aluminum smoke pan as described above, to fit under one side of the grill. After lighting the charcoal and letting it come to the proper temperature, place the covered aluminum or cast-iron smoke pan holding corn kernels and/or wood chips directly on the coals, on one side. The other side will hold the food directly on the grate. Cover and cook for about 45 minutes, depending upon the recipe, size of the grill, and amount of food.

A note on cooking times: In my recipe testing, most fish that had been grilled over charcoal took about one-third *less* cooking time than those cooked over gas because of the more intense heat from charcoal. So take into consideration the time for gas grills as opposed to charcoal grills and adjust the cooking times, or you may burn your carefully prepared meal.

The following applies to either a gas or a charcoal grill. Using either a cast-iron smoke pan or an aluminum foil "pan," pour in 2 to 3 cups of whole corn kernels and cover. Set the pan on top of the heat source, either directly on top of the charcoals or over the cast-iron gas burners. The box should be centered under the grate. After about 10 minutes, when the smoke begins to rise, place the food on the grill, directly over the smoke. When you use charcoal, you may need to occasionally shift aside spent charcoal ashes and replace them with new coals if the smoking time exceeds, say, an hour. For most fish recipes, 45 minutes to an hour should be enough for a hot smoke, however.

You will see the corn become a solid, blackened mass, a wafer that when cooled down is light as a feather and can be picked up and snapped in half. Why? This is the sugar burning off within the corn, leaving its residue.

Continue to smoke until the mass is totally black. It will not adversely affect the food, as charred wood and charcoal do not influence taste as they burn. If you need to continue smoking beyond the time the corn has expended itself, remove the pan with protective mitts or gloves, lift out the burned wafer with a metal spatula or simply dump it out into a metal or other heatproof container, add more corn kernels, and return the pan to the grill.

The wafer may continue to smolder when you are finished, so be sure to put it into a metal container or clean aluminum paint tray lined with aluminum foil. Once it has cooled, it can be easily and safely discarded.

There you have it. Enjoy soft smoke on a grill.

Flavoring Tips

Adding flavors to the grill during the cooking process will often enhance the end result. One example is nestling half a stalk of fennel into dried corn kernels during a smoke grilling (see Bluefish Smoked over Fennel, page 26).

Often when simply grilling and not smoking, I'll toss a handful of wood chips into the fire, just to impart a slight wood flavor, nothing heavy. You can try bundling a few thick stalks of rosemary and laying them directly on charcoal or even on the cast-iron burners of a gas grill under a fillet for further taste. Bundles of thyme, oregano, and sage work well, too. They will burn quickly, so you might want to have several ready, presoaked in water for about 10 minutes.

Use your imagination: Do lemon peels impart flavor when burned? Orange? Do you have an abundance of dried mushrooms around, as I often do during the season? Try mixing a handful with the corn kernels in the smoke pan and see if it builds upon the flavor of the corn. If you have a cedar shake around (unpainted, untreated, and clean), split it into slivers and throw them into the fire for a flavor not unlike cedar-planked Pacific salmon. Do you have an extra spray bottle around? Mix white wine, water, lemon juice, a little olive oil, and some chopped herbs and mist your fish while grilling it, to flavor as well as moisten. Try flavored oils, such as hot chili oil and tarragon oil.

Be creative; it's up to you. Make your grill work for you.

Chapter 2

Appetizers

IF YOU HAVE EVER PAID CLOSE ATTENTION to people's eating habits you may have noticed a peculiar phenomenon right around the dinner hour: When people are hungry, they want to eat, now. Appetizers serve a twofold purpose: 1) to satisfy an immediate hunger and; 2) to set the tone for what will follow.

I recall an episode when, in our first restaurant, we had contracted to prepare food for a summer gallery opening nearby. The hosts kept cutting costs, considerably, until they settled on providing only a few bowls of cold pasta salads. Not enough for such a large crowd, we thought, but, of course,

could not object, even though we hinted that there might be problems with the small quantities. More important, they had also eliminated all of the appetizers. Instead they chose to buy their own: pretzels with mustard . . . for friends who would be arriving soon after noon the day of the opening. Later that day the door barged open to the restaurant with a frantic demand for more food! Naturally, they had soon run out and had hungry guests. With great dispatch we assembled more food and sent it over to the gallery.

What lesson is there to learn from this? Even though the quantity of food was too small for the number of guests, sufficient appetizers would have helped save the day. In this particular case there was not enough of either. The main course might have been good enough food, but those guests probably never even remembered it.

So, keep your guests satisfied, take the edge off their hunger, and then take them into a well-anticipated meal. Keep in mind that a delicious beginning should pave the way to what your friends will ultimately remember, good food from beginning to end, much the way a musical introduction leads its listeners toward a satisfying finale.

Quenelles

Quenelle is a French word for dumpling, traditionally made with pike. This is a good recipe to use with leftover grilled or smoked fish of most any kind.

1 **pound cooked fish fillets**

2 **egg whites**

2 **cups heavy cream**

1 **tablespoon capers**

1 **tablespoon fresh tarragon**

1 **teaspoon freshly ground black pepper**

1 **teaspoon prepared mustard**

½ **teaspoon salt**

ADVANCE PREPARATION:
Cook fish fillets

1. Place the fish fillets and egg whites in the bowl of a food processor. Pulse seven or eight times, until thoroughly mixed, then scrape down the sides.

2. Add the cream, capers, tarragon, pepper, mustard, and salt and purée for 15 to 20 seconds, or until thoroughly combined.

3. Transfer to a mixing bowl with a spatula. With a soup spoon, scoop out a heaping mound and transfer to another soup spoon, making an egg shape. Place on wax paper or parchment paper and repeat with the remaining mixture.

4. Bring water to a boil in a large saucepan or wok over medium-high heat. Reduce the heat until the water is at a slow boil and, with a slotted spoon, gently lower the quenelles into the water. Cook 8 to 10 minutes, turning once.

5. Transfer to wax paper and set aside.

6. If using in Fish Drop Soup (see page 25), use immediately. Quenelles may be kept refrigerated, covered, for up to 2 days.

SERVES 4-6

Quenelles can be used as hors d'oeuvres with Romesco Sauce (see page 230), Dill Mustard Sauce (see page 231), or Green Sauce (see page 231).

Fish Drop Soup

You may use any white fish, such as pollack, flounder, pike, or bass, or a combination, in this recipe. This soup is garlicky and the turmeric and eggs give it a rich, sun-yellow appearance. Quenelles are an optional addition, but I recommend it if you have the time for that little "extra" people pay attention to.

1 tablespoon olive oil
1 small onion, finely chopped, about ½ cup
6–8 garlic cloves, minced (or to taste)
1 tablespoon Shrimp Paste (see page 229)
1 teaspoon freshly ground black pepper
1 teaspoon ground turmeric
2 cups Fish Stock (see page 141)
2 cups dry white wine
1 teaspoon fish sauce
1 pound fish fillets, cut into bite-size pieces
Quenelles (see page 24); optional
2 eggs, beaten lightly
2–3 scallions or chives, finely chopped

1. Heat the oil in a 4-quart saucepan over medium-high heat. Sauté the onion and garlic in the oil for 3 to 4 minutes, or until softened; add the shrimp paste, pepper, and turmeric.

2. Reduce the heat to low and stir for 1 minute.

3. Pour in the stock and wine and bring to a boil over medium-high heat.

4. Reduce the heat to low, add the fish sauce, and simmer for 5 minutes.

5. Add the fish pieces, cover, and cook for about 10 minutes, or until the fish becomes firm. Add the Quenelles, if using, after the fish has cooked for 6 to 7 minutes.

6. Remove the cover and slowly dribble the eggs into the soup with one hand while whisking with the other.

7. Scatter the scallions over the soup, ladle into warm bowls, and serve immediately.

SERVES 4–6

Bluefish Smoked over Fennel

If you like bluefish and fennel, this is the perfect summer marriage. Serve with Ratatouille (see page 221) or Basic Salsa (see page 233) on the deck of your Block Island cottage, where the blues run wild in early September.

2–2½ pounds bluefish fillets
2   tablespoons sea salt
2   tablespoons sugar
1   teaspoon cayenne pepper
¼   cup milk
½   fennel bulb, split lengthwise

METHOD: Smoke grilling
ADVANCE PREPARATION:
Marinate fish for 30 to 45 minutes

1. Place the fillets in a container. Mix together the salt, sugar, and cayenne and rub on the fillets on both sides. Pour the milk over the fillets, cover, and refrigerate for 30 to 45 minutes.

2. Preheat a grill for smoke grilling, laying the fennel in the bottom of the smoke pan and covering with about 2 cups of dried corn kernels and/or wood chips.

3. Remove fillets from the refrigerator and drain.

4. Lay the fillets on an oiled grate over the smoke pan and close the lid. Turn the fillets after 20 minutes and close the lid. Keep a close watch; flames may need to be doused periodically. Cook for 45 minutes, or until the fillets are firm to the touch. Serve immediately.

SERVES 4

To Drink

An iced Gin Rickey (see page 236) made with freshly squeezed lime juice

Rosemary-Smoked Herring

The aroma of rosemary permeates the herring fillets, creating an intense flavor. You can substitute fresh chub or whitefish fillets if you prefer.

2 pounds herring fillets
2 tablespoons sea salt
2 tablespoons sugar
6 large sprigs rosemary
Dill Mustard Sauce (see page 231)
Lemon slices

METHOD: Smoke grilling
ADVANCE PREPARATION:
Marinate fish for 1 to 2 hours

1. Lay the fillets in a container and rub them with the salt and sugar. Surround the fillets with two sprigs of the rosemary and refrigerate for 1 to 2 hours. Stir after 1 hour.

2. Preheat a grill for smoke grilling, laying two sprigs of rosemary in the smoke pan covered with dried corn or wood chips. Above it, on the grate where you will place the fillets, lay a bed of the remaining sprigs of rosemary.

3. Remove the fillets from the refrigerator, brush off excess salt and sugar, rub, and lay the fillets on the rosemary bed on the grill. Close the lid.

4. Turn the fillets after about 20 minutes. Keep a close watch; flames may need to be doused. Cook for 45 minutes, or until the fillets feel firm to the touch. Serve with Dill Mustard Sauce and lemon slices.

SERVES 8-10

To Drink

Chilled champagne
or a German
Riesling

Smoked Bonito
with Green Sauce

I love bonito raw, but short of that, try smoking it and swabbing a piece with Green Sauce for a real treat.

2 **pounds bonito fillets**

2 **tablespoons sea salt**

2 **tablespoons sugar**

1 **tablespoon coarse black peppercorns**

2 **tablespoons fresh parsley, finely chopped**

Juice of ½ lemon

Pumpernickel squares

Green Sauce (see page 230)

METHOD: Smoke grilling
ADVANCE PREPARATION:
Marinate fish for 30 to 45 minutes

1. Place the fillets in a container. Mix together the salt, sugar, peppercorns, and parsley. Rub the fillets with the mixture on both sides, cover, and refrigerate for 30 to 45 minutes.

2. Preheat a grill for smoke grilling.

3. Remove the fillets from the refrigerator, brush off most of the rub, and drizzle the lemon juice on top.

4. Lay the fillets on an oiled grate over the smoke pan and close the lid. Turn the fillets after about 20 minutes and close the lid. Keep a close watch; flames may need to be doused periodically. Cook for 45 minutes, or until the fillets feel firm to the touch.

5. Serve warm on pumpernickel squares with the Green Sauce.

SERVES 4-6

Smoked Salmon Pâté

This could be a tartare except for the few minutes of a gentle smoking. Mirin is a sweet rice wine available at Japanese markets and in some supermarkets.

1 **pound salmon fillet**

1 **cup mirin or fruity white wine**

Juice of 2½ lemons (about ½ cup)

½ **cup green olives, pitted and sliced**

⅓ **cup olive oil**

2 **tablespoons finely chopped fresh dill**

2 **tablespoons finely chopped red onion**

2 **tablespoons finely chopped fresh thyme**

Toast or croutons

Lemon wedges

METHOD: Smoke grilling

ADVANCE PREPARATION:

Marinate fish for 1 hour

1. Soak the salmon in the mirin and ¼ cup of the lemon juice for 1 hour, covered and refrigerated.

2. Prepare a grill for smoke grilling.

3. Remove the salmon from refrigerator and drain.

4. Place the salmon on the hot side of the grill over the smoke pan. Close the lid and cook for 8 to 10 minutes, or until the fillets turn a pale pink.

5. Transfer the salmon to a cutting board. Chop or flake the salmon into small pieces and place them in a large mixing bowl.

6. Mix the remaining lemon juice, olives, oil, dill, onion, and thyme with the salmon pieces until all ingredients are thoroughly combined. Serve on toast or croutons with lemon wedges.

SERVES 6-8

To Drink

A good micro-brewed ale, preferably a local one

Smoked Salmon Spread

Plan ahead: Make enough salmon for dinner and for this appetizer.

You may find small squares of pumpernickel or rye bread in the deli section of your supermarket. If not, cut whole grain bread into 2-inch squares, cut each piece in half diagonally, and add a generous amount of this salmon spread. Toast the bread if you'd like.

Juice of 1½ lemons (about ¼ cup)

¼ cup mirin

2 tablespoons rice wine vinegar

½ pound Smoked Salmon (see page 112), cut into chunks

½ cup kalamata olives, pitted and sliced

2 tablespoons olive oil

2 tablespoons finely chopped fresh oregano

2 tablespoons finely chopped scallions

1 tablespoon finely chopped fresh parsley, plus extra for garnish

Pumpernickel or rye bread squares, cut in half

Lemon wedges

ADVANCE PREPARATION:
Smoke salmon, and marinate fish for 1 hour

1. In a small bowl, whisk together the lemon juice, mirin, and vinegar.

2. Place the salmon chunks in a glass baking dish and pour the mixture over them. Cover and refrigerate for 1 hour.

3. Pulse the olives, olive oil, oregano, scallions, and parsley in the bowl of a food processor five or six times, until finely chopped.

4. Remove salmon chunks and marinade from the glass dish. Add them to the food processor bowl and pulse three or four times, until coarsely chopped. Be careful not to overprocess and purée the mixture.

5. Spread the salmon mixture on the bread halves and garnish with the extra parsley. Serve with the pumpernickel squares and the lemon wedges.

SERVES 8-12

Curried Trout Timbales

You may use any other smoked fish for this recipe. Bake in muffin tins that have been buttered or use nonstick tins.

Timbales may be made ahead of time, covered, and refrigerated. To reheat, warm in a 250°F oven for 8 to 10 minutes.

6   ounces Smoked Rainbow Trout (see page 65), skinned and boned

Juice of 1½ lemons (¼ cup)

¼   cup fresh thyme, stemmed

6 to 8 wild ramps or chives

1   teaspoon curry powder

¼   teaspoon garam masala, found in the spice aisle of many supermarkets

1   cup heavy cream

3   eggs

ADVANCE PREPARATION:
Smoke trout

1. Preheat the oven to 350°F.

2. Pulse the trout, lemon juice, thyme, ramps, curry powder, and garam masala five or six times in the bowl of a food processor, until blended. Scrape down the sides and purée for 15 seconds.

3. Add the cream and eggs. Purée until thoroughly mixed.

4. Pour the mixture into six muffin cups.

5. Place tins in a roasting pan filled with water about two-thirds up on the muffin cups, then transfer to the oven. Bake for 25 to 30 minutes, or until a toothpick inserted in the center of the timbales comes out clean.

6. Remove from the heat and let sit for 10 minutes to allow the mixture to firm up. Run the tip of a blunt knife around the sides of the cups to release the timbales. Gently turn them upside down over a large plate.

7. Serve immediately or cover with plastic wrap and refrigerate.

MAKES 6 TIMBALES

Though one small timbale is the perfect appetizer or side dish, try serving Texas muffin–sized timbales with a salad for an afternoon luncheon.

Tickled Pink Oysters

This cognac and cream "bisque" simmers, absorbing a smoky flavor while the heat and smoke gently nudge open the oysters, flavoring them. If you double the recipe (except for the oysters), you could serve a cup of the bisque along with the oysters. See the Variation for details. Otherwise, drizzle about a teaspoon of the sauce over each oyster before serving.

You will need a disposable 8- to 10-inch aluminum baking pan or, my preference, a 2-inch-deep, 8-inch cast-iron frying pan to hold the bisque. See page 118 for a way to get even more mileage from the oysters.

1½ cups cognac or brandy

1½ cups half-and-half

½ cup clam juice

2 tablespoons cracked pink peppercorns (available in gourmet stores or via the Internet; see Resources, on page 244)

1 teaspoon paprika

24 unopened oysters

Lemon wedges

1. Prepare a grill for smoke grilling.

2. Combine the cognac, cream, clam juice, peppercorns, and paprika in a disposable or cast-iron pan. Set the pan directly on top of the smoke pan over the heat. The liquid may form a film on the surface, so whisk or stir it occasionally.

3. Place the oysters on the cool side of the grill. Close the lid.

4. When the oysters start to open, after about 15 minutes, completely pry open each one so the smoke flavor penetrates further, being careful not to spill their natural juices. Cook 30 minutes longer, or until opaque.

5. Transfer the oysters to plates, spoon a teaspoon of the sauce over each, and serve with lemon wedges.

SERVES 4

VARIATION If you decide to double the bisque recipe, do not spoon any over the oysters. Instead, strain, transfer to a saucepan over medium-high heat, and stir for 8 to 10 minutes, or until reduced by one third. Ladle into cups and serve immediately.

Everything Is Big in Big Sky Country

THE WEST: COWBOY HATS, SHIRTS, AND POETRY. And salmon flies. I could tell I was on my way by the many signs claiming the unique distinction of being "The Gateway to the West" (strangely enough, beginning somewhere in Ohio). The West is where everything is big. B-I-G.

I walked into an outfitting store in Ennis, Montana, to buy some flies. Today's outfitters don't match the romantic image of yesteryear: old oaken casks filled with sour pickles; bags of flour, beans, and other provisions sitting on the wooden floor; bolts of the latest fabric just shipped in from the East spread across the counter. An outfitter in today's West is more likely to be an Orvis-endorsed fly shop that sells T-shirts instead of imported calico. No money in five-cent pickles here.

A woman entered the store in front of me. At first she appeared to be of large stature. She wore a tall white cowboy hat, high-heeled platform western boots, and a bleached chamois shirt, fringed from shoulder to cuff. When she stood next to me at the counter, I realized she was petite, not large at all. It must have been the hat and shoes that made her appear much more grand. The flair of her outfit created a bigness, a drama to her presence.

I stepped up to the counter to inquire about the cost of the giant salmon flies on display. "Reasonably priced for such beautifully tied flies," I offered.

"Glad someone thinks so," the clerk responded. "You just passed Ted Turner on your way in who was grousing about the prices."

Driving toward the Rockies, one is dwarfed by the towering mountain ranges. Distance takes on a different meaning to an easterner used to the tightly knit, manicured hills of New England.

Bob Black Bull, a Blackfoot Indian from Browning, pointed to a bluff off to the east, across the prairie. "See that? It's called Sweet Grass Hills. Know how far away that is?"

"No," I answered, "but I'll guess 50 or 60 miles."

"Ha," he laughed, "that rise of land is 136 miles away."

What else is big? Buffalo. One pleasantly cool day, while fly-casting across the twisting Gibbon River in the confines of Yellowstone Park, I was absorbed in fishing and nearly jumped when I looked up. Upstream, not far away, were three buffalo lying in the tall, cool grass watching me. I wondered if they were waiting to see just how far I would dare to intrude into their space. A bright yellow flyer handed out to visitors entering the federal park reads: WARNING! MANY VISITORS HAVE BEEN GORED BY BUFFALO! I envisioned myself returning home to say that while fishing in Montana, I'd ended up in the hospital because I needed to have a buffalo horn extracted from my butt. I calmly backed out of the creek, very, very slowly.

What else is big? Driving across the Great Plains on the way into the Lewis and Clark National Park I passed several enormous ranches, one of which my host said he worked on several years before as a ranch hand. "This one is 40,000 acres, the one across the road is also 40,000 acres." About 10 miles farther up the road he pointed out the 100,000-plus-acre working ranch. It is generally understood that each head of cattle requires a little over 10 acres of land to graze comfortably. One cannot miss Ted Turner's Flying D Ranch of 107,520 acres, which he uses for his private game preserve and extensive buffalo ranch just south of Bozeman. That's big thinking. Bigger, certainly, than my puny 1¾ acres back home.

I asked a friend in Augusta what he thought was big in his state. "Tall tales. Everyone has them," he told me. He was right. I was introduced to an old-timer, Chester, who accompanies outfitters on

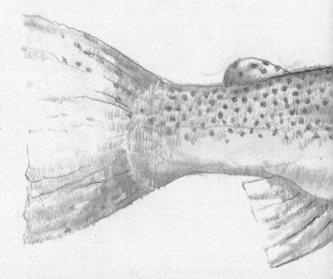

fishing and hunting trips into the Bob Marshall Wilderness. "I've heard a lot about you," I said.

"Lies, all lies," he joked. "Don't believe any of 'em."

One tale describing Chester's wilderness ingenuity told how he had stayed in camp, being the official woodcutter now that he is getting on in years, and had devised a strange-looking contraption made of barbed wire suspended over bait, a trap for bear (legal or not, I didn't ask). Hunters returning to camp, examining the trap, said they couldn't figure out how it worked. Chester replied, "Guess the bear don't either, cuz I ain't snared one yet."

How big is the West? Jim Bridger, an explorer in the mid-1800s who guided the cavalry through the Rockies, said the area was so big that you could yell into a canyon at night before going to sleep and the echo would wake you in the morning.

Anything else of size? The flies used for fishing are *big* in the West. Especially the giant stone or salmon fly that is so eagerly awaited each summer. I bought several imitations at the endorsed fly shop and was hardly able to fit them into my fly box. I became convinced of their use when I witnessed the hatch later, on the Madison River. At first I believed the hatch to be birds, or possibly bats coming out to feed on insects, they were so large. A nearby fisherman handed me a fly he had tied to imitate the *Pteronarcys californica*, a finely tied fly and nearly indistinguishable from the actual insect. The fisherman was a retired geologist who began his trip in Maine and was fishing his way up to a remote lake in British Columbia. I caught several fine 20-inch rainbows and browns with those 3-inch flies on the Madison.

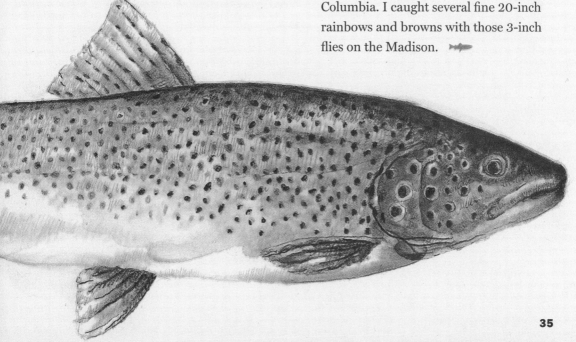

Smoked Shad Roe–Potato Balls

These roe and potato balls make a good appetizer or an interesting side with eggs at a Sunday-afternoon brunch.

½ smoked small shad roe, about ½ pound (see Smoked Shad Roe on page 101 for instructions)

2 cups mashed potatoes

1 egg

¼ cup fresh thyme, stemmed

3 tablespoons melted butter

1 teaspoon salt

1 teaspoon freshly ground black pepper

3 tablespoons vegetable oil

Romesco Sauce (see page 230) for serving (optional)

Horseradish Sauce (see page 229) for serving (optional)

ADVANCE PREPARATION:

Smoke shad roe

1. Pulse the shad roe, potatoes, egg, thyme, butter, salt, and pepper five or six times, or until thoroughly blended, in the bowl of a food processor. Scrape down the sides and transfer the mixture to a plate.

2. With your hands, form the mixture into balls about 1½ inches in diameter. Set aside.

3. Heat the oil for 1 minute in a large skillet or wok over medium-high heat. Carefully lower the balls into the oil with a spoon. Roll them around until all sides are browned, 3 to 5 minutes.

4. Remove and blot on paper towels. Serve immediately with Romesco Sauce or Horseradish Sauce, if using.

MAKES 12-15 BALLS

To Drink

Chilled mimosas or orange juice with seltzer and freshly squeezed lime

Smoked Whitefish
with Stir-Fried Shiitakes and Green Tomatoes

In early summer, before the tomatoes ripen and they are still green, pick a few for this recipe. Their tangy sourness adds diversity, balanced against the soy and oyster sauces.

You will need to smoke the fish beforehand and keep it refrigerated. To smoke whitefish, follow the directions for smoking lake trout on page 52. Remove it from the refrigerator an hour before flaking and add the flaked fish to the wok at the last minute, stirring gently so it does not break into smaller pieces.

1   tablespoon olive oil

2½ cups sliced shiitake mushrooms

¾   cup asparagus tips

¾   cup coarsely chopped green tomato

½   sweet white onion, coarsely chopped

4   garlic cloves, finely chopped

2   tablespoons unsalted butter

2   tablespoons orange flower water

1   tablespoon oyster sauce

1   tablespoon low-sodium soy sauce

1   teaspoon coarsely ground black pepper

¾   pound smoked whitefish, flaked into bite-size pieces

½   pound pasta, cooked and drained

1. Heat the oil in a wok, then sauté the mushrooms, asparagus, tomato, onion, and garlic for 4 minutes, until thoroughly heated.

2. Add the butter, flower water, oyster sauce, soy sauce, and pepper. Continue sautéing for 4 to 5 minutes, or until hot. Add the smoked fish pieces and toss thoroughly.

3. Ladle over the pasta.

SERVES 4 AS AN APPETIZER OR 2-3 AS A MAIN COURSE

ADVANCE PREPARATION:
Smoke whitefish

Smoked Salmon Pizza
with Mixed Wild Mushrooms

Choose whatever mushrooms you find, even morels. Shaggy manes would not be a good choice, because they cook down into a black liquid. Portobellos or criminis will work if you do not have access to wild mushrooms. This dish is great with a simple green salad.

4 tablespoons olive oil

½ pound wild mushrooms (shiitake, oyster, horse, or boletus), sliced

4–6 scallions, all but ½ inch of tops, finely chopped

3–4 garlic cloves, finely chopped

2 tablespoons fresh thyme, stemmed and chopped, plus 6 sprigs

Dough for a 12-inch pizza (see page 39), or purchased dough

2 small ripe tomatoes, sliced into rounds

Salt and freshly ground black pepper

8 ounces Smoked Salmon (see page 112)

2 cups shredded mozzarella

½ cup grated Asiago

1. In 2 tablespoons of the oil, sauté the mushrooms, scallions, garlic, and the 2 tablespoons of thyme in a medium-sized saucepan over medium-high heat for 6 to 8 minutes. Remove from heat and set aside.

2. Preheat a grill.

3. On a cutting board sprinkled with flour and cornmeal, roll out the dough into a thin, 12-inch circle and pinch the edges all around. Transfer to a perforated pizza pan.

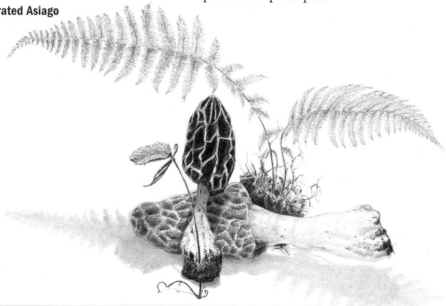

4. Lay the tomatoes on the dough and top with the mushroom sauté. Evenly spread, in order, the six sprigs of thyme, salt and pepper to taste, salmon, and cheeses over the top.

5. Transfer the pan to the grill. Turn down the heat, or, if using charcoal, set the pan away from the direct heat. Close the lid. Cook for 10 to 12 minutes but check several times, especially if using charcoal, which cooks much faster than gas. Tip up the edge of the dough to see if it has become slightly browned.

6. Move the pan to the warming shelf, close the lid, and cook for an additional 5 minutes, or until the cheeses are melted. Total cooking time should not be more than 20 minutes, but could be less.

7. Transfer to a cutting board, slice, and serve immediately.

MAKES ONE 12-INCH PIZZA

Non-Rising Pizza Dough

This dough does not need time to rise, so it is perfect for those unexpected occasions when friends stop by. This dough will be crispy and crunchy. Remember not to use baking soda; use baking *powder*.

1¾ cups all-purpose flour
2 tablespoons baking powder
1 teaspoon salt
⅔ cup water
⅓ cup olive oil
Handful of flour and cornmeal mix (about ¼ cup of each)

1. Combine the flour, baking powder, and salt in a large mixing bowl. Add the water and drizzle in the oil. Mix thoroughly.

2. Sprinkle a cutting board with the flour and cornmeal mixture and place the dough on it. Knead for 3 to 4 minutes, forming a ball, and roll out into an ⅛-inch-thick circle. Crimp the edges and fill with your favorite ingredients.

3. Bake or grill according to the recipe instructions.

MAKES DOUGH FOR ONE
12-INCH PIZZA

Gravad and Smoked Salmon
with Cilantro-Mint Rub

Gravlax is salmon; *lax* is *gravad* (cured in sugar, salt, and dill and pressed down with weights). I've elaborated on a tradition by using cilantro and mint and then mildly smoking the salmon. If you choose to stick with tradition, you need not smoke the salmon — simply cure it for up to 3 days in the refrigerator.

Serve with Dill Mustard Sauce, although a friend, after tasting the salmon, said it didn't need the sauce — it was delicious as it was.

Allow enough time to cure the salmon, overnight or at least 12 hours.

1   **small lime, washed and halved**

4   **cups loosely packed cilantro, stemmed**

1   **cup light brown sugar**

¾   **cup finely chopped mint leaves**

¼   **cup coarse salt**

1   **teaspoon cayenne pepper**

¼   **cup tequila (add to marinade, optional)**

2–3 pounds salmon fillet

Dill Mustard Sauce (see page 231)

Pumpernickel or rye bread, cut into small squares

Chopped dill for garnish

Finely chopped red peppers for garnish

Lemon wedges for garnish

1. Pulse the lime, cilantro, sugar, mint, salt, cayenne, and tequila if using in the bowl of a food processor for 30 seconds. Scrape down the sides with a spatula and pulse 1 minute longer.

2. Lay the salmon skin-side down on a piece of plastic wrap. With a spatula, cover the fillet thoroughly with the rub. Wrap tightly in three layers of plastic wrap. Place on a flat plate or baking dish, weight the fillet down with one or two clean, foil-wrapped bricks or large soup cans, and refrigerate 12 hours, turning once. The fillet will expel liquid, so you may need to drain once.

3. Preheat a grill for smoke grilling.

4. Remove the salmon from the refrigerator and unwrap. Lay the fillet on an oiled grill over the smoke pan for 1 hour. Transfer the fillet to the cool side of the grill. Smoke for 1 hour longer or up to 3 hours, depending on your preference for intensity of smoke.

5. Remove the fillet from the heat, slice, and serve with the Dill Mustard Sauce on the bread squares. Garnish with the chopped dill, red peppers, and lemon wedges.

SERVES 12-15

Smoked Gravlax
with an Orange-Dill Rub

As with the recipe for Gravad and Smoked Salmon with Cilantro-Mint Rub, you may choose to ignore the smoking process, cure the salmon in the refrigerator for up to 3 days, and serve as a somewhat traditional gravlax — that is, cured only, *not* smoked. But if you want to try a somewhat untraditional Scandinavian twist to gravlax, continue on.

Be sure to give yourself enough time to cure the salmon when preparing this recipe; you'll want to do it overnight, or for at least 12 hours.

---

1 **cup loosely packed dill, cleaned and stemmed**

1 **medium orange, washed, chunked, and seeded**

⅓ **cup apple cider**

⅓ **cup triple sec (or orange-flavored liqueur)**

2 **to 3 pounds salmon fillets**

Pumpernickel or rye bread, cut into squares

Dill Mustard Sauce (see page 231)

Chopped dill for garnish

Finely chopped red peppers for garnish

Lemon wedges for garnish

1. Pulse the dill, orange, cider, and triple sec in the bowl of a food processor for 30 seconds. Scrape down the sides with a spatula and pulse an additional 30 seconds.

2. Lay the salmon skin-side down on a piece of plastic wrap. With a spatula, cover the fillet thoroughly with the orange rub. Wrap tightly in three layers of plastic wrap. Place on a flat plate or baking dish weighted down with one or two clean, foil-wrapped bricks or large soup cans, and refrigerate at least 12 hours or up to 3 days, turning once a day. The fillet will expel liquid, so you may need to drain off the excess.

3. Preheat a grill for smoke grilling.

4. Remove the salmon from the refrigerator and unwrap.

5. Lay the fillet on an oiled grill over the smoke pan for 1 hour. With two spatulas, carefully transfer the fillet to the cool side of the grill. Smoke for 1 hour longer or up to 3 hours, depending on your preference for intensity of smoke.

6. Remove from the heat and slice. Place on bread squares with the Dill Mustard Sauce, garnish with the chopped dill, red peppers, and lemon wedges, and serve.

SERVES 12–15

Smoked Sable

Sable is also known as black cod. It's a fish I find highly underappreciated. It is not related at all to Atlantic cod, but is found instead in Pacific waters.

The first time I visited a New York City fish market, I tasted smoked sable and instantly wanted to move to New York. I didn't, but if you follow this recipe, you might well imagine the hustle and bustle of such a fish market and all its edible smoked treasures.

This is hot-smoked over corn on a grill, easily, simply. The smoked, slightly cooled fish may not slice as much as it will break apart. People won't mind once they taste the flavor. It will keep refrigerated for up to 1 week.

2   **pounds sable or black cod fillets**

2   **tablespoons good-quality extra-virgin olive oil**

1   **teaspoon sea salt**

2   **tablespoons freshly ground black pepper**

Lemon wedges

Dill Mustard Sauce (see page 231)

METHOD: Smoke grilling

1. Brush the fillets with the olive oil and season both sides with the salt and pepper. Set aside.

2. Preheat a grill for smoke grilling.

3. Lay the fillets on the cool side of the grill. Close the lid and smoke for 1 to 1½ hours, or until fillets are firm to the touch; do not turn. Lift the lid only occasionally to check for unwanted flames. Douse with water if necessary.

4. Remove the smoked fillets and let cool for about ½ hour; slice or break apart into bite-size pieces.

5. Serve with the lemon wedges and Dill Mustard Sauce.

SERVES 8–10 AS AN APPETIZER

Coffeepots, Scrimshaw, and . . . Help!

"Yet do I hold that mortal foolish who strives against the stress of necessity."

Euripides, 485–430 B.C.E.

WE WERE TO BE FIVE, fishermen all, driving north to Lake Umbagog at various times over several days, having agreed to meet at a specified boat launch in New Hampshire. The only way to our remote rented cabin was by boat. Two friends were to pick me up at the launch on a Monday in September, having arrived earlier in the week.

I promptly loaded my gear on board, sipped hot coffee from a thermos, and off we motored, away from the shores of New Hampshire to cross into Maine waters for a weeklong fishing trip.

After 3 restful days, two friends would cross the lake, planning to return later that same day. I wished them well, shouting a lighthearted call from the dock: "Don't forget to come back, y'hear?"

Wait just a minute. Come back? And what if . . . they didn't? We had teased each other about the vast quantity of food we had packed, "enough until ice out next spring, ha, ha," I had joked the night before over caribou stew and fig salad.

I sat down on the dock, looking out over the tea-colored Rapid River to the east. A trail lined the shore of the land-locked salmon-filled river (it would prove not to live up to its reputation as a quality fishery). But where was the trail? An old logging road was indicated on a topo map in the cabin, but there had been mention of it being heavily over-grown. Perhaps I should take inventory of my life as it stands. Now.

The rustic 1920s cabin held a sufficient level of potable lake water in a holding tank, but what about after the lake froze? Two tanks of propane were the primary source for cooking and light; I had only two extra batteries for my flashlight.

Food? Did I really have enough until May, 7 months away? Visions of Farley Mowat's *Never Cry Wolf* came to mind, a novel about a greenhorn Canadian biologist who resorted to eating mice in order to survive the winter wilderness until he was to be picked up by plane the following spring. Earlier, I had noticed several mousetraps scattered throughout the cabin but it hadn't even occurred to me they could be used as culinary implements.

The diminished salmon fishery would be of little help, a historically reliable food source from which to salt, dry, and smoke fish in preparation for upcoming lean winter months. There was an abundance of moose in the region but I had only a fishing rod, which seemed of little help as a weapon, puny, dull, and weakly flexible, certainly not intended for use as a saber. The *Bangor Daily News* spring headline might read: "Fishing-Rod-Wielding Man Against Beast Found in Wilderness!"

I also had no cell phone, which would have been useless anyway because of the surrounding mountains. Another recourse might be to wrench open a link of chain securing the two boats and canoe together but . . . no paddles or oars were to be found. The owner had locked them up or taken them with him.

I was getting hungry. I looked around and remembered the many wild mushrooms I had spotted in the woods, everywhere. Except I had left my field identification books in the trunk of my car, on the far side of the lake. Many of what I stepped around were new to me, being in a different climate and terrain and a higher latitude. I would never take a chance, considering the closest EMTs were likely a 30-minute boat ride away. If I had a boat. Perhaps the psychotropic mushrooms could help idle away the time. I needed to examine the cabin's stores.

Several quarts of milk nearly filled the gas-fired refrigerator, but dairy would not last long. Nor would the fresh vegetables. A dozen eggs: less than a week's worth of omelets. In the pantry was a quantity of rice, good; dried beans, good; plenty of cookware including ten, count 'em, ten, coffeepots. Ten coffeepots? Aluminum coffeepots seemed somewhat akin to the planeload of lightbulbs Mowat was left with, destined for, oddly enough, Canadian Inuits. Maybe I should consider bartering with local Native Americans wandering the Maine forest, trading coffeepots for jerky, broccoli for blankets.

The two-hole outhouse was sufficiently snug and close by, and someone had thoughtfully left approximately 2 months' worth of firewood. No ax was to be found, however, and I guessed my hunting knife would not suffice for splitting logs. Perhaps the moose ribs I found

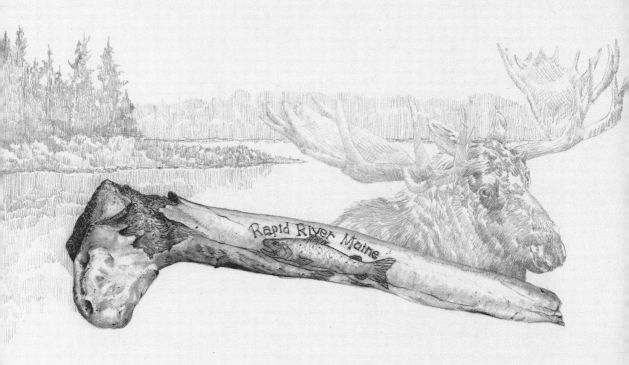

out back could serve as bone tools. Each edge was slightly tapered, the tibia or fibula forming a ready-made handle. Or possibly I could carve an atlatl, a Paleo-Indian spear-throwing device, with which to hunt moose, or spruce grouse, similar to the fat specimens I had chased up hiking the previous day. My stomach growled in anticipation of smoked fish, er, grouse, swathed in fruit chutney.

I decided to bake corn muffins and make coffee, selecting a 2-cup percolator rather than the crowd-pleasing 4-*gallon* enameled pot hanging from the ceiling. (Apparently these locals are serious coffee drinkers.) I sat down on the Adirondack-style porch in an

Adirondack-style rocker and picked up one of the moose ribs to scrape down in preparation for a morning of scrimshaw. Soon, watching two bald eagles soar overhead and hearing moose bellow nearby, I had etched an image of a fish on the polished rib bone, lettering "Rapid River, Maine" above it. I considered scratching "1805 A.D." on the back and throwing it into the forest, just for fun.

About mid-afternoon, I saw the boat in the distance, returning with more food and two friends. I knew all along they'd come back. Worried? Not me. I had food and art and craft supplies to last until ice out. 🐟

Chapter 3

Freshwater Fish

I HAD A GREAT UNCLE, my mother's uncle John, who took me fishing in his boat when I was a child. I loved him for it and for his gentle ways. (Even when, as a ten year old, I had to haul the motor to the boat.) He taught me to fish with one important ingredient: patience. We sat for hours in the hot sun angling with minnows for crappie, rock bass, walleye and, of course, sunnies, which he loved best. (Adults may too soon forget what might seem an insignificant gesture toward a child may very well result in lifelong memories.) I have never forgotten uncle John's tutelage, of good kid stuff, things children should possess forever.

Often, while I'm sitting in a boat or sautéing freshly caught fish, I think of the times we fished outside Minneapolis, coming home to eat our catch with Aunt Mary, then going out to the workshop to carve figures from old wooden vegetable crates: ducks, geese, bas-relief pheasants, and fish, which I never quite graduated to because John died before he got around to showing me how. I always look forward to eating freshwater fish, and remembering my uncle John.

Catfish
Wrapped in Collard Greens

The leaves of fresh collards measure approximately nine inches across, perfect for wrapping fish. By placing the greens into boiling water for about a minute and a half, then plunging them into cold water, you will retain their bright green color. Use a perforated pizza pan or grill wok.

8   blanched collard leaves

1   tomato, diced

1   cup seeded and sliced kalamata olives

6   scallions, finely chopped

4–6 garlic cloves, minced

1   tablespoon olive oil

Salt and freshly ground black pepper

4   catfish fillets, 8 ounces each

Lemon wedges for garnish

Cooked brown rice

ADVANCE PREPARATION:
Blanch collard leaves

1. Preheat a grill.

2. Lay four of the collard leaves on a work surface. Sprinkle half the tomato, olives, scallions, garlic, and oil and salt and pepper to taste on each leaf.

3. Place one fillet on top of each leaf; sprinkle the remaining ingredients (including more salt and pepper, if desired) over all.

4. Top each assemblage with the remaining four greens and secure tightly with toothpicks.

5. Place in an oiled perforated pizza pan, set the pan on the grill, and lower the lid. Grill for 6 to 7 minutes. Gently turn over with a spatula and grill for 4 to 5 minutes longer, until slightly browned.

6. Place one pocket on each of four plates. Remove the toothpicks before garnishing with the lemon wedges. Serve with brown rice.

SERVES 4

Sunnies Dijon

Sunfish, crappie, pumpkinseed, and bluegill — pond and lake fishers know them as a sweetwater treat. They are small after filleting (a whole fish rarely weighs a pound), so you will need several per person.

¼ cup mayonnaise

2 tablespoons spicy yellow mustard

Juice of ½ lemon (about 1½ tablespoons)

¼ cup cornmeal

1 teaspoon finely chopped fresh tarragon

1 tablespoon cracked black peppercorns

2–3 pounds sunfish fillets

Serve with Spinach Salad with Cider Vinaigrette (see below).

1. Preheat a grill.

2. Mix the mayonnaise, mustard, lemon juice, cornmeal, tarragon, and peppercorns in a large bowl.

3. Dip the fillets in the mixture until they are thoroughly coated.

4. Place the fillets on the grill and lower the heat to medium, if possible. Close the lid and cook for 6 to 8 minutes. Turn and cook 4 to 5 minutes longer, until cornmeal is slightly charred. Serve immediately.

SERVES 4

Spinach Salad with Cider Vinaigrette

For the vinaigrette:

2 tablespoons apple cider vinegar

1½ tablespoons minced fresh tarragon

1 tablespoon Dijon mustard

1 teaspoon honey

¼ cup olive oil

Salt and freshly ground black pepper

For the salad:

4 cups baby spinach leaves (packed)

1 tart apple, peeled, cored, and thinly sliced

1 cup toasted walnuts (see page 168)

1. To make the vinaigrette, combine the vinegar, tarragon, mustard, and honey in a small bowl.

2. Add the olive oil and whisk until well blended. Season to taste with the salt and pepper.

3. To make the salad, toss the spinach and apples in a large bowl. Drizzle with the vinaigrette.

4. Top the salad with the toasted walnuts, and serve immediately.

SERVES 4

Grilled Butterflied Trout

A 2-pound fish, once boned, will easily serve two people. One small butterflied brook trout will serve one person. To butterfly the fish, cut off the head and tail, remove all the bones, open it up, and lay it flat like a book. You can use any whole fish you like, including small- or largemouth bass.

You should use a fish basket for this recipe, but you can get by with two large spatulas for turning if you have to; don't forget to oil the basket and the grates before grilling.

3   tablespoons peanut oil

1   cup thinly sliced shiitake or oyster mushrooms

6–8 garlic cloves, finely chopped

1–2 serrano chiles, seeded, deveined, finely chopped

1   cup shredded white cabbage

1   small carrot, peeled and julienned

½   cup fish or chicken stock

¼   cup low-sodium soy sauce

Juice of 1 lemon (about 3 tablespoons)

1   butterflied trout (2 pounds)

1   teaspoon fresh oregano

1   teaspoon salt

1   teaspoon freshly ground black pepper

Cooked white rice

1. Preheat a grill.

2. Heat 2 tablespoons of the oil in a large skillet or wok over medium-high heat. Stir-fry the mushrooms, garlic, and chiles for 3 to 4 minutes; add the cabbage and carrot, and stir-fry 4 to 5 minutes longer, until the vegetables are thoroughly heated.

3. Pour in the stock and reduce by one third, about 5 minutes. Add the soy sauce, stir, and reduce heat to low to keep warm.

4. Drizzle the remaining 1 tablespoon of oil and the lemon juice over the butterflied fish and season with the oregano and the salt and pepper.

5. Secure the seasoned fish inside a wire-mesh basket. Lay the basket on the grill and cook for 4 to 5 minutes; turn and cook 5 minutes longer, or until the meat is opaque.

6. Remove fish from the basket, divide it into two servings, and spoon the warming sauce on top. Serve immediately with the white rice.

SERVES 2

Steelhead Trout
in Red Wine Sauce

You can substitute two rainbow trout if you have not been fortunate enough to hook into a steelhead (which is after all, a rainbow trout) from Salmon River in Pulaski, New York, in the dead of winter.

A large roasting pan is helpful for this recipe but a large skillet (big enough to hold a whole fish) will work as well.

If you wish, you may fillet the fish for ease of handling. If you do this, however, decrease the grilling and warming time by at least half.

---

2 tablespoons olive oil

1 small stalk celery, finely chopped

1 small leek, white part only, cleaned and finely chopped

1 small green bell pepper, seeded and finely chopped

½ pound mushrooms (oyster, shiitake, or boletus)

1 cup Beaujolais or other hearty red wine

6 tablespoons fresh oregano, finely chopped

6 tablespoons fresh thyme, stemmed and finely chopped

1 teaspoon tomato paste

1 whole steelhead trout (3 to 4 pounds)

1 cup heavy cream

1 teaspoon salt

2 teaspoons coarsely ground black pepper

Lemon wedges

Serve with couscous and plenty of good bread to soak up the juices.

---

1. Preheat a grill.

2. Heat the oil in a roasting pan or large skillet over medium-high heat, then add the celery, leek, bell pepper, and mushrooms. Stir and simmer for about 15 minutes.

3. Add the wine, 2 tablespoons of the oregano, 2 tablespoons of the thyme, and the tomato paste. Reduce by half, 10 to 12 minutes. Remove from the heat, cover, and set aside.

4. With a brush or cooking spray, coat the trout evenly with some oil and place on an oiled grill. Close the lid and cook for 8 to 10 minutes. With two spatulas, carefully turn the trout and cook 6 to 8 minutes longer, until the fish is firm to the touch.

5. Meanwhile, return the red wine sauce to the burner over medium heat. Add the cream and stir frequently to prevent burning. Reduce the liquid by about one third; this should take 15 minutes or so.

6. Transfer the fish to the pan of red wine sauce and coat the trout with the sauce. Cover and simmer over low heat for about 5 minutes, until thoroughly heated. Sprinkle the remaining oregano and thyme and the salt and pepper over the top and transfer to a serving platter.

7. Debone the fish and divide onto plates. Serve with the lemon wedges.

SERVES 4

Grilled Freshwater Perch
with Blood Orange Salad

For this refreshing lunch dish, you could substitute any small freshwater game fish for the perch.

2 pounds perch fillets (4 to 8 fillets, depending on size)

Juice of ½ orange (about 4 tablespoons)

1 tablespoon pure maple syrup

½ teaspoon sea salt

Chopped scallions for garnish

Blood Orange Salad (see page 224)

Cooked bulgur or pearl barley

ADVANCE PREPARATION:
Marinate fish for 30 minutes

1. Combine the fillets, orange juice, maple syrup, and salt in a container. Cover and refrigerate for 30 minutes.

2. Preheat a grill.

3. Remove the fillets from the container, pat dry, and place on an oiled grill. Cook for 3 to 4 minutes. Turn over and cook 4 minutes longer, or until the fillets are firm to the touch.

4. Garnish with scallions. Serve immediately with Blood Orange Salad and bulgur.

SERVES 4

Smoked Lake Trout
with Olive-Mustard Sauce

Lake trout are particularly fatty fish, especially the "fats" that live at depths close to 400 feet in the Great Lakes. The species that lives nearer the surface has less fat and is better suited for the following recipe. Serve with a good crusty bread to sop up the sauce and a tossed green salad.

1–2 pounds lake trout fillets

1   tablespoon olive oil

1   medium onion, coarsely chopped

½   small tomato, diced

½   cup Gaeta or kalamata olives, pitted and halved

½   cup dry white wine

¼   cup fresh thyme, finely chopped

2   tablespoons Dijon mustard

1   teaspoon fresh oregano, finely chopped

1   teaspoon freshly ground black pepper

Lemon wedges

METHOD: Smoke grilling

1. Prepare a grill for smoke grilling.

2. Lay the fillets on the cool side of the smoker. Close the lid and smoke for about 45 minutes. Turn and continue smoking 45 minutes longer, or until the flesh is firm to the touch.

3. Turn off the heat, place the fillets on the top warming shelf in the grill, and close the lid.

4. To make the sauce, in the oil, sauté onion, tomato, and olives in a large, uncovered saucepan over medium heat for 4 to 5 minutes. Stir.

5. Slowly add the wine, thyme, mustard, oregano, and pepper. Stir and simmer, uncovered, for 4 to 5 minutes, or until reduced by half.

6. Divide the trout into four pieces; lay on warm plates and spoon sauce on the side. Serve with the lemon wedges.

SERVES 4

Grilled Smallmouth Bass
Wrapped in Cornhusks

This technique is best when corn is just coming in, during midsummer. Slice off the corn and use the green husks for wrapping. Don't be alarmed when the cornhusks become charred — they should.

The use of fresh cornhusks will help moisturize the "wraps." If you need to use dried husks, found in Mexican markets for use in making tamales, soak them in water for about 30 minutes before using. But for this recipe, freshly picked is best.

2 **ears fresh corn**
2 **pounds smallmouth bass fillets, cut into four pieces**
4 **tablespoons unsalted butter, cut into chunks**
Juice of 1 lemon (about 3 tablespoons)
Salt and freshly ground black pepper
Lemon wedges

1. Preheat the grill.

2. Carefully peel away the cornhusks and set aside. Pull all silk off each cob.

3. Holding the cobs upright, slice downward with a sharp knife, cutting off the corn in rows. Discard the cobs and set the cut corn aside.

4. Spread out and press flat two or three husks per fillet. Sprinkle a layer of corn on the leaves and lay a fillet at right angles to the husks, one on top of each "packet."

5. Cover the fillets with the remaining corn. Dot the corn with the chunks of butter.

6. Sprinkle the lemon juice over each fillet and season with salt and pepper.

7. Fold the husks over the top of the packets on all sides (to form an envelope shape) and secure with toothpicks.

8. Lay on the grill for about 6 minutes; turn carefully with a spatula and cook 6 minutes longer, or until husks are slightly charred.

9. Serve immediately with the lemon wedges.

SERVES 4

Grilled Walleye
with Grapes and Shaggy Mane Mushrooms

I consider walleye, a member of the perch family, the king of sweetwater, as do many people in the Midwest and near the southern waters of Canada.

Don't be put off by the pitch-black color that appears when shaggy manes cook down. They add a dramatic background to the white of the walleye. Lay the fish on top of the sauce so it appears afloat in a black sea.

1½ to 2 pounds walleye fillets

2½ cups shaggy manes, cleaned and sliced, (6 to 8 mushrooms; you may substitute oyster or shiitake mushrooms)

½ cup frozen white grape juice

½ cup orange-flavored liqueur

4 tablespoons unsalted butter (½ stick)

1 cup globe (or black) grapes, sliced in half

2 tablespoons freshly ground black pepper

Zest of 1 orange (1 to 2 tablespoons) for garnish

METHOD: Grilling

Serve with short-grained white rice and steamed asparagus with slivered almonds.

1. Preheat a grill.

2. Brush the grill and skin side of the fillets with oil. Cook the fillets for 4 to 5 minutes. Turn and cook 3 to 4 minutes longer, or until flesh is firm to the touch. Transfer to the warming shelf and keep warm.

3. Meanwhile, to make the sauce, sauté the mushrooms in the butter in a non-reactive saucepan until the mushrooms are soft. Add the grape juice and the liqueur. Turn up the heat to medium-high and cook for 5 to 6 minutes, or until the liquid is reduced by about one third.

4. Add the grapes and pepper and ½ of the zest and toss for 1 to 2 minutes.

5. Divide the walleye into four pieces. Ladle the sauce onto four plates and lay the fillets on top.

6. Garnish with the rest of the orange zest and serve immediately.

SERVES 4

Wild Mushroom Caution

In spite of scary, sometimes unattractive names for *eumycota,* wild mushrooms have been relished for centuries and across continents. Spring and fall are good times for finding quality specimens. But never rely upon guesswork when picking and eating wild fungi.

With all due caution, one should respect something that can be potentially harmful. Some foods — nuts, berries, plants, dairy products, and so on — can cause allergic reactions in some people. One should not be casual about ingesting foods of the wild. Indeed, I once kept wild mushrooms in my refrigerator that I skirted around for several days, trying to identify them through various guidebooks and spore prints. After some deliberation, checking reference books, and deciding that they were ultimately safe, I sautéed one, eating a very small sample before finally consuming them all.

A mycologist friend once told me, quite straight-faced, that when one eats wild mushrooms, one should always leave a small piece on the kitchen counter. Stupid, I inquired why. So the hospital can confirm the cause of death, he said joking. Relating that particular anecdote to another hunter/gatherer, he said that whenever he and his wife eat wild mushrooms, they leave a note on the counter that simply states: "We ate mushrooms."

Go, seek fresh wild mushrooms. With caution.

Smoked Puffballs

Puffballs are a wild, porous mushroom, making them likely candidates for absorbing smoke. The final result is a loamy, earthy aroma with just a hint of the flavor of corn or whatever wood is used: maple, grapevines, sassafras, fruitwood.

Puffball mushrooms

1. Prepare a grill for smoke grilling.

2. Slice the puffballs into pieces ½ inch thick and 2 to 3 inches long.

3. Lay them on the cool side of the smoker. Smoke for about 1 hour, or until lightly browned and dried, turning once about halfway through.

4. Store in an airtight container at room temperature for up to 1 year. Reconstitute following the instructions on page 58 and use in tomato sauces or soups.

Smoked Walleye
with a Dried Mushroom–Pumpkin Seed Rub

This recipe is simple to make; prep time is about 10 minutes. But first you must dry mushrooms, or buy them, and toast pumpkin seeds. If you take the time to do this a day or so ahead, the last-minute preparation consists of merely rubbing the pulverized mix into the flesh of a fillet and then smoke grilling it. Serve with Ratatouille (see page 221) and a green salad.

¾ cup toasted pumpkin seeds (see page 168)

½ cup dried mushrooms (see page 58)

¼ cup olive oil

1 teaspoon sea salt

1 teaspoon freshly ground black pepper

1½ pounds walleye fillets

Juice of ⅓ lemon (about 1 tablespoon)

Lemon wedges

METHOD: Smoke grilling

1. Prepare grill for smoke grilling.

2. In the bowl of a food processor, pulse the pumpkin seeds, mushrooms, oil, and salt and pepper six to eight times, or until thoroughly blended. Set aside.

3. Brush or spray oil on the underside skin of the fillets and lay them on a cutting board. Drizzle the fillets with the lemon juice. Using your hands or a rubber spatula, press the rub into the flesh of the fillets, covering all surfaces.

4. Gently lay the fillets on the cool side of an oiled grill. Close the lid and smoke for 1 to 1½ hours without turning, until the fillets are firm to the touch. Lift the lid only to check for unwanted flames.

5. Divide the fillets onto four plates and serve with the lemon wedges.

SERVES 4

VARIATION Mix the rub with yogurt and use as a dip, or mix with aged goat cheese, tomato paste, or just about anything else you find appealing.

Smoked Burbot
with Wild Mushroom, Plum & Mint Sauce

You will need to plan ahead by smoking the burbot and keeping it refrigerated, or plan carefully to end the smoking just before preparing the sauce. Remove the burbot from the refrigerator an hour before using.

Initially, I used wild horse mushrooms for this recipe, but white-button mushrooms also work well.

Burbot, sometimes called ling, is similar to cod or monkfish in its consistency. Those fishers fortunate enough to catch burbot (they are rarely found in fish markets) love them. Serve with brown rice.

2½ cups wild mushrooms, cleaned and stemmed

1¾ cups black plums, seeded and sliced (4–5 medium plums)

1 cup fresh mint, coarsely chopped

4 tablespoons butter (½ stick)

¼ cup apple cider

¼ cup tawny port

Salt and freshly ground black pepper

1 pound smoked burbot fillet

Cooked brown rice

ADVANCE PREPARATION:
Smoke the burbot

1. Sauté the mushrooms, plums, and mint in the butter for 3 to 4 minutes in a non-reactive saucepan over medium-high heat.

2. Add the cider, port, and salt and pepper to taste and sauté 4 to 5 minutes, or until the liquid is reduced by one third.

3. Add the smoked burbot, turn the heat to low, and simmer for about 5 minutes, until the fish is thoroughly coated.

4. Remove the burbot from the pan, divide it into four servings, and serve immediately with the brown rice.

SERVES 4

Drying and Reconstituting Mushrooms

YOU MAY DRY ANY MUSHROOMS, commercial or wild, even those forgotten in the refrigerator for days. I bought shiitakes from a local mushroom grower but had not used them. A week later I looked inside the bag and found them nearly dried.

I grabbed the nearest container with perforated sides and bottom to allow for the circulation of air. The inside of my salad spinner was perfect. I set it out on my porch in the sun for 2 days. They finished drying quite nicely and I used them in a soup. A strainer or colander would also have been suitable.

When I dry mushrooms correctly, I use the following method. Cut mushrooms into slices as thin as possible; they will dry quicker and take less time to reconstitute. The exceptions are the extremely small specimens, such as young morels and black trumpets, which you can hardly see against the dark ground in the first place; leave them whole. Shelf mushrooms, such as chicken of the woods, need to be very thinly sliced.

How to Make a Screen for Drying Mushrooms

To make a screen 24 inches by 30 inches, nail together four 1-inch by 2-inch pieces of pine and then staple a piece of window screen (available at any hardware store) over the frame. I've had my screen for years and it works fine. An old house screen might also work if it is first cleaned thoroughly.

Spread your mushrooms on top of a screen (see sidebar), leaving space between each piece to allow air to circulate. Simple as pie. They will diminish in size but many mushrooms become more potent in flavor.

Mushrooms are best dried in the open sun, but you need to keep watch for insects or a neighbor's curious cat. To avoid problems if I can't keep constant vigilance, I straddle the mushroom-filled screens across the backs of two chairs facing apart on my screened-in porch and position them toward the sun, sometimes following the course of the sun throughout the day by moving the chairs.

In most cases, 2 to 3 days is enough to thoroughly dry thinly sliced mushrooms. To expedite the process, turn on a fan and face it toward the mushrooms for several hours.

During fall and winter months, I make good use of the pilot light in my gas oven. I have a commercial range and know the pilot light is higher and hotter than most households need, heating up my kitchen in summer months *too* high for my comfort. But it's perfect for drying mushrooms, keeping a consistent 100 degrees. (It's also great for drying cherry tomatoes, split in half and drizzled with olive oil and herbs.) I once spread a basket of fall brown oyster mushrooms on a baking sheet in the evening and by the next morning, they were perfectly dried.

Transfer the dried mushrooms to a plastic or glass container you can seal tightly; zipper-lock bags are especially good because you can squeeze the air out of them, thus taking up less space in the pantry. No need for refrigeration. I've kept dried mushrooms for up to a year.

I'm constantly hanging larger specimens from the chestnut beams that line my living room around the ceiling, intermixed with the bamboo fly rod, stuffed lake trout, dried bittersweet vines, and various other dust collectors. (If you do this, dust off the dried mushrooms in the spring before you reconstitute them.)

To reconstitute dried mushrooms, simply immerse them in a liquid for 20 minutes to an hour, depending upon the density of the mushroom. You may use water or dry or sweet sherry or port for a more robust soak — say, when making a sauce. Also, red or white wine is fine; I've used stale beer, milk, or cream (again in anticipation of a particular sauce). The limits are boundless when you know that all you're really doing is returning the moisture — most of a fungi's composition — that was lost to drying.

Smoked Walleye
with Red Pepper Sauce

To simplify your tasks, prepare the red peppers ahead; they will keep refrigerated for several days. When you are ready, take them out of the refrigerator 1 hour ahead and finish with the following recipe.

1½ pounds walleye fillets

6 ounces (½ bottle) beer

¼ cup fresh basil, coarsely chopped, plus more for garnish

½ teaspoon sea salt

1 tablespoon coarsely ground black pepper

2 cups Roasted Red Peppers (see below)

¼ cup fish or chicken stock

2 tablespoons port wine

Chopped fresh red bell peppers for garnish

ADVANCE PREPARATION:
Marinate fish for 1 hour

1. Place the fillets, beer, basil, salt, and pepper in a plastic or glass container. Cover and refrigerate for 1 hour.

2. Prepare a grill for smoke grilling.

3. In the bowl of a food processor, add red peppers, stock, and wine. Pulse four or five times. Scrape down the sides with a spatula and purée.

4. Transfer the mixture to a 2-quart saucepan and simmer over medium heat for about 15 minutes, or until reduced by about one third. Remove the saucepan from direct heat but keep it warm.

Roasted Red Peppers

4 large red bell peppers

¼ cup fresh basil, coarsely chopped

2 tablespoons extra-virgin olive oil

1 teaspoon sea salt

Freshly ground pink peppercorns

1. Preheat a grill.

2. Lay the peppers directly over high heat until they become entirely blackened on all sides, about 10 minutes. Rotate them continuously while cooking.

3. Cut off the stems and lay the peppers flat on a cutting board. Scrape or cut away all veins and seeds. Cut the peppers into 1-inch strips.

4. Layer the peppers in a plastic or glass container with the basil, oil, and salt and the pepper to taste. Cover and refrigerate up to 2 days if not using as a sauce.

MAKES ABOUT 2 CUPS

5. Pat dry the fillets and place on the grill, centered over the smoke pan, for 15 minutes. Close the lid but keep watch so you can douse occasional flames with water. Turn the fillets and cook 25 to 30 minutes longer, or until firm.

6. Divide the fillets into four servings. Ladle the warm red pepper sauce onto plates and place the fillets on top. Garnish with the remaining basil and red peppers and serve immediately.

SERVES 4

Scrambled Eggs
with Smoked Shad Milt

Roe are fish eggs and milt is the sperm. Both are considered delicacies, but not everyone appreciates fine foods. One male shad will produce only a small amount of milt, so you might wait until you have collected milt from several fish before taking the time to smoke the creamy packages. I often smoke the roe and milt at the same time as shad fillets. The fillets may be frozen but the roe and milt are best if used fresh.

Smoke-grill milt on the cool side of the grill for 45 minutes to 1 hour or smoke in a smokehouse for 2 to 3 hours on oiled aluminum-foil trays pierced with holes.

2 tablespoons unsalted butter
6 eggs, beaten
¼ cup half and half (or whole milk)
1 tablespoon fresh tarragon, finely chopped
Salt and freshly ground black pepper
½ cup smoked milt (about 6 ounces)
Basic Salsa (see page 233)

> **ADVANCE PREPARATION:**
> Smoke the shad milt

1. Melt the butter in a large skillet over medium heat.

2. Scramble the eggs, cream, tarragon, and salt and pepper to taste in the butter. Add the milt.

3. Continue to cook for 3 to 4 minutes, or until eggs are thickened and no visible liquid remains. Serve immediately with Basic Salsa.

SERVES 2

Walleye Hash Browns

A food I have missed since moving away from the Midwest many years ago is hash brown potatoes, those crispy, crunchy, golden brown potatoes that I request in restaurants when I return home to visit. Cutting the potatoes on a mandolin works best.

Feel free to try this recipe with any easily flaked, grilled freshwater fish, but I prefer it with that upper-midwestern, sweet white-fleshed walleye. This dish goes well with scrambled eggs for breakfast.

1   **pound walleye fillet**

2   **medium Yukon potatoes, peeled and julienned**

½   **cup finely chopped red onions**

¼   **cup heavy cream**

2   **tablespoons all-purpose flour**

2   **tablespoons Dijon mustard**

2   **tablespoons grated Parmesan**

1   **teaspoon canola oil**

4   **tablespoons unsalted butter**

1. Preheat a grill.

2. Grill the fillet 4 to 5 minutes on each side, until firm and opaque. Allow to cool, then flake the fillet and set aside.

3. Gently mix the flaked fillet, potatoes, onion, cream, flour, mustard, and Parmesan in a large mixing bowl.

4. On a cutting board, shape the mass into a large patty, being careful not to break it apart. It should resemble an oversized pancake.

5. Heat the oil and 2 tablespoons of the butter in a large skillet over medium-high heat. Using two spatulas, carefully place the patty into the skillet. Sauté over medium heat until brown, about 10 minutes.

6. Gently turn the patty and dot with the remaining butter. Sauté 10 minutes longer, or until the potatoes are fully browned.

7. Cut into four wedges and serve while hot.

SERVES 4

Smoked Butterflied Largemouth Bass

After cleaning and scaling the fish, remove all bones and lay the fish out flat like a book, with the skin side on the bottom. A fish basket helps in the preparation of this recipe, or use aluminum foil pierced with holes in the bottom.

1 **whole bass, 2½ to 3 pounds, butterflied**

Curing solution of your choice (see pages 198–201)

6–8 **garlic cloves, finely chopped**

½ **cup cilantro, chopped**

2 **tablespoons tomato paste**

1 **teaspoon salt**

1 **tablespoon coarsely ground black pepper**

Basic Salsa (see page 233)

METHOD: Smoke grilling

ADVANCE PREPARATION:
Cure fish 1 hour before grilling

1. Inject the whole fish with curing solution 1 hour before cooking.

2. Prepare a grill for smoke grilling.

3. In a bowl, mix the garlic, cilantro, tomato paste, salt, and pepper into a paste.

4. Rub the paste into the fleshy surface of the bass with a spatula, covering the fish completely.

5. Oil the grate and the bass skin with a cooking spray or brush. Lay on the cool side of the grill and close the lid. Cook for about 1¼ hours; turn and cook 1¼ hours longer, or until the flesh is firm to the touch.

6. Divide each side into two servings and serve immediately with the Basic Salsa.

SERVES 4

Smoked Apache Trout

A friend returned from Arizona and presented me with a mess of Apache trout. Delicate and white fleshed, with a blush of red down the sides, Apache trout remind me of cutthroats.

4 to 8 trout fillets
Juice of 1 lemon (about 3 tablespoons)
Lemony Corn Salsa (see page 233)

METHOD: Smoke grilling

1. Prepare a grill for smoke grilling.

2. Sprinkle the lemon juice across the top of the fillets. Oil the grate and skin side (bottom) of the fillets with a cooking spray or brush. Lay the fillets on the cool side of the grill and close the lid.

3. Smoke for about 2 hours, or until the trout are golden brown. Serve immediately with Lemony Corn Salsa.

SERVES 4

To Drink

Icy-cold
Lime Margaritas
(see page 236)

Smoked Rainbow Trout

Use this recipe after a good day on the river when the fish is at its freshest. You may, of course, use any other trout, such as brook, cutthroat, or brown. This recipe is for a mild smoke. Increase the time by another hour or so for a more intense smoke flavor.

You may serve this dish for dinner, and, if you have enough, save part of the smoked trout to make Curried Trout Timbales (see page 31) for an appetizer another day.

2   whole trout, 2–3 pounds total
Curing solution of your choice (see pages 198–201)
Dill Mustard Sauce (see page 231)

1. Prepare a grill for smoke grilling.

2. Inject the whole fish with the curing solution 1 hour before cooking.

3. Oil the grate and both sides of the trout with a cooking spray or brush. Lay the trout on the cool side of the grill and close the lid. Cook for about 1¼ hours; turn and cook 1¼ hours longer, or until the fish are golden brown.

4. Remove and debone the fish before serving with the Dill Mustard Sauce.

SERVES 4

To Boil Trout

"Put a handful of salt into the water. When it boils put in the trout. Boil them fast about twenty minutes, according to their size.

"For sauce, send with them melted butter, and put some soy into it; or flavour it with catchup."

— *Miss Leslie's Directions for Cookery,*
Eliza Leslie, 1851

Smoked Pike
with Dried Cherry and Pear Sauce

I first tried this recipe on the shore of Lake Megiscane, a fly-in-only lake 400 miles north of Montreal, where no roads and no radio meant total isolation . . . and, thus, total concentration on fishing and food. It was the first of October and the weather was cold, with heavy, wet snow for an entire day, ideal for smoking fish.

You may also use this recipe with a stream- or lakeside smoker, described on pages 204–206.

After smoking and before serving, slice following the line of the spine with the tip of a sharp fillet knife. Lift off one side of the fish, then remove the backbone and discard. Pick out as many Y bones and smaller bones as possible. Be wary, however; pike is notorious for harboring dozens of tiny bones.

1   **whole pike (or walleye or perch), 1½ to 2 pounds**

4   **large ripe Bosc pears, peeled, thinly sliced**

1   **cup white vermouth (or sweet white wine)**

¼   **cup crushed black peppercorns**

4   **tablespoons unsalted butter (½ stick)**

1   **cup dried cherries reconstituted in hot water and drained (or cherry jam)**

2   **tablespoons brandy**

Cooked white rice

Sautéed broccoli rabe

1. Preheat a grill for smoke grilling.

2. Lay the fish on an oiled grate and shut the lid. Cook for 1½ to 2 hours, or until it is firm to the touch.

3. While the pike is smoking, prepare the sauce. Place the pears in the vermouth in a mixing bowl; add the peppercorns and marinate in the refrigerator for 1 to 2 hours.

4. Remove pike from the grill and keep warm. Remove pears from the marinade and set both aside.

5. Melt the butter in a large saucepan over medium-high heat. Sauté the pears and cherries for 3 to 4 minutes.

6. Add half the remaining marinade and the brandy. Cook, reducing the liquid for 6 to 8 minutes, until the sauce is slightly thickened. Stir and remove from the heat.

7. Ladle over the smoked fish and serve with the rice and broccoli rabe.

SERVES 4–6, DEPENDING UPON THE SIZE OF THE FISH

Smoked Yellow Perch
in Grapefruit Marinade

My great-uncle, who taught me to fish and also to carve, loved these little darlings. By himself, he could eat a half dozen. We often caught them at Ottertail Lake in Minnesota. Small, often only about a half-pound each, these freshwater favorites are buttery and sweet.

Serve two fillets (or more) per person, depending upon size.

¼ **cup olive oil**
½ **cup grapefruit juice**
2 **tablespoons finely chopped cilantro**
1 **teaspoon cayenne pepper**
8 **perch fillets**
Grapefruit wedges

1. Stir together the oil, grapefruit juice, cilantro, and cayenne in a large mixing bowl.

2. Place the fillets into 1-gallon zipper-lock bags or a glass baking pan. Pour the marinade over the fillets and refrigerate for 1 to 2 hours.

3. Prepare a grill for smoke grilling.

4. Remove the fillets from the marinade and place them on the cool side of the grill. Close the lid and let smoke for about 1 hour. The internal grill temperature should be maintained at 200 to 250°F.

5. Replenish the corn or wood chips if necessary. Turn the fish and smoke for an additional 1 to 1½ hours, or until slightly golden in color. Serve with the grapefruit wedges.

SERVES 4

A Pleasant Distraction

A DENSE FOG ENGULFS ME, offering a colorful panorama of morning on Thousand Acre Lake. The gray fog transposes into a yellow veil, lingering briefly before the sun emerges over the lake. I drink in the cool colors of morning.

I have fished this refuge for more than two decades, having had to hike in my first days to camp, fish, or enjoy the wilderness. Now, I paddle my birch-bark canoe across the lake to this inlet, a favorite spawning area for large-mouth bass, lying in the security of brightly painted offshore water lilies.

Nature's awakening increases in stages: Fish leap, slurping hungrily; a pair of mallards swim in circles, madly quacking; a cacophony of frogs begins a crescendo while a pair of geese splay their webbed landing gear and splash down nearby, startling my sleepy senses. Now . . . we're all awake.

The beaver lodge still stands near a dense growth of speckled alder. A shot rings out behind me, nearly causing me to tip my canoe. No, not a shot — a beaver, whacking the water with its tail. I turn too late to see the strike, but instantly the toothy creature surfaces, curiously circling me. I am no intruder, I say. I feel a sense of belonging, a connection.

Finally, the languid fog sweeps clear. I look out across the lake to see the opposite shore awash in an ocher palette, brushing the tips of majestic maple and oak. A lone silver birch glares like a light-house beacon among its dim, deciduous neighbors, brilliantly reflected in flat, aubergine water. Mountain azalea, cinnamon fern, and thick sumac line the shore. A wispy breeze jumps treetops, alights on the water in undulating ripples, breathing life into the spirit of the lake.

And so when I turn and see a wake out

in the middle, I take further notice. It appeared from nowhere, out of the fog, backlit by the rising sun. A white swath follows behind *something* out there. Something big. I reach for my binoculars. It is certainly not a fish.

Curiously, swimming in the middle of the lake is a deer. A big deer, displaying a magnificent rack. I've seen lumbering moose making their way across a Maine lake, red deer darting about Scottish highlands, caribou steeling across Labrador ranges, but never a whitetail deer swimming so casually, here in my own backyard.

I swing my canoe in its direction and pull hard. What I will do when I get there, I don't know. The sun has cut over the horizon, blinding on my left, but my course remains steady. I paddle with intent.

Now I see him clearly. A massive creature he is, head crooked forward, the only visible part of him suggesting a powerful body beneath the waterline. He turns sideways, sees me approaching. I don't want to frighten him; no, I embrace his free spirit.

I see the antlers clearly now. Eagerly, I count the tines. Ten of them! He bolts ahead, leaving me in his wake. I shoulder my paddle while a cranky blue heron flits off its perch in a huff.

Now I see them up close, his eyelashes. Long, curled upward, appearing as if glued on. Not real, too pretty. And on a champion of the wild, on this . . . guy deer. I dig in with the paddle, hoping for a closer inspection. They flirt again in the morning sun. The deer is sporting eyelashes longer than any others I have ever seen, on a human or otherwise. He is stunning, flashing an alluring device women would die for. He turns away, probably embarrassed. Poor guy, caught out here in the middle of a lake, hoping his pals don't see him.

Suddenly he turns, veers around a stump, and approaches shore. If I am to salute him for his gallant effort, I need to hurry. I glide over the surface, lodging in a mass of duckweed. I look over and eagerly watch a powerful forward lunge: Every muscle on his back, shoulders, and chest is maximized; the veins on his neck stand out as if a quivering, living

bas-relief. He emerges from the water. There is no dainty jeté here; forceful, hefty footwork is needed on this, nature's stage.

On shore now, he yanks each leg from the mud without as much as a pause, as if catapulted from the lake by an underwater cannon, charging past me while splashing mud, muck, and weeds in every direction. Water gushes off his back as he leaps, trailing roots, leaves, and the flower of a long yellow water lily from his rack. He heads toward the dense underbrush dragging his floral shawl behind him. Forging ahead with the power of a steam locomotive, he runs. He does not even stop to shake off, like my dog would have.

But he turns, and in one frozen moment, flashes his large brown eyes at me, then makes a beeline for the sanctuary of the forest, away from Thousand Acre Lake. And me.

What did I just experience? Did we make contact — the two of us? One grand, wild ungulate and one bedazzled *Homo sapiens*. Did he penetrate my psyche or did I imagine the connection? Will we meet again or did I scare him away forever by my nosy intrusion? I will never know what transpired. That look, those eyes, the illumination will last forever. For me it will.

Now, where was I? Ah, yes, the fishing.

Chapter 4

Saltwater Fish

ONE OF THE PRIMARY differences between fresh and saltwater fish is texture: few freshwater fish have the distinct firm character that saltwater fish possess. Being naturally pickled in salt (well, sort of) the meat is less likely to crumble or flake apart in cooking. Saltwater fish is good for bouillabaisse, soups, and grilled dishes. Skewered cubes of tuna will hold together under the stress of handling, say while being turned over a fire.

When buying seafood, look for a few things that indicate freshness. First, a good fish market should not smell, and neither should the fish. Go home only with fish that has a slight sheen. The flesh should be firm and translucent (opaque flesh may mean that the fish has been previously frozen). If you are buying a whole fish, choose one with eyes that are not sunken — bulging eyes mean a fish is freshly caught. Many of these tips apply to freshwater fish as well. Most important, do not waste any food, please. If you catch your own fish, do not kill a fish needlessly; when you buy, buy only what you need.

Maple Syrup Salmon Steaks

The sugar in the maple syrup will burn off and singe the exterior of the steaks while imparting a sweet flavor. And, of course, the delicious charred skin — one of my favorite parts — should be savored. Some Japanese restaurants serve it as a side dish for an additional charge.

Mirin is a sweet rice wine available in the Asian section of the supermarket.

¼ cup pure maple syrup

¼ cup mirin or white wine

¼ cup low-sodium soy sauce

2 tablespoons olive oil

Juice of ½ lemon (about 1½ tablespoons) and zest of 1 lemon (about 1 tablespoon)

2 tablespoons cracked black peppercorns

2 pounds salmon, cut into ¾-inch-thick steaks

METHOD: Grilling

ADVANCE PREPARATION:
Marinate fish 30 minutes before grilling

1. Mix the maple syrup, mirin, soy sauce, oil, lemon juice, and peppercorns in a noncorrosive container. Place the steaks in the marinade and refrigerate for 30 minutes.

2. Preheat a grill.

3. Remove the salmon steaks from the marinade, drain, pat dry, and reserve the marinade. Place the steaks directly over the flame and cook for 4 minutes; turn and cook 4 more minutes longer, or until the steaks are slightly soft to the touch. Grill a shorter time for rare, longer for well done.

4. Meanwhile, after turning steaks, heat the marinade in a small saucepan over medium-high heat until it comes to a boil, then simmer for 5 minutes. Immediately turn off the heat.

5. Ladle sauce over the salmon steaks.

SERVES 4

Columbia River Chinook
with Cherry Balsamic Sauce

I grew up on the western edge of Minnesota and my grandmother lived in Vancouver, Washington. My family traveled by Great Northern Railroad (where my father was an engineer) to visit about once a year. I eagerly looked forward to these adventures, soaring through the Rockies on the Vista Dome, watching my back for notorious train robbers and peering down at the Columbia River for a glimpse of Lewis and Clark's birchbark canoes.

We were en route, really, to two special treats: picking and eating cherries high up in my grandmother's tree until I burst and — especially — savoring the utterly delicious taste of freshly caught wild salmon. The first time I experienced *real* salmon, not from a can, but chinook from the Columbia River, I knew there was another world out there, and I wanted more of it.

1 **cup fresh cherries, washed and pitted**
½ **cup fish or chicken stock**
¼ **cup fresh thyme, stemmed**
2 **tablespoons brandy**
1 teaspoon **fresh lemon juice**
2 **tablespoons brown sugar**
1½ teaspoons **balsamic vinegar**
1½–2 pounds **salmon fillets**
Lemon wedges

1. Preheat a grill.

2. Pulse the cherries three or four times in the bowl of a food processor, until they are coarsely chopped.

3. Simmer the stock, thyme, brandy, and lemon juice in a saucepan over medium heat for 10 to 12 minutes, or until reduced by half.

4. Add the brown sugar and vinegar, stir, and simmer for 2 to 3 minutes, until thoroughly heated. Remove from the heat but keep warm.

5. Place the salmon fillets on the oiled grill and cook 4 to 5 minutes; turn and cook 4 to 5 minutes longer, until the fillets are slightly soft to the touch.

6. Divide into four servings. Ladle warm sauce onto the center of four plates, creating pools. Lay the salmon directly on top of the sauce.

7. Serve with the lemon wedges.

SERVES 4

Hoisin-Grilled Coho

Chinook and coho are naturally Pacific anadromous salmon (fish that spawn in freshwater and live in saltwater), but were introduced to the Great Lakes in 1967 to produce a freshwater sport fishery.

After the spawn, coho and chinook turn dark and perish. The meat loses all flavor by then, and if intended for the table, the fish must be caught soon after it enters its home stream, when it is still bright.

On and off for several years, some friends and I have ventured on a thousand-mile trip to enjoy fishing from the shores of Lake Superior on the Ontario side, where we have angled for coho and chinooks, among other fish, and have enjoyed many meals of freshly grilled salmon.

Hoisin sauce may be found in the Asian section of your supermarket.

Zest of 1 lemon (about 1 tablespoon) and juice of ½ lemon (about 1½ tablespoons)

¼ cup low-sodium soy sauce

2 tablespoons cracked black peppercorns

2 pounds coho fillets

½ cup hoisin sauce

Chopped chives for garnish

Chopped red pepper for garnish

ADVANCE PREPARATION:
Marinate fish for 30 minutes

1. Whisk together the lemon zest and juice, soy sauce, and peppercorns in a small bowl.

2. Pour the marinade over the fillets and refrigerate for 30 minutes.

3. Preheat a grill.

4. Remove the fillets from the marinade, drain, and pat dry. With a basting brush, brush half of the hoisin sauce on both sides of the coho.

5. Place fillets directly over the heat and cook for 4 minutes. Brush with the remaining sauce and turn. Cook for 4 more minutes, or until slightly soft to the touch. Grill fish a shorter time for rare, longer for well done.

6. Divide the fish onto four plates, garnish with the chives and red peppers, and serve immediately.

SERVES 4

Serve with short-grain brown rice and grilled zucchini with beets.

Salmon and Boletus Kebabs

If you can't find wild boletus mushrooms (also called cepes), use small porto-bellos (baby bellas or criminis, which are the same mushroom) or any other firm mushroom.

If you do not have metal skewers, try to find the heavy-duty 11½-inch wooden skewers, rather than the usual 10-inch, thinner skewers found in most markets. The heavier ones are sturdier and do not break or burn as easily. Serve two skewers per person.

¼   cup olive oil

¼   cup parsley, finely chopped

¼   cup fresh thyme, stemmed, finely chopped

2   tablespoons lemon juice

2   tablespoons coarsely ground black pepper

1   teaspoon salt

1½ pounds salmon fillets, cut into 24 cubes, 1¼ inches each

1 to 1½ pounds mushrooms, cut into 24 chunks, 1¼ inches each

8   wooden skewers (11½ inches long), soaked for 30 minutes in warm water

Lemon wedges

METHOD: Grilling

ADVANCE PREPARATION:
Marinate fish for 1 hour

Soak Your Skewers

Wooden skewers should be soaked in warm water for 30 minutes before using so they don't ignite on the grill.

1. Mix the oil, parsley, thyme, lemon juice, salt, and pepper in a large bowl.

2. Add salmon chunks, mix thoroughly, cover, and refrigerate for 1 hour.

3. Preheat a grill.

4. Remove the mixture from refrigerator, add the mushroom chunks, and toss to coat the mushrooms with the marinade. Drain in a colander.

5. Alternate salmon and mushrooms on skewers to make eight kebabs, each layered with three pieces of fish and three pieces of mushrooms.

6. Lay the soaked skewers on an oiled grill and cook 4 minutes. Turn and cook 4 minutes longer, or until the fillets are slightly soft to the touch.

7. Serve two skewers and the lemon wedges on each plate.

SERVES 4

Grilled Wild King Salmon
with Smoked Lobster-Tarragon Beurre Blanc

Pull out all stops to make this at an old-fashioned dinner party for special friends. You may prepare (or purchase) the cooked lobster ahead and refrigerate until needed. Take the meat out of the shell and wrap tightly in plastic wrap. It will keep 2 to 3 days. If you prefer, you may simply grill the lobster, but as with the smoked lobster, do not completely cook the meat because it will finish cooking in the sauce.

1   lobster, 1¾ pounds
½   cup melted butter
Juice of ½ lemon (about 1½ tablespoons)
2   pounds salmon fillets
¼   cup finely chopped red onion
3   tablespoons white vinegar
2   tablespoons water
¼   cup heavy cream
2   tablespoons finely chopped fresh tarragon
4   tablespoons (½ stick) butter, cut into
    8 pieces
Salt and freshly ground black pepper
Lemon wedges
Blood Orange Salad (see page 224)

METHOD: Smoke grilling
ADVANCE PREPARATION:
Smoke lobster

1. Prepare a grill for smoke grilling.

2. Turn the lobster onto its back on a large cutting board. With a sharp knife, make an incision down the center of the tail, almost to the tip, without cutting through the shell. With your hands, gently split apart the tail, opening up the cavity.

3. Drizzle the butter and lemon juice into the cavity.

4. Lay the lobster on its back on the grill, over the smoke pan. Close the lid and smoke for about 25 minutes, or until the meat is firm to the touch. Do not turn over the lobster.

5. Remove the lobster from the grill with tongs. Transfer to a cutting board and remove the meat from the tail and claws, reserving the coral and all juices in the refrigerator.

6. Cut the meat into ¾-inch pieces and refrigerate until needed.

7. To make the beurre blanc, bring the onions, vinegar, and water to a boil in a medium saucepan over medium-high heat; reduce the heat and simmer for 3 to 4 minutes, or until reduced by about half.

8. Add the cream and tarragon; simmer for 1 to 2 minutes, or until reduced by half.

9. Turn off the heat and whisk in the butter chunks one piece at a time, incorporating each piece until melted.

10. Strain the liquid through a sieve or cheesecloth and return to the pan.

11. Remove the lobster meat from the refrigerator and set aside.

12. Reoil the grill and lay the salmon on the hot side. Cook for 4 to 5 minutes; turn and cook 4 to 5 minutes longer, or until slightly soft to the touch. Turn off the heat and transfer the salmon to the warming shelf or set aside.

13. Add the lobster pieces and juices to the saucepan with the beurre blanc, stir, and turn up the heat to medium high. Simmer, covered, stirring several times, for 3 to 4 minutes, or until the lobster meat is thoroughly heated.

14. Divide the salmon into serving-size pieces, transfer to warm plates, and spoon the beurre blanc over the salmon. Serve immediately with the Blood Orange Salad.

SERVES 4-6

To Drink

Chilled Chablis or California sauvignon blanc

Grilled Halibut
in Coconut Milk and Soy Sauce

On his spring vacation away from lobstering off Provincetown, my friend Paul McGraff loves nothing better than to unwind on a fishing excursion to Alaska. He angles for, among other piscatorial delights, king salmon — delicious, always — but my favorite is the succulent, pearly white halibut he brings back and generously shares with friends.

I developed this recipe and served it to Paul and his wife, Marge, more than once. This is one of my favorite saltwater-fish dishes.

Low-fat chicken stock works better than fish stock in this recipe. I've tried both and discovered this peculiarity. Dark soy sauce is darker and richer than regular soy sauce and may be found in Asian markets or in the Asian section of some supermarkets.

---

4 halibut steaks, 1 inch thick, about 2 pounds

1 tablespoon vegetable oil

4–6 cloves garlic, finely chopped

¼ cup finely chopped fresh ginger

¼ cup finely chopped jalapeño peppers

1–2 anchovy fillets, chopped

¾ cup chicken stock

½ cup coconut milk, unsweetened

⅓ cup tomato sauce

¼ cup dark soy sauce

Freshly ground black pepper

½ tomato, diced

1 tablespoon pure maple syrup (or honey)

2 cups rice noodles or wheat noodles, cooked and drained

1 tablespoon sesame oil

6–8 large scallions, green tops removed, chopped

Lemon wedges

1. Preheat a grill.

2. Grill the halibut on an oiled grate for about three quarters of the actual time desired, 3 to 4 minutes per side, and keep warm on the grill's warming shelf.

3. Heat oil in a large saucepan or wok and sauté the garlic, ginger, jalapeño peppers, and anchovies over medium heat for 3 to 4 minutes.

4. Add the stock, coconut milk, tomato sauce, soy sauce, and black pepper to taste; simmer over medium heat for 7 to 8 minutes, or until reduced by half.

5. Add the diced tomato and simmer an additional 3 to 4 minutes.

6. Sauté the noodles in the sesame oil until warm. Add about one third of the sauce from the pan and mix together.

7. Lay the warm grilled halibut steaks in the pan with the remaining sauce, spooning the sauce over the steaks and turning to coat. Simmer for 1 to 2 minutes, or until steaks are thoroughly coated.

8. Sprinkle the scallions over the halibut and serve with the noodles and lemon wedges.

SERVES 4

Lemon Sorbet-Glazed Mahi-Mahi

This odd-seeming combination really does work. The sugar in the sorbet, yes, fruit sorbet from the frozen foods section of the supermarket, caramelizes when cooked down and creates a perfect citrus glaze for fish. Try other combinations using lemon or lime juice, which helps cut the sweetness of the sugar. Halibut is also good prepared this way.

2   cups frozen lemon sorbet
Juice of 1 large lemon (3 to 4 tablespoons) and zest of 1 large lemon (about 1 tablespoon)
2   pounds mahi-mahi fillets, 1 inch thick
Chopped fresh cilantro for garnish

1. Preheat a grill.

2. Melt the sorbet for 4 to 5 minutes in a 4-quart saucepan or large saucepan over medium-high heat.

3. Add the lemon juice and half of the zest, lower the heat to simmer, and reduce by one third, about 8 minutes.

Remove from the heat and set aside to cool.

4. Lay the fillets on a plate and spoon half of the cooled sauce over them, turning to coat thoroughly.

5. Transfer the steaks to the grill and cook 4 to 5 minutes. Turn, brush the reserved sauce on top, and cook 5 minutes longer, or until fish is firm to the touch.

6. Garnish with the remaining lemon zest and the cilantro.

SERVES 4

Tuna Kebabs

These savory skewers are perfect for a late summer lunch. I serve them with short-grained rice and a salad.

¼ cup lemon juice

1 tablespoon olive oil

2 tablespoons dried marjoram

2 tablespoons dried oregano

2 tablespoons dried thyme

½ teaspoon sea salt

1 tablespoon freshly ground black pepper

16 pieces tuna fillets, cut into 1½-inch cubes, about 1 pound

24 1½-inch pieces green bell pepper (about 2 large)

24 1½-inch pieces red bell pepper (about 2 large)

24 1-inch pieces red onion (about 2 medium)

16 cherry tomatoes

6 wooden skewers (11½ inches long), soaked for 30 minutes in warm water

1. Preheat a grill.

2. In a large mixing bowl combine the lemon juice, oil, marjoram, oregano, thyme, salt, and pepper. Toss together the fish chunks, peppers, onion, and tomatoes, coating all chunks.

3. On each of four skewers alternate one piece of fish, one piece of green pepper, one piece of red pepper and one piece of onion until all skewers are filled. Skewer eight cherry tomatoes onto two separate skewers. Set aside.

4. Lay all skewers except the one with tomatoes on an oiled grill. Turn after 4 to 5 minutes and add the tomato skewers to the grill. Grill fish kebabs an additional 4 to 5 minutes, or until fish is firm to the touch, and remove. For medium-rare tuna, cut grilling time in half. Remove tomato kebabs after 5 minutes.

5. Slide tomatoes off their skewers; serve each guest one fish skewer and four tomatoes.

SERVES 4

Black Cod
with Minted Orange Sorbet Sauce

Black cod, also known as sable, range from Alaska to California and have superbly tender, slightly oily but sweet white meat. They have a delicate texture and should be turned on the grill gently, with two spatulas, so they don't break apart and fall through the grates.

With most recipes that call for citrus, I almost always add the zest of the fruit — the oils — which adds yet another dimension of flavor. If you do not have a zesting tool, you may substitute a potato peeler, but avoid peeling off the white pulp of the fruit along with the skin. Then simply dice the strips.

1½ cups orange sorbet

½ cup finely chopped fresh mint

Juice of 1 large orange (about ½ cup) plus zest (about 2 tablespoons)

1½ pounds black cod fillets

METHOD: Grilling

ADVANCE PREPARATION:
Marinate fish for 30 minutes

1. Preheat a grill.

2. Melt the sorbet in a 4-quart saucepan over medium-high heat.

3. Add the mint, orange juice, and half of the zest. Lower heat to medium and cook, uncovered, for 7 to 8 minutes, or until reduced by one third. Set aside to cool.

4. Lay the fillets in a shallow container and spoon the sauce over them; turn and coat thoroughly. Refrigerate for 30 minutes.

5. Remove the fillets from the marinade and transfer to the grill. Cook 4 minutes. Turn and brush additional marinade on top. Cook 4 minutes longer, or until the fish is slightly soft when poked.

6. Divide into four equal portions, garnish with the remaining orange zest, and serve.

SERVES 4

Tilapia
and Coffeehouse Stuffing

Two separate coffee shops I patronize during winter months, seeking warming cappuccinos, exhibit generous, delightful habits: At closing time, they offer left-over bagels, scones, and croissants to their customers, rather than discard them. During frigid months in New England, I take home as many baked goods as they allow in order to feed the birds outside my window: chickadees, nuthatches, and ever-greedy, but also hungry, blue jays. I heartily confess, however, that the following recipe came about one day from an excess of leftover treats.

If you have control over the ingredients, onion, garlic, or "everything" bagels are best in this recipe, as is a mix with, say, one scone — preferably with raisins — and one croissant. The birds and I both love the unexpected mix. Adjust the baked goods according to the generosity of your particular coffeehouse.

2   bagels, cut into small pieces

1   scone, broken into pieces

1   croissant, broken into pieces

¼   small red onion, coarsely chopped

1   medium-sized orange, cut into chunks (peel included)

4   large eggs

Salt and freshly ground black pepper

4   pieces aluminum foil, cut into 15-inch squares

2   pounds tilapia, 1 inch thick, cut into four equal pieces

1   lemon, quartered (peel included)

To Drink

An amber beer, such as India Pale Ale

1. Preheat a grill.

2. In the bowl of a food processor, pulse the bagel pieces, scone pieces, croissant pieces, onion, orange chunks, eggs, and salt and pepper to taste for 10 to 15 seconds, or until the ingredients are just mixed together thoroughly but not puréed. You may have to do this in two or three batches. Set aside the stuffing in a bowl.

3. Lay out the four separate pieces of foil. Place one piece of tilapia on each and spoon a ½-inch-thick layer of the stuffing over each fillet (you'll use about ½ cup each). Squeeze a lemon quarter over each of them. You may have leftover stuffing, which can be frozen for another use.

4. Pinch together the foil at the top. Place the foil packets on the grill over high heat. Cook for about 10 minutes. You may have to check to see if the stuffing is thoroughly heated; if not, return to the grill (and turn over carefully) for an additional 4 to 5 minutes.

5. Remove from the grill and allow guests to open the packets and remove the contents themselves for a more festive presentation.

SERVES 4

Tuna Steaks
and Blood Oranges in Foil

Blood oranges hold a flavorful juice worth trying, at least once.

4 tuna steaks, 6–8 ounces each

⅓ cup low-sodium soy sauce

Juice of 1 fresh blood orange (about 4 tablespoons)

¼ cup finely chopped fresh ginger

2 tablespoons fresh lime juice

2 tablespoons pure maple syrup

Salt and freshly ground black pepper

Zest of 1 blood orange

8 blood orange slices (about 2 small oranges)

ADVANCE PREPARATION:
Marinate fish for 30 minutes

1. Combine the tuna steaks, soy sauce, orange juice, ginger, lime juice, and maple syrup in a large mixing bowl. Stir together, cover, and refrigerate for about 30 minutes.

2. Preheat a grill.

3. Tear off four pieces of aluminum foil, 12 inches by 12 inches each. Remove the tuna steaks from the marinade and place one in the center of each piece of foil. Season with the salt and pepper and cover each with the zest and two orange slices. Crimp the foil tightly together.

4. Grill for 4 to 5 minutes; turn and grill 5 minutes longer, or until the tuna is firm to the touch.

5. Unwrap each foil packet and serve immediately.

SERVES 4

Grilled Tuna Burgers

The combination of grilled tuna and plenty of fresh corn makes these fish burgers perfect for lunch outside on a warm summer afternoon.

1½ pounds fresh tuna

2   eggs, beaten

4–6 small gherkins or cornichons, finely chopped

Salt

1   teaspoon freshly ground black pepper

1   tablespoon olive oil

½   cup finely chopped sweet white onion

2   cups fresh corn

¼   cup dry white wine

Juice of 1 lemon (about 3 tablespoons) and zest of that lemon (about 1 tablespoon)

1½ tablespoons finely chopped fresh dill

Lemony Corn Salsa (see page 233)

1. Preheat a grill.

2. Place the tuna on the oiled grate and grill for 3 to 4 minutes. Turn and grill 3 to 4 minutes longer, or until the fish is slightly soft. Remove and cool.

3. Break apart the cooled tuna in a large mixing bowl, then add the eggs, gherkins, salt to taste, and pepper and mash with a large fork. Set aside.

4. Heat the oil in a large saucepan over medium-high heat. Add the onion and sauté for 2 to 3 minutes, until soft. Add the corn, wine, lemon juice, and dill and simmer for 4 to 5 minutes. Remove from the heat.

5. Thoroughly mix the liquid and the zest into the tuna. Form the mixture into four patties. Place the patties on an oiled, perforated pizza pan or in a wire-mesh basket over the grill. Brown the patties for 3 to 4 minutes; turn and cook 3 to 4 minutes longer, or until firm to the touch.

6. Serve on toasted hamburger buns with the Lemony Corn Salsa.

SERVES 4

To Drink

Chilled Lemonade (see page 236) with a sprig of fresh mint

Curried Grilled Pompano

You may substitute redfish or grouper for the firm white flesh of pompano, but know that without the delicate flavor of pompano, the dish will not be quite the same.

To use fresh lemongrass stalks, when you can find them in Asian or upscale produce markets, pound the yellow bulbous ends — which look like small leeks or large scallions — with a mallet, hammer, or heavy knife handle. You need only to pulverize it to extract its unique flavor while it cooks. If you cannot find lemongrass, substitute lemon zest, carefully peeling and avoiding the white pulp as much as possible. Galangal or Thai ginger may be found in the produce section in Asian markets and some grocery stores.

1 tablespoon olive oil

1 medium onion, finely chopped (about 1 cup)

4–5 cloves garlic, finely chopped

1 tablespoon finely chopped galangal (or ginger)

½ cup light coconut milk

2 sticks lemongrass, bruised (or 2 wide strips of lemon zest)

1 teaspoon chili powder (or hot sauce to taste)

1 teaspoon curry powder

1 teaspoon ground turmeric

½ teaspoon ground cinnamon

1½ pounds pompano fillets, about 1 inch thick

Juice of ½ lemon (about 1½ tablespoons)

Lemon wedges

1. Heat the oil in a large skillet over medium-high heat. Sauté the onion, garlic, and galangal for 3 to 4 minutes.

2. Add the coconut milk, lemongrass, chili powder, curry powder, turmeric, and cinnamon. Cook for about 5 minutes, or until the liquid is reduced by one third. Reduce heat to low.

3. Preheat a grill.

4. Lay fillets on an oiled grill, drizzle the lemon juice on top, and cook for 4 to 5 minutes. Turn and cook for 4 to 5 minutes longer, or until the fish is firm to the touch.

5. Remove the fillets from the grill, spoon the warm sauce over them, divide into four portions, and serve immediately with the lemon wedges.

SERVES 4

Striped Bass
with Cattail Shoots and Morels

Combine all of these wild foods, which appear at around the same time in the spring. See the section on cattail shoots on page 87. This dish is delicious with roasted potatoes and a salad of spring greens.

8–10 cattail shoots, green tops removed
   (or hearts of palm)

6–8 morels, cleaned and trimmed
   (or criminis)

½ cup olive oil plus 1 tablespoon

½ cup fresh thyme, stemmed and cleaned

½ teaspoon salt

1   teaspoon freshly ground black pepper

1½ pounds striped bass fillet

Salt and freshly ground black pepper

2   tablespoons butter

Juice of 1 small lemon

1. Preheat a grill.

2. Remove the tough outer layer from the cattails and slice diagonally as you would scallions. Set aside.

3. Slice the morels into bite-size pieces and set aside.

4. Mix ½ cup of the oil and the thyme and salt and pepper in a small bowl.

5. With a basting brush or spoon, coat the bass fillet and transfer it to the grill.

6. Meanwhile, heat the butter and the remaining 1 tablespoon oil in a skillet over medium heat. Sauté the morels for 3 to 4 minutes, until the mushrooms are softened. Add the sliced cattail shoots, lower the heat, and cook for 2 to 3 minutes longer. Reduce the heat and keep warm.

7. Grill the bass for 4 to 5 minutes; turn and grill for 4 to 5 minutes longer, or until the fish is firm to the touch.

8. Divide into four servings and place on warm plates. Spoon the morels and cattails next to the bass. Drizzle the lemon juice over the bass and season with additional salt and pepper. Serve immediately.

SERVES 4

Cattail Shoots

Young cattail shoots are the white bottoms, not the roots, of cattails just coming up in marshy areas or freshwater ponds and lakes in the spring, about the same time as morel mushrooms, which are probably somewhere nearby, under an ash tree possibly. Together, with grilled striped bass that are coming up the Hudson River at about the same time to spawn, they make for a special combination that is rarely equaled for freshness and unique flavors, each bite testifying to the bounties of the earth.

To harvest cattails, likely in the same way early Native Americans did, locate new greens 3 to 4 feet tall in freshwater or at its edge. In some cases waders may be helpful, or necessary. Reach down and, with both hands, pull up firm and hard. The shoots will break away from the roots and come up in your hands. All of the green tops are fibrous and tough, so field-clean them by cutting them off and discarding, along with any roots.

In the final cleaning, at home under running water, trim off the several outer layers of the white part; they, too, are tough. They look a bit like the growth rings of trees. The inner core is what you will be left with. With any luck, some may make it to the table, if you don't eat them all raw first, as I often do.

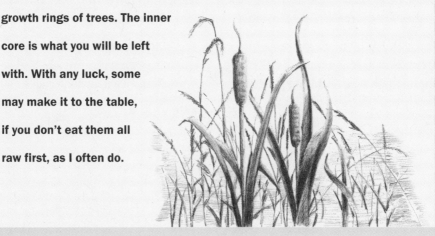

Striped Bass
with Curried Shrimp Sauce

You don't want to completely cook the bass because you will be finishing it in a skillet on the stove. Adjust the heat by adding or subtracting chili powder.

Use the Shrimp Paste recipe on page 229 or a commercial shrimp paste found in the Asian section of some supermarkets.

1   large sweet white onion, finely chopped
3–4 garlic cloves, peeled
2   teaspoons finely chopped fresh ginger
1   teaspoon chili powder
2½ tablespoons canola oil
1½ pounds striped bass fillets
1   medium tomato, diced
1   tablespoon Shrimp Paste (see page 229)
Juice of ½ lemon (about 1½ tablespoons)
Cooked white rice

1. Pulse the onion, garlic, ginger, and chili powder five or six times in the bowl of a food processor. Scrape down the sides and purée for 1 to 2 minutes, or until smooth.

2. Heat the oil in a medium skillet over medium-high heat. Add the puréed ingredients, stir, reduce heat to low, and cook for about 15 minutes, covered, stirring occasionally, until thickened.

3. Meanwhile, preheat a grill.

4. Lay the fillets on an oiled grate and cook for 3 to 4 minutes. Turn and cook 4 to 5 minutes longer, or until firm. Move to the grill's warming shelf.

5. Add the tomatoes to the skillet, cook for 3 to 4 minutes, swirl in the Shrimp Paste, and stir for 1 minute.

6. Transfer the fillets to the pan, spooning the sauce on top. Drizzle the lemon juice on top, cover for 1 to 2 minutes, and remove from the heat.

7. Divide the fish into four portions, spoon the sauce over each, and serve immediately with white rice.

SERVES 4

Bluefish
with Tomato and Basil

Anyone living on the Atlantic Coast must eat bluefish at least once in his or her lifetime. It's natural oily, strong flavor may take getting used to, however.

If you fillet the fish yourself, it must be gutted immediately after catching. Some people prefer to remove the dark meat that runs along the spine, which can be quite strong in flavor.

2   pounds bluefish fillets

Juice of 2 limes (about 4 tablespoons) and zest of 1 lime (about 2 teaspoons)

2   teaspoons sea salt

4–5 medium tomatoes (about 1½ pounds), cubed

1   cup cleaned and coarsely chopped fresh basil

¼   cup good-quality extra-virgin olive oil

1   tablespoon freshly ground pink and green peppercorns

3–4 garlic cloves, minced

Serve with Smoked Corn on the Cob (page 220).

1. Lay the fillets in a noncorrosive container and cover with the juice of 1 lime (about 2 tablespoons) and 1 teaspoon of the salt. Refrigerate for 30 minutes.

2. Mix the remaining 2 tablespoons of lime juice, 1 teaspoon of salt, and the tomatoes, basil, oil, peppercorns, garlic, and zest in a large mixing bowl. Stir well and set aside.

3. Preheat a grill.

4. Remove the bluefish fillets from the marinade, drain, and transfer to the grill.

5. Place the fillets directly over the heat and cook for 5 minutes; turn and cook 5 minutes longer, or until the fish is firm to the touch.

6. Transfer the fillets to warm plates, ladle the sauce over each, and serve immediately.

SERVES 4-6

Sea Bass in Foil
with Chickpeas and Mint

Sea bass contains 16 percent more omega-3 fatty acids — the good fat — than even the wildest salmon, a boon for lovers of sea bass.

2 pieces 12-inch-square heavy-duty aluminum foil

1 tablespoon olive oil

2 pounds sea bass fillets

1 cup mint leaves, washed and stemmed

1 medium tomato, thickly sliced

1 small sweet white onion, thinly sliced

½ cup cooked chickpeas

1 teaspoon ground cumin

½ teaspoon ground coriander

¼ teaspoon cayenne pepper

¼ teaspoon ground cinnamon

Salt and freshly ground black pepper

Present on a large serving platter over rice and steamed asparagus.

1. Preheat a grill.

2. Lay out one piece of the foil, brush with oil, and place the bass fillets on top. Layer the mint leaves, tomato, onion, chickpeas, cumin, coriander, cayenne, cinnamon, and salt and pepper to taste on the fillets.

3. Wrap the foil around the layers and crimp together at the top. Wrap the second piece of foil around the first, but crimp together at the bottom. This forms a secure packet in which the bass and other ingredients can steam.

4. Lay the packet on the grill and cook for 6 to 8 minutes. Turn and cook 4 to 5 minutes longer, or until the fish is firm to the touch.

5. Remove the packet from the heat, open the foil, and serve.

SERVES 4–6

Grouper
with Tandoori Sauce in Foil Pouches

You may substitute red snapper, tilefish, or sea bass. Adjust the heat index according to your particular tastes by the amount of tandoori powder you use. Tandoori powder, which can be extremely hot, is found in the Asian section of the supermarket. Serve this with rice noodles or pasta.

1   cup plain yogurt

¼   cup coarsely cut fresh ginger

4–5 scallions, peeled and coarsely cut
      (include all but ½ inch of greens)

6–8 garlic cloves, peeled

2   tablespoons tandoori powder

Juice of ½ lemon (about 1½ tablespoons)

½   teaspoon sea salt

4   pieces 12-inch by 18-inch heavy-duty
      aluminum foil

2   pounds grouper fillets, cut into
      four equal pieces

1. Preheat a grill.

2. Pulse together the yogurt, ginger, scallions, garlic, tandoori powder, lemon juice, and salt in the bowl of a food processor for 1 minute. Scrape down the sides and purée for 30 seconds, or until blended. Set aside.

3. With a rubber spatula, remove the sauce from the processor bowl and generously rub on both sides of each fillet. Lay the fillets on the foil, spoon any leftover sauce on top, fold over the aluminum, and crimp tightly to form a firm seal.

4. Lay the pouches on the grill and cook for 5 minutes; turn and cook for 5 minutes longer, or until the fillets are firm to the touch.

5. Remove the pouches from the heat and let guests open and discover their steaming dinner.

SERVES 4

Grilled Shad
with Morels

Use as much of the morel as possible. Cut off the ends of the stems and brush the rest to remove dirt and insects.

Make sure your shad has been fully boned, or you will spend an inordinate amount of time picking out the bones.

2   tablespoons unsalted butter

1   teaspoon olive oil

2   cups morels, cleaned and sliced into large pieces (or substitute criminis)

½   teaspoon sea salt

1   tablespoon freshly ground black pepper

1   tablespoon brandy (optional)

1   boneless shad fillet, about 1 pound

ADVANCE PREPARATION:

Prepare morels — cut off the stems, roughly slice them, and begin cooking 3 to 4 minutes before the caps. Be sure to slice the caps into large pieces, so they don't dissolve into mere fragments.

1. Preheat a grill.

2. Melt the butter in a medium-size saucepan over medium-high heat. Add the oil and sauté the morels, salt, and pepper for 8 to 10 minutes (12 to 15 minutes if large), covered.

3. Uncover, add the brandy, if using, and reduce by about one third, 2 to 3 minutes. Turn off the heat but keep warm over low heat.

4. Place the fillet on an oiled grill. Cook for 4 to 5 minutes; turn and cook for 4 to 5 minutes longer, or until the fish is opaque. Divide in half and transfer to two warm plates. Spoon the morels on the side.

SERVES 2

Monkfish Loins
in a Peanut Marinade

Fillets of monkfish, also called loins, can dry out on the grill, so don't overcook them. If the loins are small, you may need one loin for every two people. Monkfish are really ugly but . . . don't judge a book by its cover. Serve this with white rice, Cucumbers Sautéed with Fresh Cilantro (see page 225), and a green salad.

1   can (14 ounces) unsweetened coconut milk

3   tablespoons crunchy peanut butter

3   tablespoons dark soy sauce (found in Asian markets or in the Asian section of some supermarkets)

1½ pounds monkfish loins

1   teaspoon vegetable oil

4–5 garlic cloves, finely chopped

2   tablespoons finely chopped fresh ginger

½   cup apple cider

4–6 large scallions, finely chopped

ADVANCE PREPARATION:
Marinate fish for 1 to 2 hours

1. In a nonreactive container, mix together the coconut milk, peanut butter, and soy sauce. Marinate the loins in the mixture for 1 to 2 hours, covered, in the refrigerator.

2. Remove the loins from the marinade, drain, and set aside. Discard the marinade.

3. Preheat a grill.

4. Lay the monkfish loins on an oiled grate. Grill for 6 to 8 minutes; turn and grill for 6 to 8 minutes longer, or until the loins feel firm when pressed with your finger.

5. Heat the oil over medium heat in a large saucepan. Sauté the garlic and ginger for 2 to 3 minutes, or until soft. Add the cider, stir for 1 minute, then sprinkle in the scallions. Turn off the heat.

6. Divide the loins into four portions. Spoon the sauce over each and serve immediately.

SERVES 4

Monkfish-Persimmon Pockets

You may need two cabbage leaves to form each pocket for the monkfish if the head of cabbage you select is small. Choose small persimmons, which tend to be less astringent than large ones.

4   savoy cabbage leaves

1   teaspoon sesame oil

1   teaspoon sesame seeds

1   small jalapeño pepper, finely chopped

1   medium red onion cut into 16 slices (about ⅛ inch thick each)

2   fresh persimmons, each cut into 8 slices (about ¼ inch thick each)

1   pound monkfish loins, cut into 4 equal pieces

½   teaspoon cracked black peppercorns

Pinch of salt

1. Prepare a grill for smoke grilling.

2. Immerse the cabbage leaves in boiling water for 3 minutes. Remove, plunge into cold water, and drain.

3. Lay out cabbage leaves flat, brush them with half of the sesame oil, and sprinkle on half of the sesame seeds and jalapeño.

4. Lay two slices of onion and two slices of persimmon on each piece of cabbage so that the onion is against the cabbage leaf.

5. Place one piece of fish on the onion and persimmon slices. Top with the remaining persimmon and onion.

6. Brush with the remaining oil and sprinkle the remaining sesame seeds and jalapeño over all. Season with the peppercorns and salt.

7. Pull over the sides of the cabbage leaves, as for an envelope, and secure with a toothpick. Pull over ends and secure with another toothpick.

8. Place the pockets on the grill, centered over smoke pan. Cook for 10 to 12 minutes. Douse occasional flames with water.

9. Turn the pockets and cook another 10 minutes. Remove toothpicks and serve immediately.

SERVES 4

The Old Man of the Sea

MARTHA'S VINEYARD, a charming 23-mile-long island off the coast of Massachusetts, was made famous by 18th-century whaling captains and former president Bill Clinton and his family.

A favorite spot of mine, on the western side of the island off Nashaquitsa Cliffs, not far from property once owned by Jacqueline Kennedy Onassis, is a cove where I often fished in my lightweight 13-foot aluminum canoe. It was also here where Ernest Hemingway and I almost became soul mates.

It was early evening when I loaded my canoe with rod and tackle and dodged incoming breakers. A few people strolled the beach, enjoying a brisk fall evening. A slight breeze blew from the northwest, and for now, I chose to head into the wind to my right and let it gently nudge me downwind as I fished parallel to the shore; I would then paddle back upwind and repeat the process.

The sky had dimmed, gradually losing most of its low-hanging light. Wispy cirrus clouds gently fanned to the west while a pink glow crept into the horizon.

Soon, the wind changed direction, blowing offshore. Two strolling beach-combers had decided to linger, throwing sticks for their golden retriever. The couple had been watching me, possibly curious about what crazy person would be on the ocean in a canoe.

I had tied on a deep-water lure for bottom fishing and slowly trolled upwind as I paddled, supporting the rod sideways, holding it under one knee, as I often did in order to troll, while at the same time managing the paddle. Suddenly, I thought the rod was going to flip out of the canoe. I had hooked on to something solid, a snag, I believed. After tugging on the line a bit, I realized it was more than a snag. I looked out to where the line cut into the surface of the water . . . it moved! I tried to reel in but my rod dipped further, unrelenting.

The rod continued to hold fast and,

try as I might, I could not reel in the fish. I waited for something to happen: a lurch, a dive . . . anything. But nothing. Except now . . . the *canoe* moved. Very slowly it cut through the water. I was being towed! The sensation was as being winched toward a telephone pole while seated in an automobile. This would be a catch to be reckoned with.

I looked up and saw people on shore appearing farther away, peering out at me through binoculars. They appeared to be beckoning. The sun hadn't set, but it wouldn't be long now. I felt the breeze on my face; I was moving out to sea. In a canoe, no less.

The remote possibility existed that the next tract of land I encountered could be Portugal, at the same 42-degree latitude as the Vineyard. After all, I wasn't steering; I had no control. Or sextant, silly me. Spencer Tracy's weathered face appeared, lips parched, white hair bleached whiter by blistering sun, towing the 1,500-pound fish lashed to the side of *his* little vessel.

I could only guess at what I had inadvertently hooked. A monster striped bass? A sting ray, perhaps? If so, I'd

never get it over the gunwale into the canoe. Had I happened upon a descendant of the fierce great white shark Jaws? After all, the movie was filmed in these very waters. That fish *ate* a boat.

Should I be concerned about arctic narwhal this far south, the legendary unicorn of the deep, surfacing abruptly, driving its 8-foot horn through the bottom of my flimsy canoe into my rear?

What if I'd snagged a humpback whale? They'd be feeding now, storing energy for their annual migration. My canoe might be seen as krill. Perhaps I'd be spared, appearing as a mere crumb on the ocean's surface.

Would I beach my 30-ton, 60-foot whale? Maybe not; my Swiss army knife seemed hardly adequate as a makeshift lance. Possibly I could call up the spirit of Herman Melville to revive Queequeq's harpooning expertise.

Would I consider cutting the line? Of course not; was I a fisherman or not? Hemingway's spirit would smack me hard for even considering it. No, I would not cut, but it was getting darker now. Maybe just a *little* slice, to weaken the monofilament and let the beast break it off. "Not me," I'd claim if confronted. People on shore faded to stick figures in dim light. And now I really had to use a bathroom.

I had no food, no water, no radio, and apparently no sense. Had I really tossed a canoe over pounding ocean waves and jumped inside? Stable sea kayaks, yes. A tippy, crummy little 13-foot canoe, no. My parents sent me to a plains university, not the Woods Hole Oceanographic Institute. I longed for my freshwater, *shallow* trout pond back home right then.

The . . . *whatever* . . . was diligently towing me now, a breeze at my back. My course held fast on a beeline vector toward Nantucket, far away. But Hemingway and I did not have to duke it out over some honor thing. I did not have to fabricate a story, in typical fisherman fashion, about the size of my monster. Thankfully, I did not have to make any decisions. The whatever-it-was made the decision for me, on that cool fall day — the day I felt as if I were a novel in progress.

It was sudden, uneventful. Shattered was the fleeting notion of a huge advance for my manuscript: *Kon Tiki Canoe: Survival at Sea.* What ultimately remained in my thoughts after the flimsy monofilament line broke (on its own), silently, with no warning, no fanfare, no deep-throated cellos to telegraph the climax, was the pressing fact that, scary creature or not, I had nearly met Hemingway. On his terms.

I still had to use a bathroom.

Grilled Seafood Sausages

Nowadays, sausage casing is readily available. You may find it in your supermarket. If not, order it from a butcher. Any firm, white-fleshed fish will do in place of the cod. The lobster meat is not to be puréed. Instead, it is coarsely chopped so that flecks of its red color will show through the casing after grilling.

If you don't have a sausage-making attachment for your stand mixer, use a pastry bag, which is easily found in most kitchen supply stores. Use a large tip.

The sausages are partially cooked in boiling water before grilling.

½ pound cod (or halibut or pollack)

½ small apple, peeled and coarsely chopped (about ½ cup)

3 egg whites

2 tablespoons snipped chives

2 tablespoons Shrimp Paste (see page 229, or substitute ¼ pound cleaned shrimp)

2 tablespoons fresh tarragon

1 tablespoon fresh cilantro

1 tablespoon fresh thyme, cleaned and stemmed

1 teaspoon coarsely ground black pepper

¼ teaspoon sea salt

⅛ teaspoon cayenne pepper

½ cup heavy cream

¼ pound lobster meat (or substitute crab), finely chopped

¼ pound white mushrooms, finely chopped

6 feet sausage casings

Several 12-inch pieces of twine

Serve with Mixed Wild Mushroom Pasta (see page 223) and Spaetzle (see page 235).

1. Pulse together the cod, apple, egg whites, chives, shrimp paste, tarragon, cilantro, thyme, pepper, salt, and cayenne five or six times in the bowl of a food processor. Scrape down the sides with a spatula. Add the cream and purée 20 to 30 seconds, or until thoroughly combined.

2. Add the lobster and mushrooms, pulse two or three times (only until coarsely chopped), and transfer to a large container.

3. Secure the casing over the end of a sausage attachment and fill the casing. If you're using a pastry bag, squeeze the mixture into the casing until the entire bag is tightly filled, leaving no air pockets. Tie off each end with a piece of twine. Every 6 to 8 inches, tie off links.

4. Preheat a grill.

5. Bring a large pot of water to a boil. Reduce the heat to medium, add the

sausages, and simmer for 6 to 8 minutes. The sausages will feel slightly soft, being not quite done at this point.

6. Remove the links from the water and cut at the tie-off points.

7. Transfer the links to the grill and cook for 10 to 12 minutes, or until browned by the grill and thoroughly cooked. The links are done when they are firm. Serve immediately.

SERVES 6-8

Cod
with Puttanesca Sauce and Leeks

Cod is a good match with the tomato-leek-champagne sauce. Make sure the aluminum foil packets are pinched together firmly so they will not leak when you turn them over. Serve this dish with couscous and toasted garlic bread.

2   pieces heavy-duty aluminum foil, each 12 inches square

2   pounds cod fillet

1   tablespoon olive oil

2   leeks, green stalks cut off, thinly sliced

1   medium tomato, diced

¼   cup champagne (or dry white wine)

8–10 kalamata olives, pitted and sliced

3–4 garlic cloves, minced

2   tablespoons capers

1   teaspoon fresh oregano

1   teaspoon balsamic vinegar

1   teaspoon freshly ground black pepper

Salt

1. Preheat a grill.

2. Lay the cod on the foil, brush it with the oil, and layer the leeks, tomato, champagne, olives, garlic, capers, oregano, vinegar, pepper, and salt to taste on top of it.

3. Tightly crimp the foil all around. Wrap a second piece of foil around the packet, crimping it on the opposite side. Be sure the packet is secure. Lay it on the grill directly over the heat. Cook for 8 to 10 minutes; turn and cook 3 to 4 minutes longer. Open the packet and insert the tip of a knife into the fillet. If it feels firm, it is done.

4. Remove from the heat, uncover, and transfer the dish to a large serving platter.

SERVES 2-4

Smoked Tuna
with Ponzu Sauce

You may slice the tuna thin — use a very sharp knife — and serve as an appetizer.

½ cup sake

Juice of ⅔ lemon (about 2 tablespoons)

1 tablespoon low-sodium soy sauce

1½ pounds sushi-grade tuna

1 teaspoon sesame oil

½ cup bamboo shoots

½ cup shiitake mushrooms, finely chopped (or oyster or baby bellas)

3–4 garlic cloves, diced

2 tablespoons finely chopped fresh ginger

½ cup Ponzu Sauce (see page 232)

Cooked brown rice

Lemon wedges

Serve this dish with Grilled Marinated Eggplant (see page 225).

To Drink

Sake or cold Sapporo beer

1. Prepare a grill for smoke grilling.

2. In a noncorrosive container, whisk together the sake, lemon juice, and soy sauce. Marinade the tuna in the mixture for 20 to 30 minutes in the refrigerator.

3. Remove the tuna, drain, and place on the cool side of the grill. Smoke for about 45 minutes with the lid closed. The tuna will be quite rare and soft to the touch.

4. Meanwhile, heat the sesame oil in a large skillet or wok over medium-high heat. Sauté the bamboo shoots, mushrooms, garlic, and ginger for 1 to 2 minutes. Add the Ponzu Sauce, simmer 6 to 8 minutes until vegetables are thoroughly coated, and turn off the heat.

5. Remove the tuna from the heat and divide into four portions. Place on warm plates with brown rice and ladle the sauce over the fish and rice. Serve with the lemon wedges.

SERVES 4

Smoked Shad Roe

If you love shad roe in the spring, at the same time the forsythia is in bloom, be brave. Try this.

To prepare in a smokehouse, increase the smoking time to 3 to 4 hours (see page 190). Keep in mind that roe is perishable; even after smoking, it will keep only 4 to 6 days.

What to do with the roe after it's smoked? Substitute smoked roe for the smoked milt in Scrambled Eggs with Smoked Shad Milt, on page 61. Roe is very rich, so if the sacs are large, half of one is probably enough for one person.

fresh shad roe in its own sac, ½ to 1 sac per person

Lemon wedges

1. Prepare a grill for smoke grilling.

2. Generously spray the rack and the underside of the roe sacs with cooking spray. Lay the sacs on heavily oiled 12-inch aluminum squares on the cool side of the grill. Smoke for 1½ hours with the lid closed.

3. Remove carefully with a spatula and serve immediately with the lemon wedges.

VARIATION Before serving, sauté the roe in butter and a splash of white wine in a skillet over low heat for 5 to 6 minutes on each side, turning very gently.

To Drink

Cold beer or iced Gin Rickeys (see page 236)

Smoked Shad
with Gazpacho

Make the gazpacho a day ahead, if you have the time; it helps to meld the spices and flavors. If you smoke-grill the shad a day ahead of time as well, you'll be ready for a quick afternoon meal.

A good gazpacho should have large chunks of vegetables mixed into the tomato and a lot of garlic, as this one does. Adjust the hot sauce accordingly.

Juice of 1 lemon (about 3 tablespoons)

2 pounds boneless shad fillets

2 tablespoons cracked black peppercorns

1 tablespoon sea salt

1 can (14½ ounces) stewed tomatoes

1 tablespoon olive oil

2 teaspoons cider vinegar

½ teaspoon ground coriander

½ teaspoon ground cumin

½ teaspoon hot sauce, plus extra if desired

½ teaspoon dried oregano

1 English cucumber, peeled and coarsely chopped

1 small green bell pepper, coarsely chopped

1 small sweet white onion, coarsely chopped

8 garlic cloves, minced

1 medium tomato, coarsely chopped

Lemon wedges

1. Prepare a grill for smoke grilling.

2. Drizzle 1½ tablespoons of the lemon juice over the shad fillets and season with 1 teaspoon of the peppercorns and ½ teaspoon of the salt.

3. Smoke on the cool side of the grill for 1½ hours, or until the fillets have taken on a golden hue but remain soft. Remove and refrigerate for at least 12 hours.

4. To make the gazpacho, pulse the remaining lemon juice, peppercorns, and salt and the stewed tomatoes, oil, vinegar, coriander, cumin, hot sauce, and oregano in the bowl of a food processor four or five times.

5. Add half of the cucumber, half of the pepper, half of the onion, and half of the garlic. Pulse five or six times, then transfer to a large bowl.

6. Add the tomato and the remaining chopped vegetables and stir thoroughly. Cover and transfer to the refrigerator for at least 12 hours.

7. A half hour before serving, remove the shad and gazpacho from the refrigerator. Divide the shad into four portions, ladle the gazpacho into bowls, and serve with the lemon wedges and extra hot sauce, if desired.

SERVES 4

VARIATION Instead of smoke grilling, smoke the shad a day ahead in a large smoker or smokehouse for 5 to 6 hours, and refrigerate until ready to use.

Tea Leaf-Smoked Red Snapper

If you can, have your fishmonger bone and prepare the snapper for you; otherwise, clean and remove all the bones and lay out the fish flat, butterflied, with the skin side down.

Use a fish basket or aluminum foil with holes for this recipe.

6 tablespoons dried black tea leaves

3–4 star anise, crushed

4–6 garlic cloves, finely chopped

2 tablespoons ground cinnamon

2 tablespoons low-sodium soy sauce

1 tablespoon pure maple syrup

1 whole snapper, 2½ to 3 pounds, boned and butterflied

Papa's Papaya Chutney (see page 232)

Cooked brown rice

1. Prepare a grill for smoke grilling.

2. Mix the tea leaves, anise, garlic, cinnamon, soy sauce, and maple syrup into a paste. Rub the paste into the flesh of the fish with a spatula.

3. Oil the grate and the snapper skin with a cooking spray or brush. Lay the snapper on the cool side of the grill and close the lid. Smoke 1¼ hours; turn and smoke 1¼ hours longer, or until the fish is golden brown.

4. Remove the snapper from the heat, divide each side into two portions, and serve immediately with Papa's Papaya Chutney and brown rice.

SERVES 4

To Drink

Sake or chilled India Pale Ale

Yellowtail Smoked
over Fennel

Yellowtail is also called *hamachi* in Japanese restaurants and used in the making of sushi. I love it raw, but smoked its sweet flavor comes through even more. Yellowtail, a member of the *Carangidae*, or Jack family, should not be confused with yellowfin tuna.

½ stalk fresh fennel, cut in half lengthwise
2 pounds yellowtail fillets
Lemon wedges
Dill Mustard Sauce (see page 231)

1. Prepare a grill for smoke grilling.

2. Place about 2 cups of dried corn kernels in the center of a smoke pan or on an 18-inch square of heavy-duty aluminum foil. Nestle the fennel into the center of the corn. Cover and place directly over the heat source.

3. Wait until the corn and fennel begin to smoke, about 10 minutes. Lay the yellowtail fillets on the cool side of the grill, on oiled grates. Close the lid and smoke for 1 to 1½ hours, or until the fish is slightly golden. Lift the lid only occasionally to check for flames. Douse with water if necessary.

4. Remove the fillets from the heat, divide into four portions, and serve while warm with the lemon wedges and Dill Mustard Sauce.

SERVES 4

Smoked Croaker

The meat of Atlantic croaker (included in the larger group known as drum fish) has a slight lemony but sweet flavor. There are bones, yes, but they're manageable. I don't mind having guests pick away with their fingers; the backbone lifts out easily.

Serve one to two fish per person; they are often less than a pound each, including the head and tail.

½ cup olive oil
Juice of 1 lemon (about 3 tablespoons)
2   tablespoons finely chopped oregano
2   tablespoons finely chopped thyme
1   teaspoon salt
1   tablespoon freshly ground black pepper
2   pounds croaker fillets
Papa's Papaya Chutney (see page 232)

METHOD: Smoke grilling
ADVANCE PREPARATION:
Marinate fish for 1 to 2 hours

1. Stir together the oil, lemon juice, oregano, thyme, salt, and pepper in a large mixing bowl.

2. Place the croaker into a 1-gallon resealable plastic bag or a glass baking pan. Pour the marinade over the fish and refrigerate for 1 to 2 hours.

3. Prepare a grill for smoke grilling.

4. Remove the croaker from the marinade, pat dry, and place on the cool side of the smoker. Close the lid and smoke for about 1 hour. The grill temperature should be maintained at 200 to 250°F.

5. Replenish the corn or wood chips if necessary, turn the fish, and smoke for 1 to 1½ hours longer, or until the fillets are golden. Serve warm with Papa's Papaya Chutney.

SERVES 4-6

Smoked Pastrami Mackerel

You may increase the smoking time to 3 hours, or longer, for a more intense smoke flavor reminiscent of a "pastrami-style" preparation. Brining or using a curing solution is optional.

Smoked fish can be refrigerated for several days or frozen for up to 6 months.

Crack whole peppercorns by pulsing several times in a food processor or by wrapping in a cloth towel or wax paper and smacking with the flat side of a meat cleaver into a consistent but coarse rub.

Curing solution of your choice (see pages 198–201); optional
⅓ cup cracked black peppercorns
1 tablespoon dried oregano
1 tablespoon coarse salt
1 tablespoon dried thyme
2 pounds mackerel fillets
Dill Mustard Sauce (see page 231)

1. Prepare a grill for smoke grilling.

2. Inject or brine the fillets with the curing solution, if using, and refrigerate for 30 minutes to 1 hour.

3. Mix the peppercorns, oregano, salt, and thyme in a large bowl. Pack and rub the mixture thoroughly into the top side of the fillets with your hands. Set aside.

4. Oil the grate and the underside of the fillets (the skin side) with a brush or cooking spray. Lay the fillets on the cool side of the grill and close the lid. Resist the temptation to open the lid, except to add more dried corn or wood chips and to check for flames, which may need dousing. Smoke for a total of 2½ hours, or more if you wish, but do not turn. Mackerel will turn golden brown.

5. Remove the fillets from the heat and serve with the Dill Mustard Sauce.

SERVES 6-12 AS AN APPETIZER

Serve this dish with Smoked Salmon Spread (see page 30) instead of Dill Mustard Sauce.

Smoked Tuna Martini

Gin is made from juniper berries. It infuses the tuna from below while the smoke engulfs from above, creating a happy, martini-flavored smoked tuna.

You will need an 8-inch aluminum pan or a cast-iron frying pan to hold the liquid. You'll also need a wire rack, such as the kind used for roasting poultry. Oil the rack before placing the tuna on it so it doesn't stick. The rack then straddles the pan.

1   cup gin
½   cup water
Juice of 1½ lemon (about 4½ tablespoons)
1   pound fresh tuna

Serve with wasabi paste and pickled ginger, which are available in the Asian section of many supermarkets, or with Dill Mustard Sauce (see page 231).

1. Preheat a grill for smoke grilling, filling the smoke pan with dried corn kernels.

2. Mix the gin, water, and lemon juice and pour into an 8-inch aluminum pan. Place the tuna on an oiled wire rack suspended over the pan.

3. Set the aluminum pan on the grate directly over the smoke pan. Close the lid and smoke for 45 minutes. Turn and smoke 45 minutes longer.

4. Remove the tuna from the heat, cut into two or three portions, and serve immediately.

SERVES 2–3 AS A MAIN COURSE OR 6–8 AS AN APPETIZER

VARIATION To use as an appetizer, slice cold tuna thin and serve on small squares of rye or pumpernickel bread with a dollop of the Dill Mustard Sauce on top. Garnish with a small sprig of fresh dill.

Rum-Smoked Tuna

You will need an 8-inch aluminum pan or cast-iron frying pan to hold the liquid, and a wire rack, such as the kind used for roasting poultry. Oil the rack so the tuna doesn't stick to it. The rack straddles the pan and the fish essentially is steamed over rum.

A 1-pound piece of tuna will serve two or three people as a main course or six to eight as an appetizer.

1   cup rum
½   cup water
¼   cup lime juice
1   pound fresh tuna
Dill Mustard Sauce (page 231)
Small sprig of fresh dill

METHOD: Smoke grilling

1. Prepare a grill for smoke grilling.

2. Combine the rum, water, and lime juice and pour into the aluminum pan. Place the tuna on a wire rack suspended over the pan.

3. Set the aluminum pan on the grate directly over the smoke pan. Close the lid and smoke for 45 minutes. With one or two spatulas, carefully turn, then finish smoking for an additional 45 minutes.

4. Remove, cut into two or three portions, garnish with the dill, and serve immediately with the Dill Mustard Sauce.

SERVES 2 OR 3

VARIATION To serve as an appetizer, let cool in the refrigerator for about 1 hour, slice thin, and serve on small squares of rye or pumpernickel bread with a dollop of the Dill Mustard Sauce on top. This dish serves 6 to 8 people as an appetizer.

Fennel-Smoked Bluefish
with Blueberry Balsamic Sauce

The blueberries add a rich depth to this and help cut the strong flavor of the oily bluefish. You may substitute mackerel or tuna for the bluefish. Serve with brown rice and fresh corn on the cob.

2   cups fresh blueberries, washed

1   cup low-salt chicken stock

¼   cup orange-flavored liqueur such as triple sec or orange curaçao

¾   teaspoon freshly squeezed lemon juice

¼   cup fresh thyme, stemmed

1   tablespoon maple syrup

1½ teaspoons balsamic vinegar

½   stalk fresh fennel, cut lengthwise

2   pounds bluefish fillets

Chopped red peppers for garnish

Lemon zest for garnish

METHOD: Smoke grilling

1. Purée the blueberries for about 30 seconds in the bowl of a food processor. Strain through cheesecloth into a medium-size saucepan.

2. Add the stock, liqueur, lemon juice, and thyme and simmer over medium heat for 6 to 8 minutes, or until reduced by half.

3. Add the maple syrup and vinegar and simmer for 2 minutes. Keep warm over low heat.

4. Preheat a grill for smoke grilling.

5. Place about 2 cups of dry corn kernels in the center of the smoke pan or on an 18-inch square of heavy-duty aluminum foil. Nestle the fennel into the center of the corn. Cover and place on the burners or charcoal.

6. Wait until the corn and fennel begin to smoke, about 10 minutes. Lay the bluefish fillets directly over the smoke pan. Smoke 6 minutes, then turn the fillets and also rotate 180 degrees. Cook 6 to 8 minutes longer, or until the fish is firm. Remove from the heat but cover with foil to keep warm.

7. Reheat the sauce by cooking over medium heat for 1 minute.

8. Divide the bluefish into four portions. Ladle a spoonful of the sauce on the bottom of each of four plates, lay a piece of bluefish on top of each, garnish with the red peppers and zest, and serve immediately.

SERVES 4

Smoked Salmon Frittata
with Fiddleheads and Morels

This is the ultimate spring luncheon, combining fiddlehead ferns, morel mushrooms, and Vidalia onions with smoked salmon. Or it makes for a good Sunday brunch item with a small gathering of six to eight people.

My father passed down his egg-mixing technique to me, a technique I later learned was a bit French in its origin. When combining eggs for scrambled eggs, omelets, or frittatas, as is the case here, place them in a bowl (my father did it directly in the cast-iron pan), puncture the yolks, and very gently stir, not mix, the eggs. The idea is to combine them not into a yellowy mass but rather into a swirled mixture that, when cooked, leaves the whites and the yellows separated — two distinct tastes and textures. You can also use just the whites, if you prefer.

Add cooking oil to melting butter to keep the butter from burning. Also, use cooking spray to line the pan completely, all around and including the sides, as is needed for the frittata to free itself once the bottom is cooked.

If you'd like, you may use raw broken-up or flaked salmon. It will cook quite enough by the time the eggs are finished.

1 **dozen fiddlehead ferns, cleaned and sliced (or asparagus spears)**

2 **teaspoons canola oil**

1 **cup morels, cleaned, stemmed, and sliced**

¾ **cup finely chopped Vidalia onions**

½ **cup seeded, deveined, and finely chopped yellow peppers**

4–5 **garlic cloves, finely chopped**

2 **tablespoons unsalted butter**

10 **eggs**

¼ **cup finely chopped fresh tarragon**

1 **teaspoon salt**

1 **tablespoon freshly ground black peppercorns**

6 **ounces Smoked Salmon (see page 112), broken or flaked into pieces**

1. Preheat an oven or a grill to 350°F.

2. Parboil the fiddleheads for 1½ minutes. Drain and set aside.

3. Heat 1 teaspoon of the oil in a large saucepan over medium heat. Add the morels, onion, pepper, and garlic. Cook, stirring, for 3 minutes. Stir in the fiddleheads. Remove from the heat and set aside.

4. Begin melting the butter in a 10-inch ovenproof, Teflon-coated or non-stick saucepan over medium-high heat. Add the remaining teaspoon of oil to the melting butter.

5. Meanwhile, combine the eggs, tarragon, salt, and pepper in a large mixing bowl. Puncture the egg yolks and very gently swirl together for about 5 seconds.

6. Add the cooked vegetables and, without further stirring, transfer to the heated pan. Lower the heat to medium-low and cook, uncovered, for 10 minutes, or until the flavors are blended.

7. Place the pan in the preheated oven, or preheated grill for 15 minutes to achieve a slight smoke flavor.

SERVES 6 - 8

Smoked Salmon

This salmon is hot smoked. The smoked fish more closely resembles baked salmon, rather than the more familiar cold-smoked salmon, the Nova-style lox.

You may inject or brine the fillets with a curing solution (see pages 198–201), if you want, for added flavor. You may also smoke the salmon in a larger smoker or smokehouse, in which case follow the directions on page 188.

Hot-smoked salmon will keep refrigerated for up to a week. Be aware, though, that smoked salmon fresh from the smoker often doesn't last long enough to reach a refrigerator.

2 **pounds fresh salmon fillets**

1 **tablespoon good-quality extra-virgin olive oil**

1 **teaspoon sea salt**

2 **tablespoons freshly ground black pepper**

Lemon wedges

Dill Mustard Sauce (see page 231)

1. Brush the fillets with the oil and season both sides with the salt and pepper. Set aside.

2. Preheat a grill for smoke grilling.

3. Lay the fillets on the cool side of an oiled grill. Close the lid and smoke for 1 to 1½ hours. Lift the lid only occasionally to check for unwanted flames. Douse with water if necessary. Smoke longer for a more intense flavor.

4. Remove the smoked fillets from the heat and let cool slightly before slicing. Serve with the lemon wedges and Dill Mustard Sauce.

SERVES 4 AS A MAIN COURSE OR 8–10 AS AN APPETIZER

Ever Been Cold?
Go to Pulaski, New York

W E WERE TO MEET at Trump's Cabins outside of Pulaski, New York. It was February, snowing and c-c-cold. Our piscine prey was steelhead trout, the winter-migrating rainbow that runs up the Salmon River out of Lake Ontario. The feisty *Oncorhynchus mykiss* average 6 to 15 pounds here. We had engaged a guide, Trump, for a 1-day float trip. According to both Trump and Craig (our indefatigable winter camp leader), Trump is the most knowledgeable guide on the Salmon River. All other fishermen we encountered that day knew of him, due, in part, to the black letters boldly painted on his guide boat spelling: T-R-U-M-P.

I stopped at a sporting goods store in town for a few extra items: SmartWool socks and expedition weight liners, all of which were eventually layered under polar-fleece pants inside my double insulated waders. What ultimately saved my toes from frostbite were hand and foot warmers, the kind that are shaken to activate the iron, vermiculite, carbon, and salt that heat up to 156°F, intended to be slipped into mittens, socks, and boots for warmth. I believe them to be the sole reason that I did not commit hari-kari that winter day.

I am usually the first person to complain about cold feet. And I did. But so did Chris and Beezee (two other captives along for winter boot camp), who rarely, if ever, do. They followed downriver in a second boat with their own guide. The outside temperature stalled at about 0°F and when the wind blew across the water, sane people (none of whom seemed to exist this day) had to wonder why we paid our guide a substantial amount of money for continued jolts of sadism.

Silently, I reminisced about the Caribbean islands I traveled one winter, recalling warm breezes and palm trees. I shut my eyes and saw snorkeling attire and postcard-perfect turquoise water. I opened my eyes to ice floes bobbing past us and with the guides on my fly rod clogged with slush.

I had believed, erroneously, that I was quite prepared with my newly acquired gear: On the upper torso alone I wore wickable polyester fabric underwear, a Zyflex lightweight shirt, a Coolmax thermal shirt, and a Polartec-200 fleece Snap-T pullover with LYCRA-elastane cuffs, and for the outer layer, a Teflon-coated Supplex nylon parka with 200 grams olefin polyester insulation over a Gore-Tex XCR extended Comfort Range fabric with a ripstop nylon waterproof shell, all machine washable. Not enough.

On my head I tied down a microfleece hat with coyote fur earflaps and ruff. Around my neck was wrapped a Bala-clavas fleece neck gaiter and from afar I suspect that I looked like the Pillsbury Dough Boy. I was still cold.

I was reminded of my childhood days in the Midwest, when I walked a mile or so to school every day, occasionally in temperatures of fifty below. That frigid January day on the Salmon River has been indelibly etched into my temporal lobe as nearly equal to the grueling force of those Minnesota winters.

When I reached for a sandwich, it was frozen. Ever try to eat a turkey sandwich with mayonnaise, cucumbers, and tomatoes in winter conditions? Mayonnaise: teeth-shattering solid. Frozen tomatoes have no taste. Crystallized, cucumbers take on the molecular structure of bubble wrap. I set down a Styrofoam cup that contained a half-inch of steaming hot coffee; 10 minutes later, it was a hockey puck. (By the way, folks, do not drink too much coffee; you will have to eventually fumble through layers of bulky clothing to find the zipper.) The wind chill was now hovering at around 25 degrees below zero.

Our New York Sherpa told me it was warmer to stand in the river, which was 34°F. Logically, that made sense, but . . . come on! In the water? I supposed if I was fool enough to be in this predicament in the first place, I ought to listen to this man's expensive advice.

Upstate New York had already received more than 5 feet of snow . . . and it was snowing and blowing, wickedly so. Reluctantly — okay, stupidly — I removed my parka in order to get down to the feet and replace expired heat packets. (Aha, now was the time . . . nope, the zipper was frozen shut.) I am convinced that heat-packet foresight prevented me from developing frostbitten toes.

The day was saved, however, because we caught fish; well, some of us did. I hooked and lost one steelhead with the skilled assistance of my guide (he catches fish for you and then hands you the rod — part of the deal), and netted two others, a respectable 10 and 12 pounds.

Alas, Chris and Beezee did not even have a hit; feelings of desperation set in by midday. The look in their eyes told me even more: Friction from the knives being visually tossed in Craig's direction nearly heated up the air for us all.

Periodically, when I glanced toward shore, I saw them stomping around in snowbanks over their hips, attempting to reintroduce blood to their long-lost feet. I saw an ashen look on their faces that suggested they were not enjoying this outing that had been organized by their now former friend.

Later, thawing frozen tear ducts, earlobes, fingers, and toes next to the fireplace in the cabin, we discussed the fact that when one has such an uncomfortable experience, things can seem eternally fruitless (and painfully miserable) when no fish are caught. I agreed but said that as cold as I was for 12 agonizing hours on the river, the time was made somewhat enjoyable, er, tolerable by the mere fact that I *did* catch fish.

Back home 2 days later, I stopped off to see Chris and Beezee at their place of work. Chris was not in, but I asked Beezee if he had thawed out yet.

"Just barely," was his frosty reply. How was Chris? I asked. He had told Beezee it was the worst experience he ever had in his life. ➤

Chapter 5

Shellfish

OTHER THAN HAVING frozen African lobster tail for special occasions during college days in a plains state — introduced to me by my sophisticated southern belle girlfriend — I never had real lobster until moving to Martha's Vineyard in my first days of living on the East coast. Having only known the flavor of freshwater fish, I happily discovered a new food: shellfish. I scalloped with a friend at low tide in an estuary between Edgartown and Vineyard Haven, and then opened shellfish until my hands were raw. I loved every bit of those creatures so saline fresh, so wonderfully briny, that I had to invent tastebuds to accommodate the new flavors.

Lobster, corn, and potatoes, all slightly smoky from smoldering in a sandpit on the beach, only intensifies the fascination with island cuisine of a twenty-two year old from a land of agriculture.

My first job out of college was teaching at Katie Hinni's School of Creative Arts in Vineyard Haven where all of my fellow teachers were fun loving and from big eastern cities. I learned many things that summer: how to crack open lobsters with a rock and suck the juice from the legs; to eat fresh scallop roe; to dare to eat raw clams. I've become a shellfish-loving (transplanted) Easterner. Apologies to my landlocked family back home.

Corn-Smoked Lobster

This is a singular recipe where a true "corn smoke" comes through with flying colors. Have fun and blow off fireworks for the 4th of July.

Smoke a couple of extra lobsters and enjoy a Corn-Smoked Lobster Salad (see page 169) the next day at a picnic on Menemsha Beach, where I tasted my first New England lobster, which sold for $1.09 a pound at Dutcher's Dock.

If you want to serve larger lobsters than suggested, adjust the cooking time by about 15 minutes for every extra half pound.

4   lobsters, 1¼ pounds or larger
Dill Butter (see page 231), melted
Lemon wedges

1. Preheat a grill for smoke grilling.

2. Turn the lobsters on their backs on a large cutting board. With a sharp knife, make an incision down the center of each tail almost to the tip, without cutting through the shell.

With your hands, gently split apart the tails, opening up the cavities.

3. Swab the melted Dill Butter into the cavity. Lay the lobsters on their backs over the smoke pan. (You may need to do this in stages if your grill will not accommodate four lobsters at the same time.) Close the lid. Insert a meat thermometer into the thickest part of the meat, at the base of the tail.

4. Cook for about 50 minutes, or until the internal temperature reaches 130°F.

SERVES 4

To Drink

Cold beer
or Lemonade
(see page 236)

Serve with Smoked Corn on the Cob
(see page 220), potato salad,
coleslaw, more Dill Butter,
and lots of napkins.

Tickled Pink Oyster Pasta

This is, without a doubt, getting the most for your dollar. This recipe starts with an appetizer recipe, Tickled Pink Pickled Oysters (see page 32), but saves the unused smoky cream sauce to mix with pasta.

1½ cups cognac (or brandy)

1½ cups heavy cream

1   cup clam juice

2   tablespoons cracked pink (or black) peppercorns

1   teaspoon paprika

1   teaspoon cayenne pepper

1   dozen unopened oysters

Dried or fresh pasta for four people

Lemon wedges

1. Preheat a grill for smoke grilling.

2. To make the bisque, combine the cognac, cream, clam juice, peppercorns, paprika, and cayenne in a cast-iron or disposable aluminum foil pan. Set the pan directly on top of the smoke pan over the heat.

3. Place the oysters on the cool side of the grill. Close the lid and smoke for 15 minutes, until the oysters open. When this happens, pry each one completely open so the smoke flavor penetrates further. Be careful not to spill their natural juices. Cook 30 minutes longer.

To Drink

Ginger beer

4. Remove the oysters from their shells and drain the juice into the bisque. Transfer the bisque to a burner and cook, stirring, 8 to 10 minutes over medium-high heat, or until reduced by one third. Remove the bisque from the heat, strain it through a sieve into a 4-quart saucepan, and keep covered.

5. Bring water to a boil and cook the pasta according to the package instructions. Drain, then add the pasta to the saucepan along with the smoked oysters. Cook, stirring, for 1 to 2 minutes over low heat.

6. Ladle into four bowls and serve immediately with the lemon wedges.

SERVES 4

VARIATION Cook six mussels and six clams on the grill and add the meat to the sauce, as you will the oysters.

Asparagus tips or diced green zucchini add a layer of flavor and color.

Grilled Shrimp
in a Spicy Chile Sauce

This recipe may be adjusted to your individual heat preference by increasing or reducing the number of chiles.

I recommend large shrimp, 6 to 8s, or six to eight shrimp per pound, but any size will do. The number of shrimp and skewers needed will be determined by the size of the shrimp you purchase.

Use the Shrimp Paste recipe on page 229 or a jar of any commercial shrimp paste, found in the Asian section of your supermarket. Commercial paste may be very strong, so determine its potency beforehand by tasting it.

1   **quart water**

2   **large New Mexico dried chiles or ancho chiles**

1   **habanero or 2 jalapeño chiles**

2   **cups Fish Stock (see page 141)**

3–4 **garlic cloves, finely chopped**

2   **tablespoons olive oil**

2   **tablespoons Shrimp Paste (see page 229) (or use a commercial variety)**

8   **wooden skewers (11½ inches long), soaked for 30 minutes in warm water**

1   **teaspoon freshly ground black pepper**

Juice of ½ lime (about 1 tablespoon)

2   **pounds large shrimp, about 16, peeled and deveined**

Lime wedges

1. Combine the water and dried chiles in a large mixing bowl. Cover and let stand for 30 minutes. Drain the chiles and, with rubber gloves, remove the stems and seeds. Set aside.

2. Preheat a grill.

3. Grill the fresh chile for 4 to 5 minutes; turn and grill 5 minutes longer, or until softened.

4. Combine all chiles in the bowl of a food processor and pulse six to eight times. Add the fish stock and purée for 1 minute. Strain through wire mesh into a bowl and set aside.

5. Sauté the garlic in the oil for 1 to 2 minutes in a large skillet over medium-high heat. Stir in the Shrimp Paste and add the purée mixture. Reduce the heat to medium-low and simmer, covered, for about 10 minutes, or until reduced by about one third. Add pepper and lime juice.

To Drink

Cold microbrewed beer or chilled lemonade

6. Meanwhile, skewer the shrimp and grill 4 to 5 minutes; turn and grill 4 to 5 minutes longer, or until shrimp turn pink but are still slightly soft. (If using charcoal, reduce the cooking time to 3 to 4 minutes per side, depending upon the size of the shrimp).

7. Remove the shrimp from the skewers and transfer to the simmering skillet. Increase the heat to medium-high and stir for about 1 minute, just enough to coat the shrimp.

8. Remove the shrimp from the skillet, divide them onto four plates, and ladle the sauce over each. Serve with the lime wedges.

SERVES 4

Serve over short-grained white rice or orzo.

Cleaning Shrimp

Buy shrimp already cleaned so you don't run into this problem, especially if you don't have the knack for it.

"To Shell shrimps and Prawns Quickly and Easily. This, though a most simple process, would appear, from the manner in which it is performed by many people, to be a very difficult one; indeed it is not unusual for persons of the lower classes, who, from lack of a little skill, find it slow and irksome, to have resource to the dangerous plan of eating the fish entire.

"It need scarcely be remarked that very serious consequences may accrue from the shells being swallowed . . .

"Unless the fish be stale, when they are apt to break, they will quit the shells easily if the head be held firmly in the right hand and the tail in the other, and the fish be straightened entirely, then the two hands pressed quickly towards each other, and the shell of the tail broken by a slight vibratory motion of the right hand, when it will be drawn off with the head adhering to it: a small portion, only will then remain on at the other end, which can be removed in an instant."

—*Modern Cookery for Private Families*
by Eliza Acton, 1845

Jerk Shrimp

This doesn't have to be a spicy dish. You may eliminate the hot sauce entirely if you prefer. Some people buy jumbo shrimp, some buy super-colossal shrimp. Whichever size you choose, serve about half a pound of shrimp to each guest.

3–4 garlic cloves

2 tablespoons coarsely chopped sweet white onion

1½ tablespoons vinegar

1 tablespoon honey or pure maple syrup

1 tablespoon Worcestershire sauce

1 teaspoon ground cumin

1 teaspoon coarsely ground black pepper

1 teaspoon salt

1 teaspoon hot sauce

½ teaspoon ground cinnamon

½ teaspoon ground nutmeg

2 pounds large shrimp, about 16, peeled and deveined

4 wooden skewers (11½ inches long), soaked for 30 minutes in warm water

Lemon wedges

Grill skewers of vegetables, such as zucchini, green and red bell peppers, onions, and portobellos, along with the shrimp. The vegetable skewers cook about the same amount of time as the shrimp.

1. Preheat a grill.

2. To make the jerk seasoning, pulse the garlic, onion, vinegar, honey, Worcestershire sauce, cumin, pepper, salt, hot sauce, cinnamon, and nutmeg four to five times in the bowl of a food processor. Scrape down the sides with a spatula and purée for 15 to 20 seconds.

3. Toss the shrimp with the jerk seasoning until the shrimp are thoroughly covered.

4. Skewer the shrimp, four per skewer, and grill for 4 to 5 minutes; turn and grill 4 to 5 minutes longer or until shrimp turn pink. (If using charcoal, reduce the time to 3 to 4 minutes per side, depending upon size).

5. Serve immediately with the lemon wedges.

SERVES 4

To Drink

Cold microbrewed beer or iced tea with lemon

Shrimp Satays

Now that more super-sized shrimp are available these days, it is a generous gesture to serve guests colossal shrimp, if you can get past the colossal prices.

Increase the cooking time by 1 to 2 minutes per side if you use colossal shrimp. Shrimp shouldn't be served rare; nor should it be served overcooked. While it is grilling, poke it or pinch it with your fingers; it should give a little, unlike the overcooked cocktail shrimp served in most restaurants.

Don't forget, shrimp will continue to cook after it is removed from the heat, as most foods do. Your guests will thank you after they've tried a slightly *under-cooked* shrimp for possibly the first time in their lives.

Grill the shrimp on skewers or use a perforated pizza pan.

½ cup sour cream

2 tablespoons pure maple syrup

2 tablespoons low-sodium soy sauce

1 tablespoon coarsely ground black pepper

6–8 large shrimp, about 1 pound, peeled and deveined

3 tablespoons smooth peanut butter

1 teaspoon vegetable oil

10 cloves garlic (about ¼ cup), finely chopped

4 wooden skewers (11½ inches long) soaked for 30 minutes in warm water

Lemon wedges

½ cup finely chopped scallions

1. Preheat a grill.

2. Mix the sour cream, maple syrup, soy sauce, and pepper in a large bowl. Marinate shrimp in the mixture for about 1 hour, covered and refrigerated.

3. Remove the shrimp from the marinade and set aside in the refrigerator.

4. In a food processor, combine the marinade and peanut butter in a food processor for about 1 minute, or until the mixture is puréed.

5. Heat the oil over medium-high heat in a saucepan. Sauté the garlic for 2 to 3 minutes. Add the puréed mixture, bring to a boil, reduce the heat to medium, and cook 5 to 8 minutes, or until reduced by one third. Reduce heat to low, cover, and keep warm.

6. Cook the shrimp on the grill for 3 to 4 minutes, using skewers or a perforated pizza pan. Turn and cook 3 to 4 minutes longer. (Cooking time will depend on the size of the shrimp.)

7. Serve on warm plates with the lemon wedges. Ladle warm sauce over the shrimp. Sprinkle with the scallions.

SERVES 2

Scallop and Shrimp Kebabs
with Grilled Oranges

Peel oranges with a potato peeler, avoiding the white pulp just beneath the skin. The peel is wrapped around a scallop or shrimp; the packets are then wrapped in bacon.

Ever wonder what "16 to 20s" or "U to 15s" displayed in the window of your fish market means? Shrimp are measured and sold by the number of shrimp it takes to equal a pound. So, shrimp labeled by your fishmonger as "4 to 6s" means it takes between four and six whole shrimp to equal 1 pound.

Serve two skewers of scallops (three each) and one skewer of shrimp (two each) per person. In addition, each guest will receive one skewer of four orange chunks.

---

2 orange peels
24 large sea scallops
8 large shrimp, about 1 pound, peeled and deveined
Juice of 2 oranges (⅔ to 1 cup)
¼ cup soy sauce
2 tablespoons mirin
1 teaspoon cayenne pepper
1 teaspoon rice wine vinegar
1 pound bacon, each slice cut in half
16 wooden skewers (11½ inches long), soaked for 30 minutes in warm water
1 orange, washed and cut into 16 chunks
½ cup finely chopped fresh mint

Serve with sautéed greens beans and pearl barley cooked in chicken stock.

1. Peel the oranges and squeeze the juice, reserving both.

2. Mix the scallops, shrimp, orange juice, soy sauce, mirin, cayenne, and vinegar thoroughly in a large bowl. Refrigerate for about 30 minutes.

3. Preheat a grill.

4. Remove the scallops and shrimp from the marinade. Sandwich each shrimp and each scallop between two orange peels. Wrap each bundle with a piece of bacon and secure with a toothpick.

5. Skewer three scallop bundles onto eight skewers and two shrimp bundles onto four skewers. Skewer four chunks of oranges onto four skewers.

6. Pour excess marinade over all, sprinkle with the mint, and cook on the grill for 7 minutes. Turn and cook 7 minutes longer, or until the shrimp turn pink.

7. Serve each guest four skewers (two with scallops, one with shrimp, and one with oranges) or serve family-style on a center platter.

SERVES 4

Spicy Grilled Soft-Shell Crabs

Soft-shell crabs are sold in sizes ranging from "hotels," 3 inches, to "jumbos," up to 5 inches across. Three hotels or two jumbo crabs are enough for the average serving, unless you come from the Chesapeake area, where you are used to bountiful springtime feasts of the fresh molting crabs. Serve with coleslaw.

2–3 jalapeño chiles, seeded, deveined, and finely chopped
6–8 garlic cloves
½ cup tomato paste
2 tablespoons oyster sauce
2 tablespoons low-sodium soy sauce
1 tablespoon coarsely ground black pepper
1 tablespoon fish sauce
1 tablespoon pure maple syrup
Juice of ½ lime (about 1 tablespoon)
1 teaspoon tandoori powder (or turmeric)
4–6 soft-shell crabs

1. Whisk the chiles, garlic, tomato paste, oyster sauce, soy sauce, pepper, fish sauce, maple syrup, lime juice, and tandoori powder in a large bowl until thoroughly combined.

2. Add the crabs to the mixture and coat completely. Cover and refrigerate for 20 to 30 minutes.

3. Preheat a grill.

4. Remove the crabs from the refrigerator, shake off the excess marinade with tongs, and transfer to a well-oiled grill. Shut the lid and cook for about 4 minutes; turn and cook 4 to 5 minutes longer, or until crabs are bright red and firm. (Cooking time will depend on their size.)

5. Transfer the crabs to a large platter and let guests serve themselves. Have lots of napkins handy.

SERVES 2

Grilled Mediterranean Pizza
with Shrimp

I happened upon a tube of fresh, unfrozen pizza dough in the market one day, in the dairy section alongside tubes of dinner rolls and breakfast croissants, and thought I might try one — for convenience. When you don't feel like fussing with dough from scratch, try this.

You'll need a 12-inch perforated pizza pan.

I use shrimp but you could substitute chunks of lobster or langostine if you'd like. Also, any firm-fleshed fish will do, broken up into large pieces.

10–12 ounces fresh pizza dough (see page 39)

8   ounces tomato or pizza sauce

1   medium tomato, thinly sliced

½   cup pitted niçoise olives, sliced

2   thin slices sweet white onions, cut in half

8–10 large shrimp, about ½ a pound, sliced into halves

2   teaspoons fresh cracked green and pink peppercorns

1   tablespoon fresh oregano

¼   teaspoon salt

8   ounces feta cheese

4   ounces fresh goat cheese

2   tablespoons good-quality extra-virgin olive oil

Zest of 1 lemon (about 1 tablespoon)

1. Preheat a grill.

2. Roll out the dough and place in an oiled 12-inch perforated pizza pan.

3. Ladle on the sauce. Place the tomato, olives, onion, and shrimp evenly over the sauce.

4. Sprinkle the peppercorns, oregano, and salt over the pizza and crumble the cheeses on top.

5. Drizzle on the olive oil and sprinkle the zest over all.

6. Place the pizza pan on the grill, leaving the cover open. Cook for 10 minutes. Check the bottom of the crust after 5 minutes to be sure it is not burning. After 10 minutes, transfer the pan to the upper, second shelf on the same (hot) side or reduce heat to low. Close the lid.

7. Cook 10 minutes longer, or until the crust is brown and the goat cheese is melted. Remove from the heat, slice, and serve immediately.

SERVES 2

Grilled Lobster
with Tomato and Tarragon-Chive Butter

These are simply grilled lobsters, but for added flavor, after trimming the tarragon stalk, put the stalk along with a handful of corn kernels in the cool side of the grill to impart a slightly smoky flavor infused with tarragon.

2   sticks (1 cup) unsalted butter
2   tablespoons finely chopped fresh tarragon
Juice of ½ lemon (about 1½ tablespoons)
1   tablespoon chives, finely snipped
1   teaspoon freshly ground black pepper
2   lobsters, 1¼ pounds each
½   cup breadcrumbs
½   small tomato, diced
1   teaspoon capers
Lemon wedges

1. Melt the butter in a small saucepan over medium-low heat. Add the tarragon, lemon juice, chives, and pepper. Stir, then simmer for 2 minutes. Turn off the heat and set aside.

2. Preheat a grill.

3. Turn over the lobsters onto their backs on a large cutting board. With a sharp knife, make an incision down the center of each tail almost to the tip, without cutting through the shell. With your hands, gently split apart the tails, opening up the cavities.

4. If you want, remove the green tomalley from inside the lobster and add it to the tarragon butter for a richer flavor.

5. Drizzle half of the Tarragon-Chive Butter into the cavity (reserving the rest for dipping) and top with the breadcrumbs, tomato, and capers. Transfer the lobsters, shell-side down, to the grill and close the lid.

6. Grill for 15 minutes, or until meat is firm. (If using 1¾- to 2-pound lobsters, add 8 to 10 minutes.) If using charcoal, the total cooking time will be less.

7. Just before serving, warm the butter to use for dipping. Serve with the lemon wedges.

SERVES 2

Serve with Smoked Corn on the Cob (see page 220).

Grilled Stuffed Sesame Squid

A commercial fisherman friend who occasionally allows me to help him haul lobster traps; weigh, measure, and band the feisty crustaceans; swab down the deck; and stack 50-pound lobster traps — usually around 4 A.M. on a blustery, gray fall day on the Atlantic — also generously offers me super-sized squid when they're in season. Stuffed and grilled, fresh squid have no equal.

You may need to stuff more than two per guest if the squid are small.

If you are able to acquire freshly caught squid, carefully squeeze out the black ink and add some to the cooked mixture, just before stuffing and grilling, for an unusual color and a depth of flavor that never fails to delight guests.

---

8   large squid
1   tablespoon olive oil
1   teaspoon toasted sesame oil
¼   cup finely chopped fresh ginger
4–6 garlic cloves, minced
1   tablespoon sesame seeds
1   cup breadcrumbs
2   tablespoons oyster sauce
2   tablespoons coarsely chopped parsley
¼   cup finely grated aged Asiago (or substitute Parmesan)
Juice of ½ lemon (about 1½ tablespoons)
Salt and freshly ground black pepper
Vegetable oil for brushing

1. Squeeze out the ink from the squid, if possible. Cut off the head, remove the plasticlike inner sheath, and discard. Remove the tentacles, chop fine, and set aside.

2. Heat the olive and sesame oils in a large saucepan over medium-high heat for about 1 minute. Add the ginger, garlic, and sesame seeds and sauté for 1 to 2 minutes. Add the tentacles, breadcrumbs, oyster sauce, and parsley. Cook for 6 to 8 minutes, stirring frequently, or until the crumbs are browned.

3. Preheat a grill.

4. Transfer the mixture to a large bowl and mix thoroughly with the Asiago, lemon juice, and salt and pepper to taste.

To Drink

A crisp Pinot Grigio or Orvieto

5. Loosely stuff each squid with the mixture and secure the ends with toothpicks to completely close the opening.

6. Brush all sides of each squid with vegetable oil and transfer to the grill. Cook for 15 to 18 minutes, brushing occasionally. Turn, brush with oil, and cook 15 to 18 minutes longer or until the meat feels firm. (If the squid are unusually small, cooking may take only 20 to 25 minutes total.)

7. Remove from the heat, divide onto four plates, and serve immediately.

SERVES 4

Serve with grilled mixed vegetables.

Grilled Scallops
in Champagne Sauce

Use fresh sea scallops if you can. Check with Hatch's Fish and Produce Market in Wellfleet, Massachusetts (see Resources, page 224). In the fall — during the scallop months — you may find them with their own roe attached. A rare treat.

I don't promote the use of the nearly extinct black sterlet sturgeon caviar, so please use cod roe, whitefish roe, salmon roe, shad roe, or the roe I learned to love from Lake Superior, lake trout roe. My favorite? Salmon roe.

- 2 **tablespoons unsalted butter**
- 1 **teaspoon good-quality olive oil**
- 2 **medium leeks, white parts only, cleaned and thinly sliced**
- 1 **cup dry champagne**
- ¾ **cup heavy cream**
- 1 **tablespoon mixed freshly ground black and pink peppercorns**
- 16 **medium to large scallops**
- 8 **pieces thinly sliced pancetta, each piece cut in half (or substitute prosciutto)**
- 8 **wooden skewers (11½ inches long), soaked for 30 minutes in warm water**
- 2 **teaspoons stemmed and finely chopped fresh thyme**
- 3 **tablespoons fish roe of your choice**

1. Preheat a grill.

2. Melt the butter in a medium skillet over medium-low heat. Add the oil and sauté the leeks for 15 to 18 minutes, stirring occasionally, until soft.

3. Add the champagne, cream, and peppercorns and simmer for 6 to

8 minutes, or until reduced by about half. Keep warm over low heat.

4. Wrap the scallops with the pancetta slices. Skewer the wrapped scallops, leaving space between each one.

5. Lay the skewered scallops on the grill and cook for 4 to 5 minutes; turn and cook 5 minutes longer, or until scallops are soft to the touch and opaque. Set on warming shelves; turn off the heat and close the lid to keep warm.

6. Season the leeks with the thyme and stir for about 30 seconds.

7. Divide the skewers onto four plates, ladle the sauce over the scallops, and sprinkle with the roe.

SERVES 4

Serve with grilled snap peas.

Bass and Guns

MORNINGS WERE ALWAYS FOGGY, so I almost didn't see the boat on the beach. When I finally found it, I loaded it with a light jacket, bottled water, my fly rod and flies, and lunch — a sweet onion and fresh tomato sandwich — and headed out on the lake.

In spite of the predawn fog, I could hear the commercial fisherman from whom I had rented the boat pushing off ahead of me. I rowed my wooden boat in a different direction.

The fog thinned at sunup. I stopped rowing, quietly lowered the wooden oars into the antique vessel, and readied my gear. I knew the fisherman would be angling deep but I often had success surface casting for largemouth bass, so I tied on a flashy red-and-white popper.

The night before, I had enjoyed a delicious fresh bass dinner in a local restaurant, so I knew fish were here. During the day, I could usually be found on the beach sketching, writing, or reading while watching the old man go out, returning with largemouth bass. A towering mountain was to block the warming rays of the sun for another hour or so, here on what Aldous Huxley once called "the most beautiful lake in the world."

The wooden boat was cumbersome to handle and I had no anchor. I knew the Xocomil, "the wind that carries away sin," would be coming up toward noon, its usual time. I didn't want to be blown to the distant shore several miles away. I wanted to catch a fish for a stew I had planned, made with plump red tomatoes and fresh herbs I acquired from the local *mercado*. I also intended to include the magnificent onions that I relished, onions as sweet and juicy as apples. Between casts I envisioned hand-squeezing tomatoes into my cast-iron stewpot, mimicking the native women who squat around open-air fires as they prepare dinner.

Soon, the fog cleared from the emerald

lake and three volcanoes loomed in the distance: Toliman, with its twin craters; Atitlán, at 11,598 feet the highest, and also the closest; and San Pedro, which rises 9,909 majestic feet above sea level. San Pedro was rarely without its halo of thin clouds. Steam still spews from the bowels of all three volcanoes, blanketing the mountainous Central American countryside with gray volcanic ash.

Lake Atitlán (which means "place of much water"), high in the mountains of Guatemala, is a restful part of the world, inspiringly beautiful and breathtaking — masking, however, a volatile, troubled past.

The fisherman was out nearly a half-mile beyond me, dropping his long-line over the gunwale and into the water below. Half a day later he would pull in his line, holding dozens of hooks and, with luck, a few fish attached. I was convinced the fisherman must have wondered what I was doing out there, flailing a gringo fly rod in the Mayan air, appearing perhaps a bit silly.

By around noontime, I realized no bass were going to surface from the bottom of the lake for my lure, so I stopped fishing and rowed the long haul back to the palm-studded beach.

I was escaping a harsh, snowy winter and felt as if I had discovered heaven's gates here in the cool mountains of Quetzal country, a land where mountain-tops brush the bottoms of clouds. I lived in a tropical paradise at a comfortable 75 degrees in breathtaking mountains. But I never caught any bass.

It was easy enough, however, to indulge myself in satisfying meals of the flaky, delicate white meat; I enjoyed the luxury of buying fish from village boys who passed by my door most evenings. Or, better still, eating in one of the casual restaurants in town — $1.65 for an entire dinner. Occasionally I would dine in a family's home over a dirt floor and with several children watching and smiling. Meals in a private home rarely cost more than $1.

Each day I would browse the open-air market to pick out the juiciest tomatoes, ripe avocados, or my favorite — Godzilla-sized green onions for a fish stew.

I considered returning to Guatemala the following winter for another season surrounded by deliciously sweet onions and exceptionally friendly people. My mind, however, was changed the night I experienced the hard, cold end of a machine gun jabbed into the bony protuberance of my L-4 vertebra. I watched helplessly as armed militiamen escorted an Argentine friend from the cantina where we often played chess. He was incarcerated because he carried a Swiss army knife in his pocket. By chance I had left mine at home that evening.

I saw my chess mate several days later. He survived. Many did not in those years of internal wars. My Argentine chess mate and I resumed our games over a Tacana cerveza to celebrate his near miss.

We tried to ignore the stories we heard daily — reports of horrific crimes, missing tourists, and terrorist sympathizers — trying to concentrate on our game.

Perhaps someday I can return to fish in Lake Atitlán. I would relive blissful days of quiet writing and games of chess, sketching towering volcanoes in a tumultuous country where peaceful-thinking natives and Indians whose clothing and colorful culture reflect a rich inner beauty.

The faded-orange *camisa* for which I paid $5 — possibly a museum piece now — still hangs on my wall to remind me of a better winter. And the largemouth bass I catch in my favorite pond often remind me of the lake I unsuccessfully but happily fished, the most beautiful lake in the world.

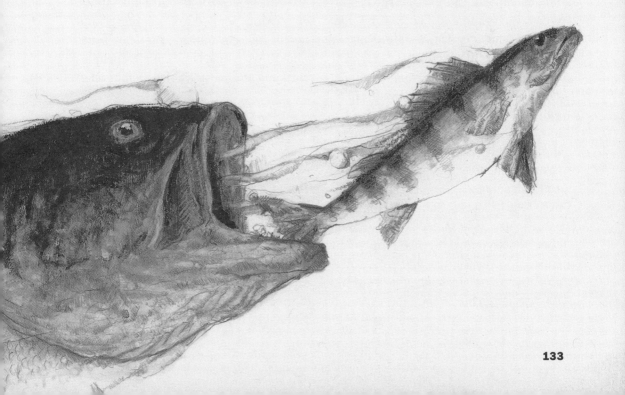

Chapter 6

Stews and Chowders

I S IT BOUILLABAISSE, bourride, burrida, cacciucco, solianka, matelote, sancochos, opera de pescado, or zuppa di pesce? Is it a stew, a soup, or . . . what? Compare fish recipes with another cook, or, better still, a fisherman, and be prepared to defend yourself. Vast geographical ranges of species of fish, saltwater and freshwater, and local vegetables, herbs, and spices are only some of the variables involved in stewing up a swirling good pot of fish with vegetables.

Southern French bouillabaisse is not bouillabaisse without the use of saffron and rascasse, a spiny rockfish that lives in the Gulf of Lion, in the Mediterranean. Craig Claiborne recommends red snapper in a Spanish bouillabaisse as the *only* fish, certainly not the combination of shellfishes that one would expect in a bouillabaisse. Bourride is enhanced with aïoli (a garlic mayonnaise) swirled into the broth just before serving; in Genoa, burrida requires the addition of porcini mushrooms to be called authentic. Italians insist squid and hot peppers are essential in cacciucco seafood stews. Solianka, originally a thick Russian stew made with sturgeon and, yes, sauerkraut, was adapted by émigrés to the United States to utilize available salmon instead of hard-to-find Russian sturgeon. French matelote is a freshwater cousin to saltwater stews, employing pond-raised eel, carp, and perch, as is a South American soup, sancochos, which traditionally includes cachama and payara, prized Venezuelan fish.

In opera de pescado, Catalonia's answer to seafood stew, dating back to the 17th century (then called zarzuela de pescado), the fish must first be fried. In Tuscany, zuppa de pesce may include cuttlefish or squid cooked in its own jet-black ink.

All ingredients in the soups and stews mentioned above, and a dozen or so not included here, appear to me to be at the discretion of the cook. Availability of

ingredients is, of course, the determining factor in preparing a regional fish stew. After all, that's how recipes have originated from the beginning of time: finding, foraging, fishing, and ultimately cooking in one's corner of the world with the ingredients at hand. Before the advent of modern-day communication and transportation systems, it was unlikely that the seven species of Mediterranean fish essential for a *true* bouillabaisse — according to Paula Wolfert, an expert on Mediterranean cuisine — could be included in, say, a Portuguese caldeirata. It just didn't happen, so indigenous fish from the Atlantic waters off Portugal were the obvious choice.

My recommendation? Meld, with consideration for taste and balance, any finfish, shellfish, vegetables, stock, wine, herbs, spices, sauerkraut, and inks in any combination that you please. But swirl in the one ingredient that will make it special: love . . . of a good fish stew.

Fisherman's Stew

I have included stews in a grilled and smoked cookbook because I like to add depths of flavor wherever I can. By first grilling some fish and adding that to stewed shellfish, I believe new layers of flavor can be achieved. Try grilling the lobster, if you want even more grilled flavor (see page 117).

3   tablespoons olive oil

4   garlic cloves, finely chopped

2   medium stalks celery, finely chopped

1   medium white onion, finely chopped

1   small carrot, finely chopped

½   pound coarsely chopped mushrooms

2   large tomatoes, seeded and diced

4   cups Fish Stock (see page 141) or clam juice or water

1   cup white vermouth

Juice of 1 lemon (about 3 tablespoons)

2   teaspoons finely chopped fresh marjoram

2   teaspoons finely chopped fresh oregano

2   teaspoons finely chopped fresh tarragon

1   teaspoon coarsely ground black pepper

1   teaspoon cayenne pepper

1   uncooked lobster (optional), 1½ pounds, cut into chunks

2   pounds grilled firm-fleshed white fish such as striped bass, cod, snapper, or ocean perch fillets, cut into 1-inch squares

8–10 large shrimp, about 1 pound, peeled and deveined

24 mussels

Chopped red pepper for garnish

Lemon wedges

1. Heat the oil over medium-high heat in a large saucepan or stockpot. Add the celery, onion and carrot; reduce the heat to low and simmer for 10 minutes.

2. Add the mushrooms and tomatoes and cook for 3 to 4 minutes.

3. Add the stock, vermouth, lemon juice, marjoram, oregano, tarragon, black pepper, and cayenne; cover and simmer 30 minutes.

4. Add the lobster (if using) and cook for 5 to 6 minutes. Add the grilled fish, shrimp, and mussels and simmer for 4 to 5 minutes, or until the mussels open.

5. Ladle into bowls, dividing the seafood evenly. Garnish with the red pepper and serve with the lemon wedges.

SERVES 4–6

Serve with crusty bread and a tossed green salad.

Salmon and Corn Chowder

I've always had an earthy, comforting feeling about corn, as well as about salmon. Coming, originally, from the landlocked corn country of Minnesota, just short of Canada — home of brilliant salmon of many species — I see the two almost as kissing cousins, homogenized in this recipe as a fall stew, reminiscent of both the harvest and the catch.

1   **pound salmon fillet**

2   **ears fresh corn**

2   **tablespoons olive oil**

1   **medium finely chopped onion (about 1 cup)**

1   **medium Yukon gold potato, diced (about 1 cup)**

2   **cups whole milk**

1   **cup light cream**

4   **tablespoons unsalted butter (½ stick)**

½   **teaspoon Worcestershire sauce**

¼   **cup finely chopped tarragon**

1   **teaspoon paprika**

Salt and freshly ground black pepper

Oyster crackers

ADVANCE PREPARATION:
Grill the salmon and the corn

---

1. Preheat a grill.

2. Lay the salmon and the corncobs on the oiled grill. Cook 6 minutes; then turn and cook 4 to 5 minutes longer. Set aside.

3. With a sharp knife, strip the corn from the cobs and cut the salmon into bite-sized pieces. Set aside.

4. Heat 1 tablespoon of the oil in a 4-quart saucepan over medium-high heat. Add the onion and potato. Cook, covered, for about 10 minutes, or until the onions are soft. Add the milk, cream, butter, and Worcestershire sauce. Simmer for about 10 minutes, or until the potatoes are soft

5. Stir in the corn, salmon, tarragon, paprika, salt, and pepper and simmer for 5 minutes.

6. Transfer to bowls and serve immediately with oyster crackers.

SERVES 6-8

Oyster Stew

If you've ever had the oyster stew at the Oyster Bar in Grand Central Station in New York, you go back, as I do whenever I can. What is amazing is how this simple dish is made in front of your eyes. I've expanded a bit on this New England chowder by grilling the oysters on the half shell first and adding to the already simmering milk and cream.

4 tablespoons (½ stick) butter, sliced into small pieces

Juice of ½ lemon (about 1½ tablespoons)

12 to 24 oysters on the half shell

2 cups whole milk

1 cup heavy cream

1 cup Fish Stock (see page 141) or clam juice

2 tablespoon paprika

½ teaspoon cayenne pepper (optional)

This is the stew for which you need Crown Pilot chowder crackers or large oyster crackers. Either one can be found anywhere along Route 1 on the rocky Maine coast from Kittery to Bar Harbor.

---

1. Preheat a grill.

2. Place a pat of butter and a drizzle of lemon in each oyster shell. Lay on the grill and close the lid. Cook for 5 to 6 minutes, or until the butter melts. Shut off the heat and leave the lid closed.

3. Meanwhile, bring the milk, cream, stock, paprika, and cayenne, if using, to a boil in a 4-quart saucepan over medium-high heat. Immediately reduce the heat to low and simmer for 10 minutes. Make sure the milk does not burn.

4. Remove the oysters from the grill and gently add them and their juices to the pot. Stir for 1 minute, transfer to bowls, and serve hot.

SERVES 4

To Drink

A cold micro-brewed lager or chilled champagne

Lobster-Tomato Bisque

This recipe falls into none of the aforementioned international exotics and has no intriguing name. It is merely a cross between tomato bisque and lobster stew.

1   tablespoon olive oil

4–6 garlic cloves, finely chopped

1   stalk celery, finely chopped

1   small sweet white onion, finely chopped

1   medium tomato, diced

1½–1¾-pound lobster

2   cups whole milk

1   cup tomato sauce

½   cup heavy cream

½   cup Fish Stock (see page 141) or clam juice

4   tablespoons (½ stick) unsalted butter

2   tablespoons finely chopped fresh parsley

1   teaspoon freshly ground black pepper

1. Heat the oil in a large saucepan over medium-high heat. Add the garlic, celery, and onion and cook, stirring, for 8 to 10 minutes. Add the tomatoes. Simmer for 4 to 5 minutes. Turn off the heat and set aside.

2. Preheat a grill.

3. Lay the lobster on its back on a cutting board. Make an incision down the center of the tail almost to the tip, without cutting through the shell; split apart the tail.

4. Grill the lobster for 15 to 18 minutes, shell-side down, with the lid closed. Transfer the lobster from the grill back to a cutting board and remove the meat and tomalley. Discard the shell and set aside the meat.

5. Bring the milk, tomato sauce, cream, stock, and butter to a boil in the saucepan with the vegetables. Reduce the heat to low. Simmer for 10 minutes, stirring often.

6. Add the lobster meat and tomalley and the parsley and pepper. Cover and simmer over the lowest possible heat for 4 to 5 minutes, or until hot. Remove from the heat and ladle into bowls.

SERVES 4-6

To Drink

A chilled Pinot Grigio or champagne

Oyster crackers are a must with this stew.

Saffron Fish Stew
with Aïoli

If you cannot find pompano (it may be expensive or out of season), substitute redfish, my first choice, or grouper. Don't skimp on quality: Use saffron and you will be delighted with this recipe, which does not require a lot of time, even though it may appear to do so.

You will not be completely cooking the fish on the grill; it will finish in the stewpot as the rest of the ingredients slowly meld into a southern French-style bouillabaisse.

6–8 garlic cloves

¾ cup finely chopped fresh oregano

¾ cup cleaned and stemmed fresh thyme

6 bay leaves

1 tablespoon coarsely ground black pepper

1 teaspoon sea salt

½ teaspoon allspice

3 tablespoons olive oil

Juice (about 3 tablespoons) and zest (about 1 tablespoon) of 1 lemon

¾ pound pompano fillets

¾ pound red snapper fillets

1 tablespoon unsalted butter

1 medium yellow onion, finely chopped

½ small green bell pepper, seeded and finely chopped

2 large tomatoes, diced (or one 14-ounce can stewed tomatoes)

1 cup fish or chicken stock

1 cup white wine

½ teaspoon cayenne pepper

1 teaspoon saffron (or up to a tablespoon if you're feeling flush)

Aïoli (see page 227)

Toasted bread

1. Preheat a grill.

2. Purée the garlic, oregano, thyme, three of the bay leaves, ½ tablespoon of the black pepper, ½ teaspoon of the salt, and the allspice in a food processor for 15 to 20 seconds.

3. Add 1 tablespoon of the oil, the lemon juice, and ½ tablespoon of the zest and pulse to combine thoroughly.

4. Lay the pompano and snapper fillets on a cutting board and with a spatula rub both sides thoroughly with the oil and herb mixture.

5. Transfer the fillets to the grill and cook for 3 to 4 minutes; turn and cook for 3 to 4 minutes longer, or until the fish is opaque. Turn off the heat, place the fillets on the warming shelf, and close the lid.

6. In a cast-iron Dutch oven, heat 1 tablespoon of the remaining oil and the butter over medium heat. Add the onion and pepper and fry together, stirring, 8 to 10 minutes. Add the tomato, stock, wine, remaining three bay leaves, the remaining ½ teaspoon of salt, ½ tablespoon of black pepper, and the cayenne. Bring to a boil, lower the heat, and simmer uncovered, for 15 minutes.

7. Add the fillets and saffron. Cover and simmer about 5 minutes, or until thoroughly heated.

8. Break up the fish in the pot with the back of a large spoon or knife. Add the remaining lemon zest and stir.

9. Ladle the stew into warm bowls and swirl in a generous dab of Aïoli, then serve immediately with the toasted bread.

SERVES 4-6

Fish Stock

Making stock may seem laborious, but the result is well worth the effort. If I'm not using stock immediately, I freeze it in pint or quart containers and thaw as I need it. This amount could last several months.

Pester your fishmonger for non-oily, white-fleshed fish frames and heads, or buy any inexpensive lean white fish. Use trimmings from cleaning your own fish. Save bits in the freezer until you have enough. You will need two 18-inch pieces of cheesecloth.

To intensify the flavor of stock or to make a court bouillon or fumet for a rich soup or bouillabaisse, return the stock to the stove and reduce the clear broth by half. Never add salt to fish stock. The seafood will have quite enough of its own.

2 tablespoons vegetable oil
2 medium carrots, finely chopped
2 stalks celery, finely chopped
1 large Spanish onion, finely chopped
1 pound mushrooms, thinly sliced
4–6 garlic cloves, minced
3–5 pounds fish frames and heads
1 cup fresh parsley
6 bay leaves
¼ cup black peppercorns
5–6 sprigs thyme
4–5 sprigs oregano
4 quarts water
1 cup dry white wine

1. Heat the oil in a stockpot over medium-high heat. Add the carrots, celery, onion, mushrooms, and garlic. Cook, stirring for 8 to 10 minutes.

2. Meanwhile, heap the fish parts on one piece of the cheesecloth and tie with string. Place the parsley, bay leaves, peppercorns, thyme, and oregano on the other piece of cheesecloth. Tie with string.

3. Add the water, wine, and cheesecloth packets to the stockpot. Bring to a boil, reduce the heat to medium, and simmer at a low roll, uncovered, for 45 minutes.

4. Remove the cheesecloth packets from the liquid, squeeze dry, and discard. Strain the remaining liquid through a colander and allow to cool for about 45 minutes. Cover and refrigerate for up to 3 days or freeze for up to 2 months.

MAKES 3½ TO 4 QUARTS

Salt Cod Chowda
with Grilled Fish and Vegetables

Chowders of all types — creamed, broth-, and tomato-based — have been around for generations of discourse, table politics, and polite discussions over which chowda is best and even how it is spelled.

I have threaded together multiple cultures into a concoction that might be chowda to some, fish soup to a few, a fishy brew to others. It doesn't really matter what the heritage, as long as it tastes good.

Salt cod must be refreshed in at least two changes of cold water for 12 hours or it will remain salty.

Grill the vegetables and fresh fish ahead and refrigerate, to save time on the day of preparation.

---

4   tablespoons olive oil

2   large green Vidalia onions or substitute large scallions

2   medium sweet yellow peppers

½   cup finely chopped mixed parsley, marjoram, and oregano

1   pound mixed seafood (cod, haddock, squid, scallops, conch, and shrimp are good fish for the mix), cut into bite-sized pieces

1   pound prepared salt cod

8   ounces blanched fatback, diced or salt pork (optional)

1¼ large white onions, diced (about 2 cups)

2   medium stalks celery, diced (about 1 cup)

2   medium potatoes, diced (about 2 cups)

4   cups water

5¼ cups low-salt vegetable stock (4 cans, 14 ounces each)

2   cups clam juice (2 bottles, 8 ounces each) or Fish Stock (see page 141)

1   tablespoon cracked black peppercorns

Lemon wedges

Croutons, crusty bread, or large oyster crackers

1. Preheat a grill (see page 13).

2. Toss together 1 tablespoon of the olive oil, the Vidalia onions, yellow peppers, 1 tablespoon of the mixed herbs, and the mixed seafood in a large bowl.

3. Pick out and drain the onions and peppers and place them on the grill. Grill for 8 to 10 minutes, until softened and slightly charred. Remove and set aside.

4. Place seafood mix in a perforated grill pan and lay it on the grill, stirring occasionally, for 8 minutes, or until the fish are firm. Remove and set aside.

5. Drain the rinsed salt cod, cut into bite-sized pieces, and set aside.

6. Heat 1 tablespoon of the remaining olive oil in a large saucepan over medium-high heat. Add the fatback and brown for about 10 minutes.

7. Remove the fatback and add the white onions, celery, and potatoes to the remaining liquid fat. Lower the heat and simmer for about 10 minutes.

8. Add 2 cups of the water, bring to a boil, reduce the heat, and cook until the potatoes are soft when pierced with a fork, about 10 minutes.

9. Add the vegetable stock and clam juice, bring to a boil, and add the salt cod. Lower the heat and simmer for 20 minutes.

10. Cut the grilled onions and peppers into bite-sized pieces, along with the grilled fish. Add to the pot with the remaining mixed herbs and the peppercorns, and simmer for 5 minutes.

11. Swirl in the remaining olive oil, ladle into bowls, and serve immediately with the lemon wedges and croutons.

SERVES 6-8

Simple Stew

This could be the simplest of all fish stews, a 119-year-old recipe:

"Bouille-Abaisse. Chop some onions and garlic very fine, fry them in olive oil, and when slightly colored add some fish cut up in slices; also a few tomatoes scalded, peeled and sliced, some salt, black and red pepper, thyme, sweet-bay, parsley, and half a bottle of white wine, and enough water to cover the fish. Put it over a brisk fire and boil a quarter of an hour. Put slices of toasted bread in a deep dish, place the fish on a shallow dish with some of the broth, and pour the balance on the bread and serve hot."

— *La Cuisine Creole*, 1885, Lafcadio Hearn

Chapter 7

Fish Wellingtons

THESE ARE THE PERFECT whip-together recipes for when you've just shouted across the picket fence, wanting to be neighborly, and suggested a cookout. Wellingtons, which are fish, vegetables, and any number of delectable seasonings grilled together in a crust, can be assembled quickly and easily and so are wonderful for those Saturday afternoons when, for example, you've noticed your neighbor returning home from a fishing trip, possessing a fine mess of brook trout you'd love to help relieve him of.

What You Will Need

Though you will use several tools and ingredients to make fish Wellingtons, there are a couple of items to which I should draw your attention right away.

Dough. You may approach this in a number of ways. You'll find a recipe for Cornmeal Dough on page 151. If you start from scratch, you need to plan ahead and let the dough rise about 2¼ hours in total. I prefer using this recipe because the dough holds together well on the grill. In addition to its stabilizing effects, I like the slight crunchiness of the cornmeal.

Another possibility is to have on hand premade pizza dough, readily available from most supermarkets. The round tubes are found in the dairy section, pre-rolled and ready for quick assembly. No fuss, no waiting for dough to rise. Just pop open the tube on the corner of the counter and out jumps the dough. You will need to roll it into the desired thickness, but essentially it is ready to use. You will need one 10-ounce tube per person. I keep a couple in the refrigerator for last-minute inspirations. I've used and compared several manufacturers' products and found them basically equal, but stay away from generic dough.

Many supermarket bakeries sell fresh premade dough, requiring no rising, and they work well too. You will need about 2 pounds of dough for four people. If you decide on store-bought dough, simply roll it out on a board sprinkled with a handful of flour and cornmeal mixed together (about ¼ cup each) and proceed as directed.

Grill Basket. You will also need a grill basket (see my discussion of this tool in Tools of the Trade, pages 15–16).

Don't forget to oil — with a basting brush dipped in cooking oil or a cooking spray — all wire grates that the Wellington comes in contact with, as well as the crust itself, or the crust may stick tight and break open when you attempt to release it. Such an event would result in dinner dropping to the bottom of the grill rather than on your guests' plates.

Once you remove the wire basket from the grill, gently turn it over and, with the back of a wooden spoon or teaspoon, carefully push back the individual pockets that have protruded through the wire mesh. Then turn it back over and do the same to the other side. By doing this, you will be able to more easily lift the Wellingtons off the wire holder with one or two spatulas. Take the extra minute to prevent a punctured crust — and a ruined dinner.

How to Do It

There are general instructions on how to make a Wellington, but individual recipes may differ, depending upon the thickness of the fillets and the particular ingredients. Never use any ingredients that will require more cooking time than the crust itself.

Each guest receives his or her own Wellington, grilled and baked in its own pouch.

A tightly sealed Wellington acts as its own oven, essentially steaming the contents and marrying all the flavors. Since equipment varies, you may need to experiment a few times. The crust should be watched carefully because it can burn quickly. I don't mind slightly charred crust; it reminds me of baked, crusty breads found in the wood-fired beehive ovens of Portugal.

The cornmeal recipe on page 151 will make four Wellingtons if you allow the dough to rise properly once, divide it, and let it rise again. After assembling the ingredients according to the instructions, leave the dough in the mixer or place it in a large, oiled bowl, brush the top with oil, and cover with a towel or plastic wrap. Allow it to rise for 1½ hours, undisturbed (if you touch it or bump it, it might slowly deflate). Remove it from the bowl, punch it down on a floured cutting board, divide in two, and cover with a towel for 45 minutes longer.

Use this time to prep your ingredients and place them in small bowls or on plates ready to assemble after rolling out the dough.

After *both* pieces of dough have risen, lift off the towel, and cut them into *four* equal pieces. Now you're ready to roll.

Before assembling the Wellingtons, get your grill going. It should be hot by the time you finish preparing them.

On a cutting board sprinkled with a mixture of flour and cornmeal, roll out each piece of dough into a not-too-thin (about ³⁄₁₆-inch-thick) round piece about 10 inches in circumference. Set aside the other pieces of dough so you can assemble them one at a time.

Draw an imaginary line down the center of the circle. You will be assembling the Wellington on only one side of the circle, the side closer to you, and, when finished, bringing the opposite side over the ingredients, covering them like a pouch, and pinching the dough tightly around the edges to contain the ingredients.

Follow the specific instructions for each Wellington recipe. For all Wellingtons, oil what will be the inside surface of each one. Make sure, however, that there is no oil within an inch of the edges. If the edges are oily, they will not stick together. Next, divide the listed ingredients, including the fish, into four servings. Layer each Wellington with one quarter of the total amount of recommended ingredients. Carefully lift the far side of the dough toward you, draping it over the half containing the ingredients, aligning it with the bottom piece.

At this point, if you are feeling particularly artistic, you may form, push, and shape the dough with the end and back side of a spoon or knife into a fish shape; include scales, head, fins, and tail for a more festive, creative presentation.

With your fingers, curl about ½ inch of the bottom edge over the top edge and pinch tightly together. If you puncture the pouch, pinch it together, or it may leak during cooking. Double-check the seams to make sure they are secure. If you want, finish edging all around with a fork.

Brush the top and bottom with olive oil and, with your hands or two large oiled spatulas, very gently lift the pocket into an oiled grill basket, making sure each pocket is separated from the others. If the grill basket you use is small and you are serving four guests, you may need to grill two at a time, in two batches. If you do so, keep the first ones warm by holding in a 200°F oven.

Lay the grill basket on the grill, reduce the heat from high to medium if using a gas grill, and close the cover. If you are using a charcoal grill, bank most, not all, of the charcoal off to the sides, leaving some in the middle before placing the grill basket on top of the heat and closing the lid.

Cook about 10 minutes; turn and cook 10 minutes longer, depending upon the specific recipe and the thickness of the fish. Using charcoal will shorten the cooking time to 6 to 8 minutes on each side — total cooking time is about 15 minutes —so stay close by.

Remove and let each guest unveil his or her own pocket of treasures.

Key West Wellington, Sunset Pier-Style
(Red Snapper, Chiles, and Lime)

In order to enhance the Key West style of fish preparation, you may need an ample supply of piña coladas to serve with this meal, toward sundown on the pier, of course.

Handful of flour and cornmeal mix (about ¼ cup each)

Dough for four 10-inch Wellingtons (page 151)

¼ cup olive oil

1½ pounds red snapper fillets

2–3 medium tomatoes, cut into ¼-inch slices

1 small habanero chile, stemmed, deveined, and minced (or more to taste)

3–4 garlic cloves, finely chopped

¼ cup finely chopped cilantro

4–6 large scallions, top ½ inch of green parts removed

1 tablespoon coarsely ground black pepper

1 teaspoon salt

4 limes, cut into ½-inch-thick slices

1. Preheat a grill.

2. Sprinkle the flour and cornmeal mix on a pastry or cutting board. Roll out four circles of dough with a rolling pin. Make each about ⅛ inch thick and about 10 inches in circumference. Brush with a small amount of the oil, leaving a 1-inch unoiled border.

3. Draw an imaginary line across the center of the dough circles. Lay a quarter of the fillets on half of each round. Top the fillets with the tomato slices, chile, garlic, cilantro, scallions, pepper, salt, and lime slices. Drizzle the oil over all.

4. Carefully lift and fold the untopped dough over the ingredients, pinch the edges tightly all around, and trim with a knife. Brush the top and bottom with olive oil and gently place inside an oiled grill basket.

5. Lay on a gas grill, reduce the heat to medium, and close the cover. Cook for 10 to 12 minutes; turn and cook 10 to 12 minutes longer, or until the pockets are browned or lightly charred. If using charcoal, move most of it off to the sides and place the grill basket in the center. With charcoal, cook 6 to 8 minutes on each side.

6. Remove the Wellingtons from the grill basket. Serve while hot.

SERVES 4

New York Wellington
with East Coast Stripers

A retired senior outdoor writer for the *New York Times* has often recounted tours of fishing on the Hudson and East Rivers, in the shadow of the city's mighty skyscrapers or even under bridges, for striped bass. Nelson Bryant, whom I interviewed on Martha's Vineyard in the late '70s — just after one of the famous Martha's Vineyard Striped Bass and Bluefish Derbies and when the bass population was strong — has consistently supported the reintroduction of striped bass into eastern waters after a substantial decline from overfishing. Thankfully, conservation has repopulated a superior sport fishery. Let's hope it stays that way.

8 tablespoons sake

2 tablespoons pure maple syrup

6 tablespoons wasabi powder whisked into 2 tablespoons water

2 pounds striped bass fillets, 1 inch thick

Handful of flour and cornmeal mix (about ¼ cup each)

Dough for four 10-inch Wellingtons (see page 151)

2 tablespoons vegetable oil

8 scallions, cleaned, with ½ inch of the green tops removed

1 avocado, peeled and sliced

1 cucumber, peeled, seeded, and thinly sliced

1 lemon, thinly sliced (you may use the zested lemon, below)

2 tablespoons mirin

2 tablespoons low-sodium soy sauce

Zest of 1 lemon (about 1 tablespoon)

1. Whisk together the sake, maple syrup, and half the wasabi paste in a small bowl. Set aside.

2. Lay the bass fillets in a large container, skin-side down, and pour the sake mixture over them. Cover with plastic wrap and refrigerate for 30 minutes.

3. Preheat a grill.

4. Sprinkle the flour and cornmeal mix on a pastry or cutting board. Roll out four circles of the dough with a rolling pin. Make each about ⅛ inch thick and about 10 inches in circumference. Brush with a small amount of the oil, leaving a 1-inch unoiled border.

5. Remove the bass fillets from the marinade. Draw an imaginary line across the center of each piece of dough. Lay a quarter of the fillets on half of each round. Spread with the

remaining wasabi paste and layer with the scallions, avocado, cucumber, and lemon slices.

6. Drizzle with the mirin and soy sauce and sprinkle with the lemon zest.

7. Carefully lift and fold the untopped dough over the ingredients, pinch the edges tightly all around, and trim with a knife. Brush the top and bottom with remaining oil and gently place inside an oiled grill basket.

8. Lay on a gas grill, reduce the heat to medium, and close the cover. Cook for 8 to 10 minutes. Turn and cook 8 to 10 minutes longer, or until the pockets are browned or lightly charred. If using charcoal, move most of it off to the sides and place the grill basket in the center. With charcoal, cook 6 to 8 minutes on each side.

9. Remove the Wellingtons from the grill. Serve while hot.

SERVES 4

A Wee Peaty Wellington
(a Marriage of Salmon and Scotch)

If I had access to peat moss, which I saw alongside the roads on the Isle of Skye, I'd smoke this Wellington with it; the aroma is so redolent of the Scottish countryside. Meanwhile, single-malt scotches are the next best thing (for flavoring).

Use any kind of salmon, especially wild king salmon from the Pacific Northwest when it is available.

Handful of flour and cornmeal mix (about ¼ cup each)

Dough for four 10-inch Wellingtons (see page 151)

2 tablespoons olive oil

1½ pounds salmon fillets

¼ cup Dijon mustard

2 tablespoons mayonnaise

1 cup fresh dill, cleaned and snipped fine

1 lemon, cut into slices ¹⁄₁₆ inch thick

Zest of 2 lemons (about 2 tablespoons)

3 tablespoons peaty Scotch whisky (such as Laphroaig)

1 teaspoon salt

To Drink

This dish goes well with Samuel Smith's Pale Ale, of course.

1. Preheat a grill.

2. Sprinkle the flour and cornmeal mix on a pastry or cutting board. Roll out four circles of the dough with a rolling pin. Make each about ⅛ inch thick and about 10 inches in circumference. Brush with a small amount of the oil, leaving a 1-inch unoiled border.

3. Draw an imaginary line across the center of each piece of dough. Lay a quarter of the salmon fillets on half of each round. Swab the fish with the mustard and mayonnaise; add the dill, lemon slices, zest, Scotch, and salt.

4. Carefully lift and fold the untopped dough over the ingredients, pinch the edges tightly all around, and trim with a knife. Brush the top and bottom with olive oil and gently place inside an oiled grill basket.

5. Lay on a gas grill, reduce the heat to medium, and close the cover. Cook 10 to 12 minutes; turn and cook 10 to 12 minutes longer, or until the pockets

are browned or lightly charred. If using charcoal, move most of it off to the sides and place the grill basket in the center. With charcoal, cook 6 to 8 minutes on each side.

6. Remove the Wellingtons from the grill basket. Serve while hot.

SERVES 4

Cornmeal Dough

The addition of cornmeal makes for a sturdy dough that is able to stand up to grilling. When the dough is rolled out onto a mix of flour and cornmeal, it is further strengthened.

1½ cups warm water (about 110°F)
1 package (¼ ounce) dry yeast
2 tablespoons extra-virgin olive oil
1 teaspoon sugar
½ teaspoon salt
3¾ cups all-purpose flour
¼ cup yellow cornmeal
Handful of flour and cornmeal mixture (about
    ¼ cup each) for rolling dough

Using a Standing Electric Mixer

1. Thoroughly mix the water, yeast, oil, sugar, and salt in a small mixing bowl. Set aside for 5 to 8 minutes, or until the mixture becomes frothy.

2. Place the flour and cornmeal in the bowl of a standing electric mixer fitted with a plastic pastry blade. With the machine on low, add the yeast mixture and process until the dough just comes together into a firm ball. Do not overprocess.

3. Transfer the dough to an oiled mixing bowl, cover it with a towel or plastic wrap, and set it aside for about 1½ hours, or until it has doubled in size.

4. Sprinkle a cutting board with the flour and cornmeal mixture. Remove the risen dough, cut it into two pieces, and place on the prepared cutting board. Cover with a towel for 45 minutes.

5. Remove the towel and divide the *two* pieces into *four*. Roll out one piece of dough at a time into a 10-inch circle for a Wellington or a 12-inch circle for a pizza. Wrap any unused dough in plastic wrap and freeze for up to 3 months.

By Hand

1. Thoroughly mix the water, yeast, oil, sugar, and salt in a small mixing bowl. Set aside for 5 to 8 minutes, or until the mixture becomes frothy.

2. Place the flour on a pastry or cutting board or in a large bowl. Form a well in the center and pour the yeast mixture into it. Slowly incorporate the yeast mixture into the flour, adding a little water if necessary. Knead until smooth, 4 to 5 minutes.

3. Transfer the dough to a large oiled mixing bowl. Cover with a towel for about 1½ hours, or until it has doubled in size.

4. Follow steps 4 and 5 for Using a Standing Electric Mixer.

MAKES DOUGH FOR FOUR 10- TO 12-INCH PIZZAS OR WELLINGTONS

Berkshire Brookie Spring Wellington
(a Spring Harvest of Brook Trout, Watercress, and Fiddleheads)

This is a recipe for spring, when everything is finally exhibiting signs of life after the last snowmelt, and everyone is eager to cook out. It's especially good on opening day, when that alluring trout stream beckons.

Use brook trout fillets preferably weighing 4 to 6 ounces each. In my fishing backyard, that is hardly the problem. You will need eight to ten fillets for two people.

The brookies are wrapped with green gatherings of wild onions, watercress, and fiddlehead ferns, all available at about the same time. A perfect marriage of spring flavors.

To blanch the fiddleheads, immerse them in boiling water for 1 to 2 minutes, then submerge in cold water that has had lemon juice added to it to retain the brilliant green color.

Handful of flour and cornmeal mix (about ¼ cup each)

Dough for four 10-inch Wellingtons (see page 151)

3 tablespoons olive oil

8–10 trout fillets, 6 ounces each

8–10 wild onions (or substitute 4–8 scallions)

½ cup fiddlehead ferns, cleaned, trimmed, and blanched

½ cup stemmed and cleaned watercress

1 lemon, cut into ½-inch-thick disks

4 tablespoons (½ stick) unsalted butter

Juice of 1 lemon (about 3 tablespoons)

1 tablespoon freshly ground black pepper

1 teaspoon salt

1. Preheat a grill.

2. Sprinkle the flour and cornmeal mix on a pastry or cutting board. Roll out four circles of the dough with a rolling pin. Make each about ⅛ inches thick and about 10 inches in circumference. Brush with a small amount of the olive oil, leaving a 1-inch unoiled border.

3. Draw an imaginary line across each circle of dough and place one quarter of the fish fillets on half of each round.

4. Divide the onions, fiddleheads, watercress, lemon, butter, lemon juice, pepper, and salt in four and layer on each Wellington.

5. Drizzle with the olive oil.

6. Carefully lift and fold the untopped dough over the ingredients, pinch the edges tightly all around, and trim with a knife. Brush the top and bottom with olive oil and gently place inside an oiled grill basket.

7. Lay the grill basket on a gas grill, reduce the heat to medium, and close the cover. Cook for 8 to 10 minutes; turn and cook 8 to 10 minutes longer, or until the pockets are browned or lightly charred. If using charcoal, move most of it off to the sides and place the grill basket in the center. With charcoal, cook 6 to 8 minutes on each side.

8. Remove the Wellingtons from the grill basket. Serve while hot.

SERVES 4

Moroccan Wellington
(Sushi-Quality Tuna with Preserved Lemons)

Preserved lemons are a staple in Morocco even though tuna may not be. Shops are stacked from floor to ceiling with jars of salted, pickled lemons and limes.

Freezing the tuna briefly before assembling will help prevent it from becoming overcooked on the grill. Freeze 1-inch-thick pieces of tuna for 20 to 25 minutes before assembling.

Handful of flour and cornmeal mix (about ¼ cup each)

Dough for four 10-inch Wellingtons (see page 151)

2 tablespoons olive oil

1 pound sushi-quality tuna, cut into 4 strips

1½ cups preserved lemons, cut into bite-size pieces (see Preserved Lemons and Limes, page 155), or substitute fresh lemons

1½ cups coarsely chopped fresh mint leaves

1½ cups diced tomatoes

3 tablespoons brown sugar

1 tablespoon freshly ground black pepper

1 teaspoon ground coriander

1 teaspoon ground cumin

1. Preheat a grill.

2. Sprinkle the flour and cornmeal mix on a pastry or cutting board. Roll out four circles of the dough with a rolling pin. Make each about ⅛ inch thick and about 10 inches in circumference. Brush with a small amount of the oil, leaving a 1-inch unoiled border.

3. Draw an imaginary line across the center of each of the circles of dough. Lay a piece of tuna on half of each round. Divide the lemons, mint, tomatoes, brown sugar, pepper, coriander, and cumin into four and layer each Wellington with them. Drizzle with the olive oil.

4. Carefully lift and fold the untopped dough toward you and over the ingredients, pinch the edges tightly all around, and trim with a knife. Brush the top and bottom with olive oil and gently place inside an oiled grill basket.

5. Lay on a gas grill, reduce the heat to medium, and close the cover. Cook for 8 to 10 minutes; turn and cook 8 to 10 minutes longer, or until the tuna is browned or lightly charred. If using charcoal, move most of it off to the sides and place the grill basket in the center. With charcoal, cook 6 to 8 minutes on each side.

6. Remove the Wellingtons from the grill basket. Serve while hot.

SERVES 4

Preserved Lemons and Limes

Buy lemons and limes in midwinter, when they are small, inexpensive, and ripe, to salt down for pickling. You will need two 1-quart glass canning jars.

2   pounds lemons or limes
Juice of 1 pound of lemons or limes
1   cup coarse salt
6   cinnamon sticks, 2 to 3 inches long each
¼   cup peppercorns

1. Wash the lemons and set aside 1 pound (about half). Cut these in half, remove the seeds, squeeze the juice, and set aside. Discard the lemons or save the zest for another recipe.

2. Cut off the tops of the remaining lemons, hold them upright on the counter, and slice down, cutting each lemon into eighths. Do not cut all the way to the bottom; they should hold together, creating a fanlike appearance.

3. Push down one lemon into a jar, facing up, and top with a layer of salt, then a layer of cinnamon, then a layer of peppercorns. Repeat layering until both jars are full.

4. Fill the jars with the lemon juice, making sure both are full, leaving little space at the top.

5. Tightly screw on the tops and refrigerate for up to 2 months. Every few weeks, turn the jars upside down (or right-side up).

6. Before using, wash excess salt off the fruit.

MAKES 2 QUARTS

Ya Sure You Betcha Wellington
(Perch Fillets with Morels)

Originally hailing from Minnesota, where the nearest saltwater is 1,500 miles away, I love freshwater sunnies or perch cooked any way. You may use fillets of perch, sunfish, crappies, rock bass, or walleye for this recipe.

Handful of flour and cornmeal mix (about ¼ cup of each)

Dough for four 10-inch Wellingtons (see page 151)

2 tablespoons olive oil

1½ pounds perch or other freshwater fillets

2 medium tomatoes, seeded and sliced

1 cup fresh morels, cleaned and sliced (or any firm, meaty mushroom)

1 sweet white onion, thinly sliced

4–6 cloves garlic, finely chopped

2 tablespoons coarsely ground black pepper

1 teaspoon salt

Juice of 1 lemon (about 3 tablespoons)

1. Preheat a grill.

2. Sprinkle the flour and cornmeal mix on a pastry or cutting board. Roll out four circles of the dough with a rolling pin. Make each one about ⅛ inch thick and about 10 inches in circumference. Brush with a small amount of the oil, leaving a 1-inch unoiled border.

3. Draw an imaginary line across the center of each circle of dough and lay a quarter of the fillets on half of each round. Layer with the tomatoes, morels, onions, garlic, pepper, and salt. Drizzle the lemon over the top and drizzle the oil over all.

4. Carefully lift and fold the untopped sides over ingredients, pinch the edges tightly all around, and trim with a knife. Brush the top and bottom with olive oil and gently place inside an oiled grill basket.

5. Lay on a gas grill, reduce the heat to medium, and close the cover. Cook 10 to 12 minutes; turn and cook 10 to 12 minutes longer, or until the pockets are browned or lightly charred. If using charcoal, move most of it off to the sides and place the grill basket in the center. With charcoal, cook 6 to 8 minutes on each side.

6. Remove the Wellingtons from the grill basket. Serve while hot.

SERVES 4

Rangeley Salmon

"THE SALMON ARE FINALLY IN. Look, down there." Pete is pointing to several dark shadows in the water. "Three of them. One of 'em's big, too." Pete and his friends watch for the landlocked salmon from a bridge over a river. The men discuss fishing and life over coffee at Fritz's Donut Shop, not far from Rangeley Lake in northern Maine.

"What do you suggest I use?" I ask.

"Black Ghost," Pete responds. "Maybe Green if you want. Really doesn't matter. They're not feeding now."

I have tied on a red-and-white streamer and after considering the mixed advice decide to leave it on.

Pete's eyes are glued to the water. He does not look up when he speaks, his face deep in concentration. Words are few here, where quiet exclamations take precedence over long declarations.

There is a vastness about this North Country: miles of apparently lost rivers and streams; dense acres of spruce, their prickly tips rising seemingly high enough to tickle clouds. Canada geese, mallards, and the ever-present crooning loons appear on the water everywhere.

A balance is felt, even in the shifting wilderness. I tread carefully, knowing my place as an outsider.

I see Pete several times a day. We acknowledge each other and continue our broken conversation, interspersed with determined casts, changing flies, and . . . waiting.

"Fishin's poor."

"Why?"

"Water's low, dry summer."

I tie on a dry fly, remind myself to pick up a Black or Green Ghost when I return to town. I cast again, allowing the lazy fly to float over gray silhouettes below. The fish are uninterested; Pete decides to move on. "Good luck." He drives off in his shiny green four-wheel-drive vehicle with a red L.L. Bean canoe strapped topside. I leave awhile later, to check out Fritz's warm, honey-glazed doughnuts.

"Any luck?" Pete asks from across the U-shaped counter.

"No, nothing after you left."

"Who's yer friend?" a man asks Pete, sipping hot coffee.

"From Massachusetts."

"Was there once. State's not big enough fer me," he says unequivocally. "After getting through Boston last year, there we were, smack in Rhode Island. Dang near missed that one too." The fisherman takes a cigarette from the pocket of his red plaid shirt. "Sure do make 'em small down they'a."

"I live on the other side of the state, in the Berkshire Mountains," I say, almost apologetically.

"Aa . . . yup, gotta live somewhey'a."

I finish my doughnut and coffee and head back for some evening fishing.

Looking toward the lake and across to Beaver Mountain, I watch the southwestern sky slowly fade to strokes of pink and deep violet, an artistic union between a flock of Florida flamingos and a Wyeth landscape. Dim sunlight flickers its waning glow through the forest as I relish my favorite time of day.

Upon returning to the river I have a choice of fishing spots; the other men are discouraged and remain behind at Fritz's. I rig up my rod and tie on my faithful streamer.

Except for the low roar of flowing river water into the lake and the occasional dive-bombing swallows, it is quiet. And then . . . I see salmon below me, four, five fish.

They appear motionless, facing headlong into the flow of the current. They

dart about, changing places in their underwater ballet. As the light grows dim, they almost disappear against the sandy bottom. I cast toward the largest of the cigar shapes when . . . bam, a strike!

I pull up my rod tight and set the hook. The salmon breaks water, furiously leaps into the air, and takes my breath away. A magnificent, silvery fish, it twists and spins into the cool Maine air as if to flaunt itself before me.

When the sudden lurch of the line startles me, I usually don't believe I have hooked a fish, particularly such a beauty, until a valuable split second has passed. This hesitation is often the opportunity a fish needs to break away. Not this time. Another graceful leap and I am reminded that I have surely hooked the mighty landlocked salmon, a fading species here.

The light is giving way quickly. This is when the sky diminishes to a blue-black hue. Even shadows disappear. The treeline fades to a blur. I hear a splash, catching me off guard. I'm rewarded by a whitish streak of brilliance, angling skyward out of the water, slicing the night like a razor. In an instant, the fish flops back into the water, now lost from my view.

I guide the line toward shore. The fish makes one last attempt for freedom and tears away, causing my reel to whir in fierce protest. I direct the line back, allowing no slack. It seems as if hours have passed even though I know it has been only minutes. Finally I reel in line and gently net the fish. Kneeling beside my catch I feel triumphant, whole.

Unknowingly, several fishermen have gathered, returning to check the day's end, and happen to witness a tourist land a fish. They call down from the riverbank to inquire if it is a landlocked salmon.

"Yes," I reply. I cradle the silver streak in both hands to show them before I release it back into its home water. The fishermen talk among themselves and return to their cars. Pete bids me a good-night: "Good fish, son, first one of the season, y'know." As he turns his back to me, headed for his truck, I hear a mumble from some of the other fishermen, "Well, whad'ya gonna do? Those Massachusetts boys're entitled too."

Indonesian Wellington
(a Cultural Blend of Sea Bass with Peanuts, Soy Sauce, and Tamarind)

This may seem strange, but all the ingredients are staples in Indonesia's mixed cuisine. Tamarind paste, actually an ingredient in Worcestershire sauce, may be found in the Asian section of your supermarket, as can dark soy sauce.

3 tablespoons peanut oil, plus more for oiling dough

4 shallots, finely chopped

4 garlic cloves, finely chopped

2–3 jalapeño chiles

1 teaspoon Shrimp Paste (see page 229)

¾ cup shelled and skinned peanuts

3 tablespoons dark soy sauce

1 tablespoon tamarind paste

1 teaspoon sugar

Handful of flour and cornmeal mix (about ¼ cup of each)

Dough for four 10-inch Wellingtons (see page 151)

1½ pounds sea bass, orange roughy, or snapper fillets, divided in four

½ small cucumber, peeled and thinly sliced

Juice of 1 lime (about 2 tablespoons)

1. Heat 1 tablespoon of the oil in a medium skillet over medium-high heat. Add the shallots, garlic, chiles, and shrimp paste and sauté, stirring, for 2 to 3 minutes. Set aside.

2. In the bowl of a food processor, pulse the peanuts for about 15 seconds, until coarsely chopped. Add the sauté mix, soy sauce, tamarind paste, and sugar and pulse 10 to 15 seconds, or until thoroughly blended. Scrape down the sides with a spatula and set aside the sauce.

3. Preheat a grill.

4. Sprinkle the flour and cornmeal mix on a pastry or cutting board. Roll out four circles of the dough with a rolling pin. Make each about ⅛ inch thick and about 10 inches in circumference. Brush with a small amount of the oil, leaving a 1-inch unoiled border.

5. Draw an imaginary line across the center of each dough circle. Lay a quarter of the fillets on half of each round. Coat one side of the fillet with the sauce, then turn and repeat. Lay the sliced cucumbers on top and drizzle the lime juice and the remaining peanut oil over everything.

6. Carefully lift and fold the untopped dough over the ingredients, pinch the edges tightly all around, and trim with a knife. Brush the top and bottom with peanut oil and gently place inside an oiled grill basket.

7. Lay the basket on a gas grill, reduce the heat to medium, and close the cover. Cook for 10 to 12 minutes. Turn and cook 10 to 12 minutes longer, or until the pockets are browned or lightly charred. If using charcoal, move most of it off to the sides and place the grill basket in the center. With charcoal, cook 6 to 8 minutes on each side.

8. Remove the Wellingtons from the grill basket. Serve while hot.

SERVES 4

Zydeco Wellington
(Louisiana Catfish)

I recommend catfish for this recipe, which was inspired by the bayous of Louisiana, but you may substitute any firm white-fleshed fish, such as turbot, grouper, or perch, if you prefer.

Tamarind paste may be found in the Asian section of your supermarket.

3   tablespoons vegetable oil

1   medium white onion, coarsely chopped

6–8 garlic cloves, minced

1   green pepper, cored, seeded, and coarsely chopped

½   cup dry sherry

¼   cup sorghum syrup or honey

¼   cup tomato paste

2   bay leaves

2   teaspoons hot sauce (or to taste)

2   teaspoons tamarind paste

1   teaspoon salt

½   teaspoon allspice

Handful of flour and cornmeal mix (about ¼ cup of each)

Dough for four 10-inch Wellingtons (see page 151)

3   pounds catfish fillets

Juice of 2 limes (about ¼ cup)

1. In 1 tablespoon of the oil, sauté the onion, garlic, and pepper for 4 to 5 minutes in a large skillet over medium-high heat. Add the sherry, sorghum syrup, tomato paste, bay leaves, hot sauce, tamarind paste, salt, and allspice. Cook, stirring, for about 6 minutes, or until thoroughly heated. Remove from the heat and set aside.

2. Preheat a grill.

3. Sprinkle the flour and cornmeal mix on a pastry or cutting board. Roll out four circles of the dough with a rolling pin. Make each about ⅛ inch thick and about 10 inches in circumference. Brush with a small amount of the oil, leaving a 1-inch unoiled border.

4. Draw an imaginary line across the center of each dough circle. Lay a quarter of the fillets on half of each round. With a spatula or spoon, coat one side of each fillet with the sauce. Turn over and repeat. Drizzle the lime juice and remaining oil over everything.

5. Carefully lift and fold the untopped dough over the ingredients, pinch the edges tightly all around, and trim with a knife. Brush the top and bottom with remaining oil and gently place inside an oiled grill basket.

6. Lay on a gas grill, reduce the heat to medium, and close the cover. Cook for 10 to 12 minutes; turn and cook 10 to 12 minutes longer, or until the pockets are browned or lightly charred. If using charcoal, move most of it off to the sides and place the grill basket in the center. With charcoal, cook 6 to 8 minutes on each side.

7. Remove the Wellingtons from the grill basket. Serve while hot.

SERVES 4

The Forerunner of Fish Wellingtons?

POTTED FISH

"Three shad or six small mackerel, uncooked; one third of a cup of salt with half a saltspoonful of cayenne pepper mixed with it, and half a cup of whole spices, cloves, peppercorns, and allspice mixed in about equal proportions. Vinegar to cover.

"Clean, remove the skin, split in halves, cut each half into three pieces, and remove all the larger bones. Pack the fish in layers in a small stone jar. (Earthenware must not be used on account of the vinegar.)

"Sprinkle the salt and spices over each layer. Add one onion sliced thin, if you do not dislike the flavor. Add vinegar enough to completely cover the fish.

"Tie a thick paper over the top, or tie a cloth over and cover with a crust of dough to keep in all the steam.

"Bake in a very moderate oven five or six hours. Remove the dough-crust, and when cooled cover, and keep in a cool place.

"This will keep some time, if the fish be kept under the vinegar; the bones will be dissolved, and it makes an excellent relish for lunch or tea."

Mrs. Lincoln's Boston Cook Book,
by Mrs. D. A. Lincoln (Boston Cooking School Cook Book, 1884)

Patagonian Wellington
(Sea Bass with Asparagus and Romesco Sauce)

Chilean sea bass works splendidly in this recipe, in spite of the fact that it is not in the bass family. It has a flaky white flesh suitable for grilling. You may substitute grouper if you'd like.

Try this recipe in the spring when the daffodils are up and so, too, are wild alliums: Onions, ramps, leeks, chives, shallots, and wild garlic are just a few of the more than 300 species of alliums.

I tried this recipe with my former restaurant partner, Carole Clark, one spring evening at her home in Livingston, New York. She had some leftover romesco sauce in her refrigerator from the previous night's dinner and she suggested that it might make a good combination with the sea bass. We agreed: It was better than good.

I foraged around her property just before sundown and found some of the necessary wild alliums I would include for this perfect combination.

You may make the romesco sauce ahead and keep refrigerated until ready to use.

Handful of flour and cornmeal mix (about ¼ cup of each)

Dough for four 10-inch Wellingtons (see page 151)

3   tablespoons olive oil

1½ pounds sea bass fillets, 1 inch thick

¼   cup Romesco Sauce (page 230)

6–8 wild onions, cleaned, ½-inch greens removed (or 3–4 scallions)

6–8 fresh asparagus spears, blanched

1–2 medium plum tomatoes, seeded and sliced

½   cup fresh basil leaves

2–4 wild garlic cloves, cleaned, tops removed (or 3–4 cloves, finely chopped)

1   tablespoon coarsely ground black pepper

½   teaspoon salt

Juice of ½ lemon (about 1½ tablespoons)

Zest of 1 lemon (about 1 tablespoon)

1. Preheat a grill.

2. Sprinkle the flour and cornmeal mix on a pastry or cutting board. Roll out four circles of dough with a rolling pin. Make each about ⅛ inch thick and about 10 inches in circumference. Brush with a small amount of the oil, leaving a 1-inch unoiled border.

3. Draw an imaginary line across the center of each of the dough circles. Lay a quarter of the fillets on half of each round. Brush with the Romesco Sauce, covering the fish completely. Layer the fillets with the onions, asparagus, tomato, basil, garlic, pepper, and salt. Drizzle the lemon juice over all and sprinkle with the lemon zest.

4. Carefully lift and fold the untopped dough over the ingredients, pinch the edges tightly all around, and trim with a knife. Brush the top and bottom with the rest of the olive oil and gently place inside an oiled grill basket.

5. Lay the basket on a gas grill, reduce the heat to medium, and close the cover. Cook for 10 to 12 minutes; turn and cook 10 to 12 minutes longer, or until the pockets are browned or lightly charred. If using charcoal, move most of it off to the sides and place the grill basket in the center. With charcoal, cook 6 to 8 minutes on each side.

6. Remove the Wellingtons from the grill basket. Serve while hot.

SERVES 4

Mediterranean Wellington
(Red Mullet with Olives, Tomato, and Feta Cheese)

You may substitute porgy, sea bream, or even grouper if you cannot locate red mullet, a true Mediterranean species.

Handful of flour and cornmeal mixture (about ¼ cup each)

Dough for four 10-inch Wellingtons (see page 151)

2 tablespoons olive oil

1½ pounds red mullet fillets

½ cup cooked chickpeas

½ cup feta cheese, crumbled

½ cup kalamata olives, sliced

¼ cup fresh oregano

½ cup sliced scallions

8 slices pancetta or prosciutto

4 lemon slices, ⅛ inch thick

4 large tomato slices, ¼ inch thick, cut in half

2 tablespoons cracked black peppercorns

1 teaspoon salt

1. Preheat a grill.

2. Sprinkle the flour and cornmeal mix on a pastry or cutting board. Roll out four circles of the dough with a rolling pin. Make each about ⅛ inch thick and about 10 inches in circumference. Brush with a small amount of the oil, leaving a 1-inch unoiled border.

3. Draw an imaginary line across the center of each circle of dough. Lay a quarter of the fillets on half of each round. Divide the chickpeas, feta, olives, oregano, scallions, pancetta, lemon, tomato, peppercorns, and salt equally and layer on top of the fillets. Drizzle the oil over everything.

4. Carefully lift and fold the untopped dough over the ingredients, pinch the edges tightly all around, and trim with a knife. Brush the top and bottom with olive oil and gently place inside an oiled grill basket.

5. Lay the Wellingtons on a gas grill, reduce the heat to medium, and close the cover. Cook 10 to 12 minutes; turn and cook 10 to 12 minutes longer, or until the pockets are browned or lightly charred. If using charcoal, move most of it off to the sides and place the grill basket in the center. With charcoal, cook 6 to 8 minutes on each side.

6. Remove the Wellingtons from the grill basket. Serve while hot.

SERVES 4

Chapter 8

Fish Salads

IN SEVERAL OF THESE SALADS, fish may be interchangeable: Try using monkfish instead of salmon; sea bass instead of cod; most any firm, white-fleshed freshwater fish, and so on. The same applies to many of the other ingredients: Feel free to exclude nuts, olives, or a particular ingredient you may not care for. Especially be aware of those ingredients to which you or someone you know is allergic. Eliminating them will not usually affect the total recipe.

Since many years ago, after having my first taste of very good-quality extra-virgin olive oil, and then later on, when I was treated to a superior balsamic

vinegar — almost wanting to devise a drink that utilized the vinegar, it was so delicious — I have tried to use only quality olive oils and vinegars, especially in foods such as salad, when the distinct tastes of simple, high-quality ingredients come through.

If you prorate the cost of, say, a twenty-dollar (or even more expensive) bottle of extra-virgin olive oil across the ounces or drizzles that you will use on salads or over steamed vegetables, it seems to me that a bottle is more than cost-effective. As when purchasing an entire 12-pound salmon, you soon forget the initial expense and simply enjoy the fish with the many ways you use it.

Here are some of the typical ingredients you might want to have on hand to compose delicious salads. Use this list as a starting point, but feel free to develop and orchestrate variations, eventually graduating to your own combinations, using any or all of the suggested recipes. Remember, as with most recipes, use your imagination and don't think that because it's in print, it's the last word. Experiment. Be imaginative, substitute, disregard. Conscientious and creative cooks devise and build upon recipes and go beyond. Don't be afraid to explore foods and their combinations. As in all art, imagination is the key ingredient to any creation.

Salad Options

mesclun (composed of a variety of greens such as baby spinach, radicchio, mustard, arugula, mizuna, tatsoi, and red oak)

any of the above greens by themselves

sprouts (bean, alfalfa, and so on)

cucumbers (English cucumbers have little or no seeds, perfect for salads)

mushrooms (some truly wild mushrooms are not recommended to be consumed raw; I suggest when using *uncooked* mushrooms, they come from a supermarket, just to be on the safe side)

fresh garlic

red onion

scallions and green Vidalia onions

sweet white onion

fresh tomatoes

galangal, also called Thai ginger (this has a bright, spicy flavor)

ginger

hearts of palm (usually canned)

extra-virgin olive oil

apple cider vinegar

balsamic vinegar

orange flower water

grated cheeses

nuts

olives, pitted, sliced, or whole

lemon juice

citrus zest (if you do not have a zesting tool, carefully peel the colored rind away from the white pith of a lemon, lime, orange, or grapefruit, and cut it into long, thin slices and dice)

Toasted Pumpkin Seeds

When toasting pumpkin seeds, make twice the amount you need because you'll eat half of them before they find their way into a recipe. Use a cooking screen to cover the saucepan; when the seeds begin to toast, they pop like popcorn and fly everywhere. Do not leave the stove; the cooking time is only a couple of minutes and the seeds burn quickly.

You may use this same recipe for toasted walnuts or almonds.

1 **tablespoon vegetable oil**
1 **cup raw pumpkin seeds**
1 **teaspoon salt (optional)**

1. Heat the oil in a large skillet over medium heat. When it crackles, add a single drop of water, being careful that the hot oil does not splatter and burn you.

2. Add the pumpkin seeds and salt, if using, and cover with the screen. Remove the screen to stir occasionally, until they begin to brown, 2 to 3 minutes. As soon as all are puffy and the same color, quickly transfer to a large plate lined with paper towels. Blot dry.

3. Store in an airtight container at room temperature; will keep for several weeks.

MAKES 1 CUP

Corn-Smoked Lobster Salad

Put together this luncheon dish after smoking a few extra lobsters (see page 117) for that July 4th family bash.

Kohlrabi was a favorite of my grandmother's, and I have never lost the taste for its crunchiness, often eating it out of hand, like you would an apple. Sliced thin, kohlrabi adds another layer of texture to salads.

To make the lobster salad:

4–6 caper berries (or substitute 8 to 10 capers)

1   small jalapeño pepper, deveined and seeded

1   teaspoon brine from jar of capers

½ cup mayonnaise

Juice of ½ lime (about 1 tablespoon)

Zest of 1 lime (about 1 tablespoon)

1   tablespoon freshly ground black pepper

1   cup julienned kohlrabi

¾ cup diced avocado

¼ cup diced grilled sweet red pepper

Corn from 2 ears of smoked corn (see page 220)

Meat from two 1¼-pound corn-smoked lobsters, cut into chunks

To finish:

2   cups lettuce

½ cup toasted pumpkin seeds (page 168)

Lime wedges

Nasturtium blossoms (optional, for garnish)

1. Pulse the caper berries, jalapeño, and brine, four to six times in the bowl of a food processor. Add the mayonnaise, lime juice, zest, and pepper and pulse six to eight times.

2. Transfer to a bowl and add the kohlrabi, avocado, red pepper, corn, and lobster. Mix thoroughly.

3. Spread the lettuce on four plates. Divide the lobster salad evenly among them and sprinkle with the toasted pumpkin seeds. Serve with lime wedges and garnish with edible nasturtium flowers, if desired.

SERVES 4 FOR LUNCH

To Drink

A crisp Pinot Grigio or lemonade with fresh mint

Calamari-Peanut Salad

One of the finest calamari meals I recall was lunch at a very simple oceanside café in a tiny village in Portugal where a dozen or so colorfully painted wooden fishing boats were lined up on the beach outside our window table, side by side, tilted all in the same direction, as if waiting to be uprighted any moment to head out to sea. The scene: perfectly set. The squid: perfectly cooked.

You will need a perforated pizza pan or grilling wok for this dish. You may eliminate the serrano chiles if you prefer a dish that is not spicy.

When calamari is tough and chewy, it was likely cooked somewhere in between the times it should be cooked, either sautéed or grilled very fast or stewed very slowly. Grilling hot and fast makes this dish work as a salad or over rice.

To make the calamari:

1½ pounds cleaned small squid, bodies cut into thinly sliced rounds, tentacles left whole

1 small red onion, thinly sliced into rounds

2–3 serrano chiles, seeded, deveined, and thinly sliced

Juice of 5 limes (about 10 tablespoons)

1 tablespoon fish sauce

1 tablespoon pure maple syrup

1 tablespoon olive oil

1 tablespoon low-sodium soy sauce

To make the salad:

1 cup baby spinach, cleaned

¾ cup arugula, cleaned

½ large cucumber, peeled, thinly sliced

To finish:

Oil for grill pan

½ cup roasted unsalted peanuts, coarsely chopped

¼ cup balsamic vinegar

Salt and freshly ground black pepper

1. Toss together the squid, most of the onion slices, chiles, 8 tablespoons of the lime juice, fish sauce, maple syrup, olive oil, and soy sauce in a large bowl and marinade in the refrigerator for about 30 minutes.

2. Arrange a layer of spinach and arugula leaves on four plates. Top with a layer of cucumber and the remaining onion slices. Set aside.

3. Remove the squid and its marinade from the refrigerator.

4. Preheat a grill. Be sure the grate is hot. Set a cooking pan on the grate and close the lid. Allow the pan to get very hot (this will take 8 to 10 minutes), but be *exceptionally cautious* and use heavy mitts or you may burn yourself on the handle.

5. Spray or brush the hot pan with cooking oil. Be very careful because it will sputter and spit. Add the squid and its marinade to the pan.

6. With mitts, hold on to the handle and shake, or with a wooden spatula, stir the mixture constantly for only 4 to 5 minutes, no more.

7. Remove the pan from the grill and divide the contents onto the four plates, topping the greens with the calamari. Sprinkle the chopped peanuts on top and drizzle the balsamic vinegar and remaining lime juice over everything. Season with the salt and pepper and serve immediately.

SERVES 4

Salmon Salad

Grill twice the amount of salmon you will need for dinner and save the rest for this salad the next day.

To make the salad:

1 **pound grilled boneless salmon**

4 **large scallions, sliced, 4 inches of tops removed**

¾ **cup sliced hearts of palm**

6–8 **cucumber slices, diced**

To finish:

4 **cups mesclun**

8 **lemon wedges**

1½ **tablespoons extra-virgin olive oil**

1 **teaspoon balsamic vinegar**

¾ **cup niçoise olives**

¼ **cup parsley, finely chopped, for garnish**

1. Remove the salmon from the refrigerator and flake into a large bowl. Add the scallions, hearts of palm, and cucumber. Gently toss.

2. Divide the mesclun equally among four plates. Mound equal amounts of the salmon mixture on top. Squeeze a lemon wedge over each salad and drizzle the oil and vinegar over all. Divide and scatter olives over the top of each plate. Garnish with the parsley and serve with the remaining four lemon wedges.

SERVES 4

Fiddlehead Fern Salad
with Orange Roughy and
Orange Flower Water Dressing

This salad has its origins in Morocco, where a traditional salad is often served with orange flower water. It comes from a land where the fragrant aroma of orange blossoms in the spring countryside wafts across the Atlas Mountains.

For a delightful summer picnic salad, grill some orange roughy ahead of time, chill in the refrigerator, and flake pieces into the salad just before serving.

Orange flower water can be found in the ethnic section of your supermarket or in a Middle Eastern food store.

To make the dressing:

¾ cup extra-virgin olive oil

4–5 teaspoons orange flower water

1   teaspoon balsamic vinegar

Juice of ⅓ lemon (about 1 tablespoon)

½   teaspoon ground cumin

2   tablespoons fresh chives, snipped fine (or substitute scallions)

1   teaspoon freshly ground black pepper

To make the salad:

1   cup fiddlehead ferns, cleaned and trimmed (about ½ pound), or substitute asparagus tips

½   medium red onion, peeled, thinly sliced

2   oranges, peeled, cut into ¼-inch slices, and halved

¼   cup thinly sliced black olives

8   cups mesclun or red leaf lettuce (about ½ pound)

To finish:

½   pound grilled orange roughy, chilled

Lemon wedges

ADVANCE PREPARATION:
Grill the orange roughy

1. Whisk the dressing ingredients in a small bowl. Transfer to a serving container and set aside.

2. Bring 4 quarts of water to a boil, add the fiddleheads, reduce the heat to low, and simmer for 2 to 3 minutes. Drain, plunge into cold water, and set aside.

3. Combine the fiddleheads with the onion, orange, and olives in a large mixing bowl.

4. Toss with the dressing and serve over the lettuce leaves with the chilled grilled orange roughy and the lemon wedges on the side.

SERVES 4–6

Mahi-Mahi and Green Papaya Salad

If you cannot buy mahi-mahi, use fresh, good-quality tuna. Find a *green* papaya and be ready for a delightful Thai surprise. Green papaya resembles kohlrabi or Jerusalem artichokes in its firm, crunchy texture, but it is far different when ripe.

Curry paste may be found in small cans in the Asian section of the supermarket and will keep for several weeks, refrigerated.

To marinate the mahi-mahi:
Juice of 1½ lemons (about 4½ tablespoons)
2   tablespoons green Thai curry paste
1   pound mahi-mahi fillets

To make the dressing:
4–6 garlic cloves, finely chopped
2   tablespoons fish sauce
Juice of ½ lemon (about 1½ tablespoons)
1   tablespoon pure maple syrup
½   teaspoon Tabasco sauce

To make the salad:
1   medium green papaya, peeled, julienned (about 3 cups)
½   small red onion, thinly sliced
¾   cup fresh bean sprouts
½   cup Jerusalem artichokes, peeled and julienned, or water chestnuts
½   cup fresh basil leaves, finely chopped
1   tablespoon peanut oil
½   teaspoon cayenne pepper

To finish:
Toasted pumpkin seeds (see page 168)

1. Preheat a grill.

2. Stir together the lemon juice and the curry paste. Add the mahi-mahi and set aside.

3. Whisk together the dressing ingredients in a large bowl. Set aside.

4. Mix the papaya, onion, sprouts, artichokes, basil, peanut oil, and cayenne in a large bowl. Set aside.

5. Remove mahi-mahi from the marinade and transfer to the grill. Grill for 4 minutes; turn and grill 4 minutes longer, or until the fish is thoroughly cooked. Transfer to a cutting board and slice into thin strips.

6. Combine the mahi-mahi with the salad and toss lightly. Drizzle the dressing over the top and sprinkle with the pumpkin seeds. Divide into four bowls and serve immediately.

SERVES 4

White Bean, Mango, and Jerusalem Artichoke Salad
with Cold Sea Bass

You may grill the sea bass ahead and refrigerate for at least 1 hour or overnight.

The sweet white meat of the bass makes a cold salad taste extra special served on the lawn at a Tanglewood concert, in the Berkshires, waiting to hear the Boston Symphony Orchestra.

To make the salad:

- 1 can (15 ounces) cannellini or habichuela beans, drained
- 1 ripe mango, peeled and sliced
- 1 cup Jerusalem artichokes, peeled and julienned
- 2–3 pepperoncini peppers, seeded, deveined, and sliced
- 4–5 chives, snipped fine
- ¼ small red onion, finely chopped
- 2–3 pickled garlic cloves, finely chopped

To make the dressing:

- ½ cup orange juice
- Zest of 1 orange (1–2 tablespoons)
- ¼ cup stemmed and chopped fresh thyme
- 2 tablespoons pure maple syrup
- 2 tablespoons extra-virgin olive oil
- 1 teaspoon coarsely ground peppercorns
- 1 teaspoon sea salt

To finish:

- 1½ pounds sea bass fillets
- 2 cups baby lettuce leaves
- Lemon wedges

1. Stir the beans, mango, artichokes, peppers, chives, onion, and pickled garlic in a large mixing bowl. Set aside.

2. Whisk together the orange juice, orange zest, thyme, maple syrup, oil, peppercorns, and salt in a small mixing bowl. Set aside.

3. Flake the sea bass into the salad bowl.

4. Drizzle in the dressing and mix gently so as not to break apart the bass.

5. Divide onto plates lined with baby lettuce leaves and serve with the lemon wedges.

SERVES 4–6

To Drink

A fruity white wine or iced tea with orange

Papaya, Carambola, and Yellowtail Salad

Make sure the papaya, honeydew, and carambola (star fruit) are ripe.

You may also use this recipe as a salsa — it tastes great with grilled fish on a warm summer day at the beach.

To make the salad:

2　cups peeled ripe papaya in large dice

1½ cups sliced carambola (about 2 small)

1　cup diced honeydew melon

¾　cup peeled and julienned kohlrabi

½　cup finely chopped mint

6–8 grilled scallions, sliced, 1 inch of green removed from the top

Salt

½　tablespoon coarsely ground black pepper

To make the dressing:

1　tablespoon olive or peanut oil

1　teaspoon sesame oil

Juice of ⅔ lime (about 1½ tablespoons)

Zest of 1 lime

To finish:

1½ pounds grilled yellowtail fillets, flaked into large pieces, refrigerated

1　cup fresh spinach leaves

Lime wedges

> **ADVANCE PREPARATION:**
> Grill the yellowtail fillets and scallions

1. Mix the papaya, carambola, honeydew, kohlrabi, mint, scallions, salt to taste, and pepper thoroughly in a large mixing bowl.

2. Whisk the dressing ingredients in a small bowl and drizzle on the salad.

3. Add the yellowtail pieces and toss again, but gently, so as not to break up the fish.

4. Lay out the spinach leaves on four plates, top with the fish salad, and serve immediately with the lime wedges.

SERVES 4

Pollack with Jicama and Melon Salad

Pollack is a sweet whitefish sometimes mistaken for, or sold as, cod and often used in the making of fish-and-chips. It's perfectly suited for this salad.

Jicama is a Mexican tuber much like kohlrabi or parsnips in texture. After peeling away the brown outer layer, julienne or slice thin and use in a rémoulade, sautéed in butter with fresh herbs, or in the following recipe. This same recipe may also be used as a dip with tortilla chips.

1¾ cups peeled, thinly sliced jicama

1 cup diced ripe melon

¾ cup finely chopped red onion

¼ cup finely chopped cilantro plus extra for serving

2 garlic cloves, diced

Juice of 2 lemons (about 6 tablespoons)

2 tablespoons olive oil

Salt and freshly ground black pepper

2 pounds fresh pollack fillets

Lime wedges

1. Stir the jicama, melon, onion, cilantro, garlic, lemon juice, oil, and salt and pepper to taste thoroughly in a large mixing bowl. Cover and refrigerate for 1 hour.

2. Preheat a grill.

3. Remove the salad from refrigerator and set aside.

4. Lay the fillets on the grill. Cook about 4 minutes; turn and cook about 4 minutes longer, or until the fish is thoroughly cooked.

5. Divide the fillet into four servings. (For a cold dish, chill the pollack.) Top the pollack with generous amounts of the salad and serve immediately. Have fresh lime wedges on the side of each plate and more chopped cilantro for guests.

SERVES 4

To Drink

Chilled Lime Margaritas (see page 236)

Shad, Wild Chicory, and Cattail-Shoot Salad

Grill more than the amount of shad you would normally use for dinner and refrigerate it for a salad the next day. And then picnic at North Lake in the Catskills, where you can admire the overlook to the Berkshire Mountains, as did some of the Hudson River School painters in the mid-19th century.

Wild chicory is up around the same time as shad are in, in my area of the Northeast, and the two make a delightful combination, along with cattail shoots. If you cannot buy or pick chicory yourself, triple the amount of baby spinach leaves.

The meat of shad is quite delicate, so be sure not to handle it too vigorously or it will break apart.

I discuss cattail shoots on page 87.

To make the salad:

1	pound grilled boneless shad fillets
2	cups chicory, washed and dried
1	cup cattail shoots, cleaned, sliced (or substitute hearts of palm)
1	cup radicchio, washed and dried
1	cup baby spinach greens, washed and dried
½	small red onion, thinly sliced
1	pear, peeled and thinly sliced
½	cup walnuts, broken or halved

To make the dressing:

1½	tablespoons orange flower water
1	teaspoon balsamic vinegar

To finish:

¼	cup finely chopped parsley
1	lemon, sliced and cut in half

ADVANCE PREPARATION:
Grill the shad fillets

1. Cut or flake the shad into small pieces and set aside.

2. Toss gently the chicory, cattail shoots, radicchio, spinach, onion, pear, and walnuts in a large bowl.

3. Divide the salad onto four plates. Lay the shad across the top of each.

4. Drizzle the orange flower water and vinegar over the top. Garnish with the parsley and serve with the lemon wedges.

SERVES 4

Grapefruit Salad
with Smoked White Fish

Use any firm-fleshed smoked white fish for this summery, tart salad. If the grapefruit is too tart, soak the peeled sections in sugar water sprinkled with cinnamon for about 15 minutes beforehand.

To make the dressing:

½ cup grapefruit juice

2 tablespoons good-quality olive oil

1½ tablespoons malt or cider vinegar

1 teaspoon sugar

Salt and freshly ground black pepper

To make the salad:

1 large pink grapefruit, peeled and cut into sections

¾ cup pecans

¾ pound smoked white fish, flaked

8 cups mesclun

To finish:

2 tablespoons grapefruit zest

1. Whisk together the grapefruit juice, oil, vinegar, sugar, and salt and pepper to taste. Set aside.

2. Divide the grapefruit, pecans, and whitefish onto four plates. Top with the mesclun greens.

3. Drizzle the dressing on top, sprinkle with the zest, and serve.

SERVES 4

In the Smoker

Chapter 9

Smoking

I T COULD HAVE BEEN IN A CAVE sometime about 7000 B.C., during the Neolithic period, when someone first noticed that fish gathered from a nearby stream and stored on a high granite shelf lasted longer when it was stored in line with the smoke that curled up toward the roof — and had a different flavor from fish simply grilled over the fire.

During the 8th century, Norsemen often dried, smoked, or pickled fish in a favorite preservative — sour whey, which is still in use.

There are references to smoked fish in Scotland dating back to the 16th century, when fish were often heavily smoked. The fishing village of Findon (known as Finnan) produced smoked and flavored haddock, called haddies. We can still find Finnan haddie today.

It has also been said that in Scandinavia, smoked fish was discovered when a wooden shed, where numerous haddock were salted and hung to dry, caught fire, almost burning to the ground. Salvaging what they could, the fishermen noticed the wonderful taste of the fish, which had been smoked for the first time. Here might have been the commencement of a new industry.

Native Americans smoked their foods over the campfire — a makeshift smoker. The scarcity of food in midwinter demanded advance planning. In this instance, smoking techniques evolved from necessity.

The growth of railroads and the shipping industry in the mid-19th century allowed for the transportation of foods that were once too perishable, including fish. It became possible to deliver fish from the oceans inland for the first time ever. Smoked fish products, which had been heavily salted and smoked, bone dry and chewy, were now flavorful, moist, and tender.

The simplest smoker was merely an armful of green boughs laid tepee-style around smoldering green logs. Under these branches (suspended over the fire on a rack of green saplings) lay the catch of the day. Smoke was contained by the branches as the awaiting meal was tended to a golden finish.

Through time our attitude toward smoked foods has shifted from the pragmatic to the hedonistic. Our contemporary yearnings for the days of old have evolved to sophisticated culinary tastes that range from having smoked salmon on a Sunday-morning bagel (certainly not a Northwest coastal tradition) to inviting friends over for a festive meal of grilled arctic char wrapped in cornhusks.

Our needs have become wants and wishes. We demand quality and can now readily obtain it most anywhere good food is produced: in fancy food stores, fresh markets . . . and our own backyards. What was once an arduous function of survival has now become a social function providing entertainment.

How the Smoke Began

The first time I built an outdoor smoker, it was just to salvage a couple of dozen fish I had gathered over time that were taking up space in my freezer. It was also for fun, of course. Unfortunately, not knowing a thing about smoking, I had chosen an old woodstove as my containment for capturing smoke and flavoring food — a stove in which I had primarily burned end cuts from a local contracting firm that specialized in the construction of New England log homes. Log homes

are built almost exclusively from soft woods. I had fueled that stove with pinewood over several years. So, of course, the inside reeked of pine pitch, a flavor reminiscent of . . . turpentine. If you ever taste food smoked with the essence of turpentine, you'll quickly learn to avoid conifer woods for smoking, believe me. I couldn't *give* those trout away! They sparkled with a lovely golden hue but tasted horrible.

After quickly learning the undesirable effects of how *not* to smoke foods from an old woodstove with a turpentine patina, I went on to build a larger wooden box from 2-inch maple tongue-and-groove flooring, a perfect material for quick assembly and solid construction. Inside, I fastened hardwood brackets to hold the racks that slid in and out, supporting the food. The top of the smoker was a hinged lid that opened backward and in which I had drilled a vent hole for draft, covered by a piece of aluminum. In the center of the bottom of the box I had cut an opening into which I attached a 6-inch stovepipe, available from any hardware store. The entire structure rested, conveniently, on the upside of a hill behind my house from where I piped a smoke conduit underground from a firebox, about 6 feet below it, on level ground. The firebox was made of firebrick and built to accommodate approximately the same size log as I used in the woodstove in my home — 18 inches long — convenient because I did not have to adjust sizes for either use.

Why, you might ask, does one pipe smoke up and into the smoker? Why not just put the smoking chamber directly over the fire? Because most, though not all, outdoor smokers utilize a "cold" smoking technique.

A "cold smoke" is a method by which food is mildly smoked in a cooler environment and for a longer period of time than with a "hot smoke," during which the internal temperature of the food is maintained at a higher level.

Smoking began long before the modern inventions of refrigeration and freezing. Raw and uncooked foods, such as fish and, say, venison, were found to last far longer in that saddlebag after being cured and smoked. A flattened fillet of fish or a string of jerky pounded with berries for flavor and smoked for durability was lightweight, easily accessible, and downright tasty. Life was more mobile way back then, and people needed foods that lasted. Indeed, smoked foods did last.

Today we have the convenience of cooling and freezing devices (and yes, you can freeze smoked foods), but what we offer in this book is the flavor of our ancestors' ways, the redolence of another time, to conjure up an abstract image of other peoples and their magic smoke. We'll regress, if only for a while, during festive times, over dinner with friends, at holidays. Autumn is a good time to crank up the smoker; during these cool months you can smoke fish without fear of spoilage. With the holiday season approaching, you'll feel satisfied putting up foods, warming beside glowing embers, and having your clothes and hair smell of smoke all day long.

Shall we purchase smoked salmon from the highlands of Scotland? No need; we have cultivated the techniques ourselves. We purchase a portable smoker to take camping or use on the patio or we build home smokers up past the barn or in the backyard. Whether in the country or in the city, the downhome taste is from another time.

Fuel: Wood Chips, Wood Chunks, Logs, or . . . Dried Corn

A rule of thumb for fetching wood from the forest for smoking, as opposed to buying wood chunks and chips: Avoid conifers, or trees with needles that stay green year-round. Deciduous trees, those that shed their multicolored leaves in autumn, are what we want for the smoking of food. Most any hardwood, such as oak, maple, birch, ash, cherry, alder, and pecan; fruitwood, such as apple, peach, and plum; and even grapevine, which I snip from my arbor each fall, is desirable. The earliest standbys, hickory and mesquite, which were introduced to the home smoking community in the mid-20th century, are best suited for hearty hams and Canadian bacon. I believe these woods to be too harsh for delicate foods such as fish, cheeses, and, in some cases, mushrooms and fruit. A notable exception comes from the Pacific Northwest, where cedar planked salmon has been a favorite for centuries.

One of my favorites, an old combination that you should try if you're able to locate the not-so-ubiquitous items, turns out to be a mix of sassafras — which is spottily available in my area of the Berkshires of western Massachusetts — and dried corncobs, gently coaxed from the feed bin of your neighboring hog farmer by a promise of something delectably smoked in return. The combination is fragrant and imparts a sweet, down-home flavor reminiscent of the outdoors. I became hooked on the combination some 25 years ago.

In the absence of sassafras and corncobs, though, and in order of preference, I like fruitwoods and grapevines. While on camping or fishing trips, I cut my own black birch, which is often readily available (at least in the northern latitudes), a longtime favorite of several fishing friends who have learned to put up with my fussing over their outdoor meals in the spring or fall in some desolate location.

Wood chips and chunks will vary by species, size, source, availability, and quality. If you have no resource other than purchased wood, these days you should have little problem locating something suitable for your needs. When I must, I buy chunks in 20-pound bags from Nature's Own (see Resources, page 244). Chunks work best in the large smoker or smokehouse, ranging in size from about 5 × 2 × 2 inches to slightly smaller, 3 × 1½ × 1½ inches, or even "mini," which I've never ordered from this company. Most chips found in hardware stores, feed supply stores, or most anywhere else these days may be smaller, and that's fine too.

If you plan and build your own smokehouse, I suggest using medium-sized chunks; they don't burn as quickly. Over the course of an 8-hour smoking, you may have to add wood three, four, or five times, depending on size. Smaller pieces must be added more often.

Some years ago I discovered an unexpected source for wood chips for smoking foods. In a nearby village was a small woodworking company that manufactured pool cues for the billiard industry. The company's maple sticks and one-of-a-kind cues were lovely to behold. I still have some that I salvaged from its rubbish, using the decorative handles to make barbecue tools. The preferred byproducts for me, however, were maple chips, the result of turning the front maple section on a lathe. The maple hardwood pieces — larger than sawdust, about pea size — made the perfect resource for my smoking operation. I was careful never to use the exotic turnings used for the handle, as exotic woods can be toxic.

I soaked the kiln-dried chips in water and dropped a couple of handfuls onto a baking tray situated over my heat source, a propane burner. My free maple chips sufficed for many years, but the company has moved elsewhere, so now I'm back to buying bagged wood when I'm not using the bountiful resources provided by the woods that surround me. Or dried corn.

So if you are resourceful, keep a lookout for unexpected free wood. Make very sure the wood you use for food is *pure* hardwood, not pine, and not exotics such as rosewood, vermilion, and mahogany — those used in the manufacture of fine woodworking, pianos, furniture, and pool cues. Also, do not use any woods that have had any type of protective finish applied to them, including varnish, paint, and preservatives. Ask if you don't know.

As you'll see, I've become a convert to another source of smoke: dried corn kernels. I've come to prefer the flavor of food, especially fish, subjected to this specific smoky environment. As mentioned in my discussion of corn smoking on a patio grill (see pages 18–22), I often lay a chunk or two of apple, maple, or sassafras on the bottom of the pan before adding the corn kernels. Once the corn has finished smoldering, which it will do before the largest chunks of wood have burned down — unless you use very small chips, which will burn at about the same rate — the chunks will continue to burn, thus increasing the length of time for smoking without having to add to the smoke pan as often. Also, you can mix varieties of wood with the corn for more interesting combinations of flavor.

Smokers of All Makes and Sizes

Let me count the ways. One, two, three, four, five, six, seven, eight . . . . There are many, many devices — kettles, buckets, grills, torpedoes, towers, boxes, vertical aluminum smokers, split 50-gallon steel barrels, stainless-steel gas grills, charcoal grills, under a piece of canvas, in a stand-up smokehouse — with which to smoke foods with electricity, wood, gas, and charcoal and with wood chunks, chips, sawdust, corn kernels, herbs, spices, and . . . I'll stop here.

Let's start with electric smokers.

Electric Smokers

I've successfully smoked fish many times on electric smokers with satisfying results. The torpedo-shaped containers are tall and narrow, somewhat limiting for elongated whole fish or fillets, but they work well for shorter fillets and for vegetables.

Essentially they work like this: On the very bottom of the smoker is an electric coil. Some of the lower-end models offer no control switches; when they're plugged in, they're on; when unplugged, they're off. The coil ignites the corn or wood chunks or chips. Above these a pan contains water, beer, or whatever flavoring liquid you choose, with herbs and spices. On one or two levels above this are the racks that hold food. Keep the cover closed and check a convenient side door to see when more corn or wood chunks are needed, which over the course of 3 or 4 hours of smoking will probably be at least once. The internal temperature should be kept at 225 to 250°F.

Another electric smoker design, a tall aluminum box with a hinged front-access door, fires up sawdust in a pan on the bottom of the chamber. Some offer the ability to hang foods; others supply only shelves. These are great for smoking fillets of freshwater perch, walleye, or various other fish that fit neatly into the size limitation of under about 12 inches. Follow the manufacturer's instructions for best results.

Some people feel the need to moisturize the air inside a smoker. Water smokers are quite popular and I have enjoyed the versatility of flavoring with various kinds of liquids in the water pan. The heat source, either charcoal or electric coils, is at the bottom of an aluminum box. Directly above the heat is a pan in which water, beer, cider, wine, or water with herbs and spices is placed, under the grills holding the food to be smoked. The constant steam keeps fillets moist while flavoring them beyond the usual smoke flavor.

Gas Grills for Smoke Grilling: By the dozens

Two burners, four, six, or more. The more efficient units, those that enable the operator to light only one or two burners at a time, to more closely control heat, are desirable and come in prices ranging from less than $100 to, yes, many thousands of dollars.

Split grates that slide back and forth come equipped on most models, allowing for various combinations of use such as setting down a smoke pan directly on top of two burners and leaving the other side (the side on which the food is smoked) off, the technique required for indirect smoking. Look for options such as side burners, where you can simmer a pan or two of sauce, and shelves on which to lay cooking tools. Most models also include closed storage bins underneath the grill area.

Manufacturers of stand-up grills have caught on to America's love of the outdoors and so are building grills that also serve as smokers. Look for a slide-out stainless-steel drawer in which to put corn, wood chips, or small hardwood twigs. These drawers are convenient and are easily wiped out after use. The drawers offered by inexpensive models, I feel, are often too small, but high-end models offer a larger capacity. The six- and even eight-burner models offer many more square inches of grill space, perfect for entertaining on a grand scale. Some of these come as slide-in countertop units that can be set into a custom-designed base, which might also include a work counter and sink, all down beside the pool.

Charcoal Grills for Smoke Grilling

I like the qualities of charcoal fuel; charcoal burns hotter than most gas burners, except for some high-end grills whose BTUs reach up into the professional strata. Charcoal emits more of a distinct flavor. You should consider using "lump" or "chunk" charcoal, irregularly shaped charcoal pieces. Lump charcoal will usually light in half the time as regular briquettes and quickly rise to higher temperatures, hotter than ordinary briquettes. Some lump may consist of wood from flooring and furniture, pallets, and construction material, so read labels before purchasing. The best lump charcoal is manufactured from 100 percent pure hardwood, preferably sugar maple.

Ideally we'd like to see companies that do not cut down trees solely for the purpose of making charcoal. Some environmentally conscious companies use trunks and branches that do not meet lumber specs and are kiln-dried to remove harmful creosote and resins. Grain alcohol should be used as fuel in the production, not petroleum, which imparts a distict flavor and may leave residue.

Briquettes may be composed of sodium nitrate, nitrogen oxide, borax, sulfur, lignite, and a petroleum binder. If you have a choice, lean toward lump, or chunk, charcoal for a cleaner, healthier burn. Charcoal is messy, of course, but you're outdoors, involving yourself in things organic.

Gas and Charcoal Grills?

Recently I've noticed advertising from a company (Char-Broil) that manufactures a grill with a basketlike unit that sits inside the bowels of the grill for use with charcoal. The basket is easily removed for use with gas burners, with which the grill also comes equipped. I have not used this grill but I speculate as to its true usefulness. I wonder what one has to give up for this kind of versatility. It is relatively inexpensive, though, and perhaps worth a try.

Japanese Egg-Shaped Smokers

These smokers are shaped like an egg and that's exactly what one company calls them, The Big Green Egg. Some are plainly colored (green), but not all: The Kamado is elaborately covered with high-fired ceramic tiles. Either Japanese design will perform the job of intense smoking. The walls of these smokers are super thick, so smoke doesn't escape except through a tightly controlled venting system. The porcelain-coated smoker can be tightly sealed with a clamp, and high temperatures (upward of 750°F) are easily obtained.

A charcoal fire ignites with a sheet or two of newspaper and goes a long way. Smoking in these types of smokers is fun — perfect for family meals. These unique smokers will sear foods quickly if you're grilling. The most attractive of outdoor cooking equipment, Japanese smokers are not as expensive as one would think. They are offered in a variety of sizes.

A Wok on the Stove

This is not a new concept. The Chinese have smoked fish with tea leaves for a long time. Line a large wok with a layer of heavy-duty aluminum foil, on which you may use tea leaves, corn kernels, small wood chips, sawdust, or any combination of these. Include herbs if you want. A half cup or less of any combustible organic flavoring will do, but start out with small amounts so the smoke doesn't overwhelm the house; you can always add more. But first! Open windows and turn on a fan.

Locate a wire-mesh rack, such as one used for roasting chickens, a round perforated pizza pan, or even a round wire-mesh spatter guard that will sit inside the wok above the smoke. Some Chinese recipes suggest simply using several chopsticks laid side by side for the platform. Lay fillets of fish or large skewered sea scallops across the rack. I like marinating them in soy sauce, white wine, lemon, maple syrup, and wasabi powder for 15 minutes first.

Turning the burner to high heat will begin the smoking quickly. Cover the wok with a lid, then turn down the heat just enough to keep the wok hot and smoldering. Smoke for about 15 minutes, or until the flesh of the fish turns opaque. If the smoke becomes too heavy, remove some of the tea leaves, corn, or wood.

Oven Smoking

Using a roasting pan or an ovenproof wok (be sure it doesn't have a wooden handle) lined with aluminum foil, follow the instructions for smoking with a wok on the stove, except without a cover. A large roasting pan will accommodate a large piece of fish, such as a side of salmon. Smoke the fish in a 500° oven.

Barrel Smokers

Custom-made smokers are available throughout the country. They can be designed according to your specific needs and built with space enough to smoke food for a contingent of hungry backwoods loggers. Brinkmann makes several ready-made steel units that look as if life began as a 50-gallon holding drum and saw its transformation into smoking units. Imagine a barrel lying on its side resting on a stand, cut in half and hinged. Welded to one side is a smaller chamber for burning logs (simple sawdust is an underachiever in these units). Once the wood begins to smolder, smoke is conducted upward and into the food chamber. Simple, straightforward, and for about $150 or so, quite a good value. The company's high-end models on wheels sell for upward of $8,000 and trail behind a vehicle. If it's serious smoking you're after, these fit the bill. These smokers are usually found wherever outdoor cooking equipment is sold. You can see photographs and learn more on Brinkmann's Web site (see Resources, page 244).

Lake- or Streamside Smokers and Large Steel Smokers

See pages 204–214 for information devoted exclusively to building these two smokers.

Smoking Fish in a Smokehouse

The following information is applicable for use with the Manikowski Smoker and the Rose Smokehouse, described on pages 210–218, or with a smoker of your own design. This information is not applicable to smoking on a grill.

Over the years, in my note taking throughout a daylong (or longer) smoking session, I've tried to stand back and analyze some of the reasons that smokings can vary from time to time. At first I noticed that while doing a smoking on a warm, humid day in summer months, I would have poor results. Why? I guessed it was due in part to the fact that I had little control over the air circulation. It often took longer, by several hours, and occasionally the results did not seem as good as they had at other times. Brisk fall days or days when the temperature was not too hot seemed better suited for smoking foods.

With continued observations and upon reflection, I believe I began to understand some of the many variables involved. Some. The process takes time, patience, and experimentation.

Food smoking is a human invention. No other species on the planet incorporates any similar activity into its food gathering, preparation, and strategy for survival. We are a resourceful, problem-solving species.

In essence, humans developed an artificial environment, intentionally or unintentionally, whereby smoke is pumped into an enclosed chamber or room, surrounding food for preservation (historically) or (today) for gastronomic purposes.

Smoke introduces millions of microscopic molecules into the air, mostly carbon and trace solids, which create a "fog" full of volatile oils that are released from smoldering wood (or corn kernels). These are the devices we use to create specific flavors. By compacting the air inside a smoke chamber with this flavoring fog, one is essentially controlling that space. Other variables, such as barometric pressure, are also involved.

Cool air is dense air; atoms are compacted and can't hold much water vapor. Warm air is more spread apart and contains fewer molecules. So inside a smoker, where there is warm air, there is room for additional atoms — carbon atoms from the smoke. If the air inside the smoker becomes heavier because of increased density, it then takes more energy to move that air up and out of the chamber. This may explain why on warm, humid days air circulation is less active and has less initiative for movement (very much the way I feel on a humid summer day).

Cool, dry conditions seem to be better suited for smoking. With proper ventilation from vent holes in the fire pit and by air being pulled through cracks and crevices in the firebrick, upward movement takes place. This airflow moves through the chamber toward the vent openings at the top of the smoker, causing cooler air, now unburdened by the weight of natural water vapor, to push through the smoker, persuading the warmer air out ahead of it. (Warm air rises.) This movement of air helps greatly in the evaporation of excess moisture in fish, and venting is crucial to remove this moisture-laden air.

Relative humidity also must be taken into consideration, even though it cannot be controlled when we build outdoor smokehouses, unlike indoor commercial stainless-steel facilities, where conditions are tightly controlled.

If the relative humidity is too high, an increased percentage of moisture will linger in the air, keeping fish from drying out, which is what we are partially intending with the help of fire and smoke. If high relative humidity prevents fish from drying out, it could result in a product too moist, too . . . mushy. The organic protein may also become more susceptible to harmful bacterial growth, especially on warm days. So if the air temperature is high, say, over 90°F, and the relative humidity stays about 75 percent, don't even bother smoking; wait until another day. A relative humidity of about 60 percent is the best condition for smoking fish.

Those are a few weather-related aspects of the process; here are some other aspects.

Salt. When fish was preserved for long journeys to inland towns and cities by the Romans and Egyptians, salt

and/or air drying was critical. Today we don't need as much salt, but we do need some for preservation purposes. Nowadays doctors advise against its overuse, citing blood pressure concerns, but some salt is necessary.

A Food and Drug Administration study in March 2001 recommended that "a 3.5 percent level of NaCl (sodium chloride) be included in concentrations used in the smoking of fish. Along with a proper temperature control of 40°F (during refrigeration) it is reasonable to conclude that the salt and cold" will keep levels of *C. botulinum* under control.

Increasingly, I have decreased proportions of salt in my curing solutions and brines by more than 50 percent of what I once used. Should you choose to experiment with various brines, start with about 1 pound of salt per gallon of water — and add other ingredients if you like. A medium brine contains 2 to 2½ cups of salt per gallon of water and a heavy brine contains 3½ to 4 cups of salt per gallon of water. These proportions are far, far too salty for me, though.

You might begin with the curing solution recipes on pages 198–201 and adjust recipes according to your own tastes. Be aware, however, that a certain amount of salt is crucial for the retarding of bacterial growth; neither smoke nor heat alone will control that aspect of the smoking process. You may notice that I use wine in some recipes, but you don't need to. Substitute water for the wine, if you want, in direct proportions.

The temperature of food in a smoker is the next important factor we need to consider. Basically, there are two kinds of smoking: cold smoking and hot smoking. To obtain a cold smoke, temperature in the smokehouse must be maintained at about 90°F to 100°F in the beginning, then raised toward the end of the smoking period to reach 165°F for at least 30 minutes. (At 120°F for too long a time, unwanted bacterial growth can take place, so it is best to stay above, or well below, that temperature for cold smoking purposes.)

The extended time for proper cold-smoked foods is often too long (days rather than hours) for most home smokers' interests, so I'll focus primarily on hot smoking techniques here. (For information about detailed cold smoking methods as dictated by the Food and Drug Administration, write to the FDA at U.S. Food and Drug Administration Office of Seafood, 200 C Street, Southwest, Washington, DC 20204.)

In hot smoking, fish is cooked to an internal temperature of 180°F to prevent spoilage and bacterial growth. Cooking in a 300°F oven for about 30 minutes either before smoking or at the end will achieve that result if your smoker will not reach those temperatures or if you are unsure whether it has. Most smokers and smokehouses, however, can achieve even higher temperatures. An instant-read thermometer is an essential item for any smoking session. Keep it nearby at all times.

A typical cycle in the smoking process will slowly bring up temperatures so that within 6 to 8 hours the internal temperature of the fish should be 165°F to 180°F. The temperature inside the smoking chamber should stabilize at 200–225°F or so, depending on how the fire pit is controlled.

By adjusting vent openings, increasing or decreasing the fire, and decreasing or increasing the amount of fuel, over time you will learn the subtleties of your individual smoker and how to control its internal temperature and air circulation. Every smoker, whether it is a 50-gallon barrel suspended under a tree limb, an old refrigerator, or a state-of-the-art smokehouse, will react differently according to its own characteristics and to the skill that each individual brings to the craft.

Upon completion of a smoking, which could take 6, 8, even 12 hours, fish need to be cooled down. An electric fan is the best tool for this job. It should be directed toward the fish, whether hanging or on racks. A pellicle will form, a shiny membrane of water-soluble protein, which indicates that the fish is ready to take down or remove from the racks and refrigerate. Yes, refrigerate: Remember, unless you boost the salt percentage in a formula and smoke the fish for a couple of days in anticipation of packing victuals for an extended kayaking trip to the Northwest Territories, you are smoking a product that will keep for days, not weeks.

I prefer to inject fish with brine only because of the convenience. Once I've steeped the curing solution and let it cool, I strain it through several layers of cheesecloth to eliminate all unnecessary food particles. You may soak fish if you prefer, of course. Just be sure you have a large container and keep the fish covered in the refrigerator while brining.

I like at least 1 hour of brining, although I have injected fish just before smoking with good results. You'll ultimately be the judge of formula and timing, on which you will keep notes.

I've used many types of syringes over the years, from a 10 cc medical syringe to one the Morton Salt Company calls a "meat pump," but only recently has outdoor cooking enthusiasm led to manufacturers' (legal) marketing of 60 cc Seasoning Injector syringes for basting and injecting. They are inexpensive, easily found in kitchenware stores, and a perfect size for our purposes. (A fishing friend and doctor must be relieved that I don't bother him anymore, begging for syringes.)

A side of salmon weighing about 2½ pounds needs about 30 ccs injected evenly throughout the fillet. It will leak, so set it in a container or directly on the plastic wrap in which you will keep it tightly wrapped. Smaller fillets may fit into zipper-lock bags, which I find quite helpful in marinating foods. Inject small fillets of, say, 1 to 1½ pounds with 10 to 15 cc. The smallest of fillets, weighing less than 1 pound, should cure enough

Nitrates and Nitrites

The continued use of nitrates and nitrites in curing foods is being investigated by the U.S. Department of Agriculture and the Food and Drug Administration. I am glad to see that this is under government consideration. I have eliminated saltpeter (potassium nitrate and sodium nitrite) from my curing solutions for years. Unfortunately, it is all too easy to find nitrates and nitrites in most commercially prepared dry curing mixes. Among other things, nitrates relax blood vessels and lower the demand for oxygen by the heart, so it is assumed that people with heart problems or weakened immune systems should avoid these preservatives.

with simple brining. Unused brine will keep for several weeks tightly covered in the refrigerator.

Before placing fillets in the smoker, drain and pat dry to eliminate any excess liquid. If you have room, you may lay them flat in the refrigerator for 30 minutes or so.

Oil all racks as well as the skin side of the fish. It will make for easier release once the fish has cooled down after smoking, in about an hour.

To release fillets or whole fish from stainless-steel racks, onto which they *will* stick, prop up the rack carefully at a slight angle so you can get to the underside, and with the backside of a teaspoon or butter knife, gently push against the skin until it loosens. Be sure to support a fillet with one hand, or the hand of a helper, so it does not release and fall. You might also need to coax it some by running a wide spatula underneath the skin. If the skin is persistent and will not release, carefully run the spatula between the skin and the meat and lift off the meat, without the skin. Warm fish directly out of the smoker will likely break apart, so let it cool down first. After you do this once, you'll develop your own technique.

An alternative method is to lay each fillet on a separate piece of cheesecloth, also brushed or sprayed with oil; it oftentimes releases with less difficulty.

Keep notes, measure temperatures inside and outside of the smoker and inside the fish, check the humidity, note the weight loss — which will be 12 to 15 percent of the original weight — and adjust the components of the operation as needed the next time you fire up the smoker.

No doubt there are as many ways to smoke foods as there are people who do the smoking, so go ahead, invent and innovate as your ancestors did — personalize your design, skills, and techniques. Smoking is a culinary craft, one easily learned and greatly rewarding. Soon enough, you will belong to the elite smoke masters society.

Some Beginning Guidelines for the Manikowski Smoker

Small shrimp, scallops, and small fish fillets weighing a pound or less *may* take 2 to 3 hours to flavor, up to 4 hours for a more intense flavor, in a large smoker or smokehouse. Be watchful of shrimp so they don't dry out, which they have a tendency to do.

An entire side of salmon weighing 2 to 3 pounds is a substantial-size fish and could be the largest you will ever smoke. This fillet will take approximately 8 hours to smoke. Longer times *may* be necessary for larger items, shorter times *possibly* for smaller ones. Larger whole fish, say, a 20-pound whole striped bass, *may* take 10 to 12 hours, or longer.

In planning a smoking session, I position smaller items toward the front so that as time goes on, I can remove those items first. Let me give you an example. Recently I smoked four wild king salmon fillets about 2½ pounds each, a whole shad of about 3 pounds, several shad fillets of about 1 pound each, and two shad roe sacs of about ½ pound each. I removed first the shad roe, the smallest, at around 3 hours, the shad fillets at 4½ to 5 hours, the whole shad at 6 hours, and, finally, the salmon at 8 hours. As you can see, the smallest came out first, the largest, last.

This all depends, too, on many variables, such as placement in the smoker (if the fish is low and close to the smoke hole where it is the warmest, it might cook faster), temperature of the fish prior to smoking (if the fish was icy cold when it was put into the smoker, it could take longer), and intensity of heat (if your fire runs hot, things may take less time). The weather of the day, outside temperature, and humidity all must be considered.

Food takes longer to smoke in a large smoker or smokehouse than in a smaller one and much longer than food smoked on a grill because of the size difference. A large smoker takes more heat and smoke to fill the larger space. Also, cold smoking takes longer to complete because the food is farther away from the heat source.

Use this book as a beginning and then follow your own taste and instincts. In time, you will know when a fillet is done by poking at it with your finger and taking its temperature.

Which Fish to Smoke?

Most any species of fish can be smoked, but fish high in oil are best suited because the oils within the flesh self-baste during the smoking process. Salmon, trout, tuna, and mackerel are ideal for smoking, with or without brining. These fish contain the highest levels of fat and oils.

Whitefish, chub, and herring, favorites in the Great Lakes regions, smoke well and are flaky and sweet. Lake trout, freshwater fish that swim and live in similar cold-water temperatures, lend themselves greatly to smoking because of their high fat content. Years ago, I started a relatively small smoked fish company, importing all four of these smoked, vacuum-sealed fish from a Lake Superior commercial fisherman, picking up my supply at the Fulton Fish Market in New York. Of these four, my best-selling smoked fillets were lake trout. It was a challenge to introduce a relatively unknown fish to East Coast palates that were, and still are, somewhat stuck on most of the following smoked species.

Fish and Mercury

According to the FDA, give careful consideration before consuming seafood with high levels of methyl mercury. The fish with the highest levels (about 1 part per million) are: tilefish (golden bass or golden snapper) at 1.45 ppm, swordfish at 1.00 ppm, shark at .96 ppm, and king mackerel at .73 ppm.

The FDA recommends that children, as well as women of childbearing age, eat no more than 12 ounces of fish per week. As I discussed on pages 2–3, a healthful balance of nutrients can easily be maintained by rotating and varying the fish species you eat.

Sable (also called black cod) and sturgeon have to be my two favorite smoked fish. New York delicatessens, a few of which for several years bought my lake trout, now charge extremely high prices for these once inexpensive fish. Incidentally, please do not support the further decimation of the Caspian Sea sturgeon, which has become nearly extinct from overfishing for meat and, on a larger scale, for caviar.

Bluefish is an extremely oily fish with a relatively strong flavor that some people find unpleasant unless it is smoked. Smoking seems to diminish that intense flavor. I ate more than my share of bluefish while living on Martha's Vineyard, and still enjoy it peppered and smoked pastrami-style.

Yellowtail is a fish I have rarely seen anyone turn down when smoked, it is so delicious. It is also delicious raw and is often used as sushi.

Preheating a Smoker

If you have been ambitious enough to have constructed a smoker out back behind the house or barn or somewhere away from any wooden buildings or trees or shrubs, you will begin a smoking in the following way.

Logs of wood take time to burn down to a bed of coals hot enough to accept the placement of green logs on top, which will only smoke and not burn, so give yourself 1 to 2 hours to thoroughly preheat the firebox.

After a deep bed of red-hot coals is ready (4 to 5 inches deep), lay two to four green logs on top, each 4 to 6 inches in circumference. They must be green or they will ignite and burn quickly, not giving off the necessary smoke. If you don't have access to green wood, soak logs in a container large enough to accommodate them — a large, clean garbage can often work very well. Soak them in water a day or two ahead to retard burning. Remember, you want smoke, not fire.

Once the green or wet wood starts to smoke, you're on your way. Just before setting the logs on top of the hot coals, you will want to place the food to be smoked on the shelves and situate them properly. Otherwise, the thick cloud of smoke that develops might prevent your seeing inside the smoker.

If you are using propane for your heat source, follow these directions:

To begin a smoking using corn and wood chunks combined (or either one alone), lay two to four large chunks of wood in an aluminum sheet pan over a propane fire and pour 6 to 8 cups of corn kernels around them; spread them evenly. It will take 30 minutes or more to ignite and begin smoking. Look for a thick cloud of smoke rising from the air vents, cracks, and crevices. You're smokin' now. (If you have neighbors, you may want to alert them to your culinary intentions to prevent fire trucks from showing up. Really.)

One load of corn and wood should last 1½ to 2 hours; then you'll need to add more. You may have to empty all the charred remains into a metal container and start a fresh smoke if it burns down completely. Also, remember to keep a container of water or a hose nearby to douse flames in the pan. Once upon a time, during a smoking, my pan of corn and wood chunks ignited. There was just a tiny flame visible between cracks in the firebrick. After running to find an empty bottle or watering can, filling it under the faucet, and getting back to the fire pit, flames were shooting out from under the cover. So be prepared. It will save you time in the long run, and possibly a ruined session or worse. The process does need frequent tending. I check things every half hour or so.

In the beginning, take notes for future reference on the amounts of corn or wood used, how often you added it to the pan, overall timing, internal temperature of the foods, and weather conditions. You'll find that future smokings will become easier when you come equipped with information.

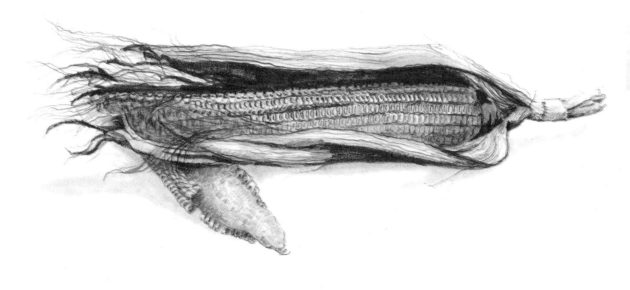

Corn: Food or Fuel? A Short History

CORN. IT HAS MANY GUISES — tamales, polenta, ugali, tortillas, grits — but it's all the same, isn't it? Well, sort of.

When Christopher Columbus stumbled across the golden kernels in a new land, he found it unique to the European palate. He filled his seaman's bag for the return trip to western Europe. Thus the grain, which had been harvested in Peru by the Inca (who took their corn seriously), traveled to western Europe and was introduced as maize, meaning "our life," "our source," "life giver," and "bread of life."

Italians also value corn. Even though polenta was once considered peasant food, it is now exalted, served along with succulent *uccelli* (small birds) and smoked wild boar chops; smothered with fresh tomato, Asiago, and escargots; sliced, fried, broiled, grilled, and sauced to death.

An overview of corn-eating cultures shows diversity and pragmatism. In the mountains of Guatemala, people pound corn flour to a pulp on a stone *metate.* The pulp is then fried over a wood fire on a griddle to make tortillas. Mexican *nixtamal* is made by soaking corn in water and slaked lime, then partially cooking it; this removes the tough indigestible kernel. The nixtamal is used in making *masa* (corn-based dough), which gets shaped into tortillas and cooked. The finished tortillas can be stuffed with pork, turkey, or vegetables. Southerners often start the day with a plate of steaming hominy grits. Nothing equals a mushy lot of *ugali* (cornmeal porridge) to someone from Kenya, where this is a staple.

Corn has been labeled *milho* by the Portuguese, *millat* in southwestern Europe, and in Romania *mamaliga* is cornmeal mush. Pueblo elders associate blue corn with the East — place of the rising sun; yellow corn with the South — home of new life; white corn with the North — place of strength; and red corn with the West — where the sun travels and where there is long life.

Over thousands of years, maize husks were used by Native Americans to make foot mats, beds, bags, and moccasins. Aztec, Incan, Anasazi, and Mayan mythology idolized the plant, which was derived from a wild grass originally grown in Central America. The next thing you know, we'll be powering automobiles with it. We already do, with ethanol.

In researching corn, I could not have fathomed the thousands, yes, thousands of uses I found. Here are a few:

Flint corn is hard (Indian corn) and used to make hominy. Dent corn is used mostly to make processed foods but is also grown for livestock. Flour corn is starchy and finely ground for baking. Popcorn is, well, popcorn. And, of course, there is the indubitable sweet corn, enjoyed on the Fourth of July, dripping with lots of butter.

Those notorious southern states made fame with their uniquely American invention of bourbon, which must be made from at least 51 percent corn; beer manufacturing converts starch to sugar; corn oil is widely used in cooking; we thank William K. Kellogg for Corn Flakes; high fructose corn syrup is used in carbonated beverages; aspirin is covered with a starch paste derived from corn; sorbitol is used in toothpaste. (Did you know that of more than 10,000 items on grocery store shelves on average, more than 2,500 use corn in some form?). Finely ground corncobs are relatively dust-free and absorbent, so they make useful carriers for pesticides, fertilizers, soaps, and even cosmetics; gelatinized corn flour can control the rate of water loss during the drying of gypsum wallboard; tetrahydrofurfuryl alcohol is a resin developed from corncobs, useful in paint and varnish; and the porcelain part of spark plugs even contains a corn product.

And I use dried corn kernels to smoke fish.

Basic Curing Solution

Straining this solution is important if you want to avoid clogging your syringe or "seasoning injector."

Pour the finished solution over a layer of cheesecloth inside a metal strainer to be sure you've eliminated the pieces of peppercorns and spices that otherwise clog needles.

This solution will keep for 1 to 2 months in a nonreactive container, covered and refrigerated.

1 cup water

1 cup dry white wine

1½ cups sugar

¾ cup salt; use a mix of kosher and iodized table salt

¼ cup pickling spices

1 tablespoon cracked black peppercorns

1 teaspoon cloves

½ teaspoon cayenne pepper

8-inch-square cheesecloth (or a large coffee filter)

1. Bring the water and wine to a boil in a 4-quart saucepan over medium-high heat.

2. Add the sugar and salt and continue boiling until they dissolve; reduce to a simmer.

3. Put the pickling spices, peppercorns, cloves, and cayenne into a cheesecloth pouch or coffee filter. Tie with a string and immerse in the liquid. Cover and simmer about 5 minutes. Turn off the heat and let it sit for about 30 minutes. Remove the spice pouch, squeeze dry, and discard.

4. Strain the liquid through a layer of cheesecloth, cover, and refrigerate. Do not use until completely cooled.

5. Inject with or immerse fish fillet in the curing solution for 1 to 2 hours or up to 12 hours.

MAKES ABOUT 2 CUPS

Bourbon Cure

This is a cure on the sweet side, so if you inject or brine your fillets, do so for only 30 minutes to an hour before smoking or grilling. Bourbon Cure keeps for 1 to 2 months covered in the refrigerator.

¾ cup bourbon

½ cup salt

¼ cup corn syrup

¼ cup triple sec

¼ teaspoon cayenne pepper

⅛ teaspoon vanilla extract

1. Bring all of the ingredients to a boil in a 4-quart saucepan over medium heat. Reduce the heat and simmer for 10 minutes, covered.

2. Remove from the heat and allow to cool. After an hour, or when completely cool, place in tightly covered jars and refrigerate until needed.

MAKES 1¼ CUP

Cures in the Rough

Using a large container, mix 1 gallon of water with 2 cups of coarse salt and stir until the salt is dissolved. Gently lower one egg (in its shell) into the solution. If it sinks, add more salt, a little at a time, until the egg rises to the surface. Take out the egg, and add about the same amount of brown or plain sugar as salt to the solution. Add spices (such as juniper berries and black peppercorns), herbs, or other flavoring ingredients you prefer.

Or try this: After dissolving the salt and sugar in water, add 1 tablespoon garlic powder, 1 tablespoon onion powder, 1 teaspoon cayenne pepper, and 1 teaspoon finely ground white pepper. Stir until dissolved. This recipe is handy when you are outdoors and have little access to supplies. Ground spices such as these are lightweight and thus easy to travel with.

Either of these recipes works well when you are immersing fish in the cure, instead of injecting.

Sorghum Chardonnay Cure

A friend from Georgia sent me a jar of sorghum for the holidays and I've enjoyed coming up with recipes to use with my newfound sweetener.

Sorghum is prepared from a canelike plant and is a little on the rough side, I believe, hinting at a slight sweet-sour character, not unlike the B grade of maple syrup, which I prefer over the esteemed grade A.

This cure will keep for 2 to 3 months in a nonreactive container, covered and refrigerated.

3   cups water

1   cup sorghum (or substitute grade B maple syrup or brown sugar)

½   cup salt

1   teaspoon mustard powder

½   bottle chardonnay, about 1½ cups

1   jar (1.5 ounces) pickling spices

8-inch square of cheesecloth

1. Bring the water to a boil in a 4-quart saucepan over medium-high heat.

2. Completely dissolve the sorghum, salt and mustard powder, in the water by whisking for a minute or so.

3. Add the wine and simmer, uncovered, for 2 to 3 minutes, until the liquor is cooked off.

4. Meanwhile, pour the pickling spices onto the cheesecloth and tie up with a string or twisty. Immerse the pouch in the solution and reduce the heat to low. Cover and simmer about 5 minutes. Turn off the heat and let sit for about 30 minutes. Remove the spice pouch, squeeze dry, and discard.

5. Strain the liquid through a layer of cheesecloth into a container and refrigerate, covered. Do not use until completely cooled.

6. Inject with or immerse fish fillets in the curing solution for at least 1 hour and up to 12 hours. Longer curing results in stronger flavor.

MAKES ABOUT 5 CUPS

Peppered Dill Rub

This rub is an attractive addition to cured, smoked fish, especially when used on red salmon. Nearly any fillet of fish can be smoked, and any fillet can be seasoned with this rub just before putting it into the smoker. You may *want* to inject the fillet with the Sorghum Chardonnay Cure (see page 200) the night before smoking; you do not, however, *have* to use this cure, nor any cure at all. The finished product might be considered by some to be a "pastrami" style of curing.

1   cup black peppercorns
4   cups cleaned and stemmed fresh dill

1. Blend the peppercorns in the bowl of a food processor for 1 to 2 minutes, or until they are coarsely pulverized.

2. Add the dill and pulse four or five times, until the dill is blended with the peppercorns.

3. Scrape down the sides with a rubber spatula and transfer to a container. Lay out a fillet on a cutting board and, with your hands or the spatula, rub the mix into the fillet until most of the surface is covered.

4. Wrap in plastic wrap and refrigerate at least 2 hours and up to 12 hours.

MAKES ABOUT 1 CUP, ENOUGH FOR ONE 4- TO 5-POUND FILLET

Lake Megiscane, Quebec

WE WERE IN THE NORTHERN HEART of Quebec, staying in a remote cabin accessible only by floatplane; the nearest road was days, or possibly weeks, away through deadfall and blow-down forest.

The first day there, Lou Blanchette — an old friend of some 25 years who has been with me through countless camping, canoeing, hunting, and fishing trips from Maine to Costa Rica — comfortingly tolerated my unease when I experienced severe disorientation. Heading back to camp in a small boat, I became convinced we were lost. I had been lost once before in 6 million acres of the Adirondack Forest in upstate New York for about 45 seemingly endless minutes. The feeling returned instantly now, coursing through my spine with the jolt of gripping adrenaline. Lou has always possessed a laid-back personality that makes anyone feel immensely comfortable and secure, an attribute especially welcome at a time such as this.

We had not thought to bring matches, food, water, compass, or topo map; we were only scouting the area in the first hours. The forlorn feeling of knowing that John, our pilot, would not be back with the plane for a few days merely cemented my uneasiness. As it turned out, we were not lost at all, but even so, Lou's casual remark that it could have been "an experience" helped justify my worries somewhat, considering the biting wind blowing off the October lake.

A few long minutes later, we spotted the cabin a mile or so away and I breathed a sigh of relief. Lou? Shrugged his shoulders and said "Let's eat" in his casual manner.

Eat we did. For the rest of the week. Randy Adams, one of my other two traveling companions, along with our guiding light, Craig Moffett, politely asked one evening whether it would be all right if we did *not* eat dinner. A compliment I accepted, considering the snow and rainy weather had kept us inside much of the week, cooking and eating. And eating.

Thus, I agreed to concoct not the

usual ambitious meal, which included a selection of wines, delicious cheeses, and vintage port, but instead a warming pot of pea soup, one of the signature meals we prepare on these, often annual, outings. I spent the afternoon working on something to accompany the soup, however, something I first developed some 22 years earlier on the shores of Lake Superior: cured and smoked freshly caught fish, in this case the ubiquitous northern pike — referred to in these Canadian parts simply as pike.

After several futile days angling for a different delicious freshwater fish of my youth, walleye — sometimes also called walleyed *pike* — we finally settled for a 30-inch *Esox lucius.*

To prepare and build our lakeside smoker, Lou and I cut and sized four green birch saplings intended for the structure's posts, serving to support the wire grate I had brought along, wired securely to notches at the top of each post. After setting up the smoker on the beach, we felled a small cherry tree with which to smoke and flavor the fish, kindled a fire bed, and laid the green cherry logs on top. After injecting the pike with my curing solution, I positioned it on the grill, over the smoke, and covered the entire structure with a seasonally tanned piece of cotton canvas. The concept, of course: to encapsulate food in a smoky environment.

The first time I tried this technique at a remote campsite on the shore of Lake Superior in Ontario, I was pleased with the outcome. It was surprisingly efficient and over the years I have built them in my backyard, at streamside, and beside magnificent North American lakes.

We ate well that evening and all week in spite of the rains and snow of early October, never getting lost and gaining a few extra pounds. And John, our pilot, did come back for us. ⤙━

Chapter 10

Lake- or Streamside Smoker

THIS IS A SIMPLE SMOKER that I devised years ago at a Canadian riverside, which you can build easily by yourself or with the help of fishing friends or family members in an afternoon. The end result, a tasty dinner, is a just reward for minimal effort. I have built ones at a campsite, streamside, and even in my own backyard.

The smoker requires only a few simple items. First, a large piece of cotton duck canvas or banner cloth, measuring approximately 60 inches by 76 inches, which should be available at upholstery or art supply stores. Do not use plastic, which melts. An oven or instant-read thermometer is useful as well. Next, you will need a stainless-steel grate, measuring about 22 inches by 17 inches, to fit under the canvas. You can find a suitable grate at an appliance store or tag sale. You might also borrow a grate from your outdoor grill or one of the shelves from your own oven. If you decide to do the latter, however, I suggest that you not repeat my mistake: I once took the top shelf from the oven while hurrying out the door on a fishing trip and then neglected to bring it back. I can still hear my ex-wife's complaints today, some 25 years later. Finally, you will need a saw or ax to cut some saplings and logs.

A grill smaller or larger than the one I recommend is perfectly fine, but you will need to adjust the canvas size accordingly. You will also need a 2- to 3-foot-long piece of nongalvanized wire, which will be cut into four pieces to hold the grill in place. To support the grill, collect four green saplings to serve as posts. You will also need three or four green logs cut to the same size as your grill to provide the smoke. Any hardwood would be suitable. If I can find it, I like black birch or sassafras, but maple is most abundant where I live. Fruitwoods such as apple are also excellent. Do not use resinous pine, or your smoked fish will have the distinct flavor of turpentine.

The curing process, which precedes the smoking, is used primarily for taste, not necessarily preservation, although the technique will keep any smoked foods longer, refrigerated, than foods that have not been cured. Years back, salt was used extensively to keep foods from deteriorating, much like the salt cod of the Scandinavians and Portuguese, but added little else, in my estimation. The excessive salt had to be rinsed off before using. Over the years I've eliminated a good deal of the salt called for in a curing solution, preferring various other ingredients that add character and flavor to the food — such as pickling spices, fresh herbs, and wine.

The day before smoking, simmer the cure over a low heat. Only after it has cooled can it be injected into the body of the fish. Any leftover brine will keep indefinitely, covered, in the refrigerator. (See recipes on pages 198–201) The curing solution will be injected with the help of a "seasoning injector," a 20 cc to 35 cc syringe with a #16-18 needle attached, or a meat pump, available from Morton Salt Co. All syringes may be reused many times if cared for properly and not bent or damaged. Immediately after using, flush out with clean water.

For posts, look for saplings that are 2 to 3 inches thick and about 28 inches long. Use only green hardwoods, which contain more moisture and so will not burn as readily near the open flame. Taper the bottoms of each sapling so that they can easily be driven into the ground.

Using a saw, ax, or sharp knife, cut a notch about 6 inches from the top of each post to act as a ledge on which to support the grill. Lay the grill on a cleared, flat area away from buildings, dry wood, leaves, or kindling. Mark the locations for the four posts, set the grill aside, and drive in the posts about 6 to 8 inches into the ground *(Fig. 10.1)*. Surround the fire area with some stones, if available.

Figure 10.1. Driving in the posts

With the grill resting in the notches on the posts, twist pieces of wire around each post and through the grill (see *Fig. 10.2*). The grill should rest at least 18 inches above ground.

Kindle a fire for about 45 minutes, or until a solid bed of coals is glowing but not flaming. Place green logs on top of the coals, beneath the grill. Set them close together to keep the flames contained and to prevent them from rolling off the coals. With the logs positioned

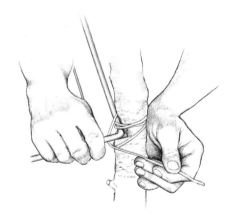

Figure 10.2. **Attaching grill**

correctly, flames from periodic flare-ups will be deflected to the sides.

Soak the canvas thoroughly in water. I once looked out my back window to see that flames had destroyed an entire piece of canvas as well as the six trout I was preparing to serve guests for dinner. Keeping the canvas moist will save you from having to endure a similar experience. If you are near a lake or stream, immerse the canvas for several hours to soak it thoroughly. If you are near enough to a building, you can use a hose or a bucket of water. Keep the water source handy, as you will need to wet down the canvas several times throughout the smoking process.

Lay your cleaned and cured catch on top of the grill *(Fig. 10.3)*. Cover the entire structure with canvas, and let the smoking begin. You will need to lift the canvas from time to time to see how your dinner is progressing *(Fig. 10.4)*. Doing so, however, may cause the fire to flame up. Gently toss some water on the fire to control the flames.

The temperature under the canvas will likely register between 200 and 300 degrees. An ideal temperature is 200 to 250 degrees, but it can be difficult to control the temperature in this kind of an environment.

I can think of no better way to enjoy a moonlit lake than with a meal of hot smoked lake trout, salmon, or pike.

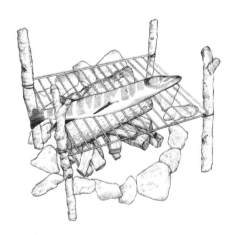

Figure 10.3. **Placing fish on the grill**

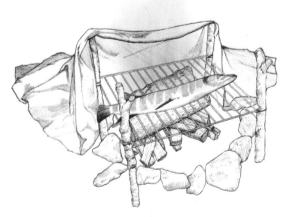

Figure 10.4. **Lifting the canvas**

Tied Tight, Tied Right

MARTHA'S VINEYARD is an island rich with grand waterfront homes lining East and West Chop cliffs; seafood restaurants; and quaint B&Bs. Up-island are the rural townships of Chilmark and West Tisbury, with a surprisingly lush countryside of working farms.

An attraction for visitors and Islanders alike is the many ways one can fish on and around the island. A small body of freshwater, Seth's Pond, is where I discovered voracious pickerel and largemouth bass — two species most Island fishermen often overlook, being saltwater-minded out there.

Fishing off Lobsterville Beach one morning, I found myself surf casting next to a fellow angler for several hours. He toyed with a feisty fish on 2-pound test for all the while I fished nearby, drove to the village of Menempsha for a bite to eat, and returned to the beach. There he was, still battling his quarry. He proudly set a world's record that day with a 6-pound bonito on 2-pound test, in my book one of the mightiest of fighting fishes, pound for pound, muscle for muscle.

A favorite spot of mine, Herring Creek, often yielded productive days of fly casting with flashy sand eel imitations across the swift tidal channel that flows in and out of Lake Tashmoo. It was there that I first learned to store a can of wasabi powder and a bottle of soy sauce in my glove compartment, to accompany fresh sashimi. Lunch followed the ebbing noon high tide.

Depending on the tide, the channel was pleasant to work; it was within sight of both Katherine Cornell's former home and a view of the nest of a vigilant osprey that often waged piscatorial war with me over our mutual food interests.

The road to Lambert's Cove is intentionally unkempt, meant to be difficult to maneuver. The sandy road keeps at bay outsiders and those unwilling to brave rugged terrain. I braved it often:

The fishing and the absence of people were worth the effort.

One day I stopped to pick up a hitch-hiker on his way to the cove, a fisherman, I surmised, judging by the gear he toted. He was a producer for a Boston television station and we fished side by side for the afternoon.

We were not alone, however. Nearby, one other person fished the inlet. Three of us stood within sight of one another, quietly absorbing the sunny calm. Until . . . until the tranquillity changed. Quickly, dramatically.

In truth, I did not see all that actually happened. I caught only the end of the incident. I had been intent on my own pursuit of the mighty *Sarda sarda,* focused, and only peripherally aware of the neighboring fishermen.

When bonito hit a fly, it is as if dyna-mite has exploded underwater, causing an upward cascade of fury. Powerful, with intent, the fish ignore a fisherman's hold in its attempt to escape. This particular fish appeared determined to swim back out through the channel to the ocean. And that it did.

Watching a fellow angler expertly play a fish, enjoying the leaps and dives we so hope for in this sport, we were ready to move aside and make way for him running back and forth on the rocks. I began reeling in my line to get it out of his way when I heard the grunt, a com-motion, a splash. I turned my head toward the fisherman and in that fleeting instant he stood dumbfounded, already stupefied at the edge of the water, the osprey glaring down at all of us.

Our friend stood looking down, staring at the blank rod in his hands. The bonito had stripped the reel from its mounting bracket, then nimbly yanked it entirely off and away from the rod itself. The reel had stayed firmly attached to the line and had tumbled through each eyelet, ripping them off their thread and lacquer holds, destroying them too. The fisherman stood stonelike, holding a wrecked graphite rod in his hands that had been stripped clean of reel and line. The osprey flicked its head for a curious glance and dipped at the splash left behind when the reel hit the water, assuming sand eel activity.

My fishing/hitchhiker companion and I left later, after things had quieted down, the tide sliding out of the channel. We retreated to his beach house for tea, discussing the sweetness and bitterness of another's misfortune. Applauding at the same time the mighty knot that man must have tied, attaching the backing line to his reel. A knot that held magnificently. ><>

Chapter 11

The Manikowski Smoker

I FIRST DESIGNED a steel smoker for Konkapot Restaurant in the early 1980s. Up to that point I had been using a dilapidated smoker behind my house that I had made years before from maple flooring. It was far too small for commercial use. In some areas, the health department will no longer permit wood to come in contact with food in commercial businesses. I wanted a smoker that was utilitarian, professional, and easily maintained. Stainless steel is a healthier, and easier to clean, alternative.

Working out the kinks of several different designs over the years, I eventually came up with this purely functional concept (see *Fig. 11.1*). A big advantage of the design is that this smoker can be divided into two separate sides. When smoking small amounts, I can use only one side. Or I can use one side for food that needs to be hung while smoking, such as ham, and the other side for fillets and other smaller items that need to rest on racks. A metal divider can be slid down into a channel to separate the two sides, or easily lifted out if I need more space. This smoker can hold up to 500 pounds of food at one time. If you do not require this amount of space, you can make your own smoker smaller.

Basic Construction

The floor of the smoker has two 6-inch openings, one in the center of each chamber, to which are attached 6-inch stovepipe coming from the fire pit several feet away. Because the heat source is far enough away from the food itself, one may "cold"-smoke or, by turning up the heat, "hot"-smoke as well, though not as readily as with a patio grill, where the heat is directly under or near the food.

Do not use galvanized stovepipe for food-processing purposes, as it can emit toxic fumes when heated. Ceramic pipe will last a very long time, a lifetime, and inexpensive standard black stovepipe will last for many years. If you keep the

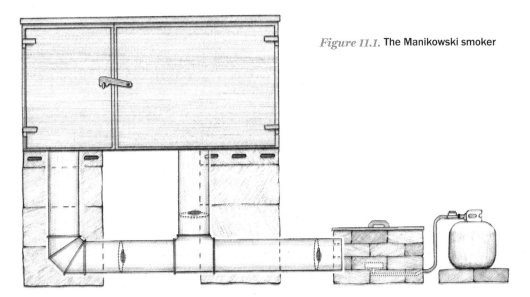

Figure 11.1. The Manikowski smoker

smoker and the fire pit covered when not in use, everything will last even longer.

A lid on top of the smoker and two doors in front allow for multiple access points. It is better to open front doors to check temperature and food. Opening the top allows too much smoke to escape.

I'll admit that I took a slightly backward approach to designing this smoker. I began by visiting refrigeration and plumbing suppliers, and located six large stainless-steel shelves that had been built for a walk-in cooler but were never used. I bought all of them, envisioning large areas on which to work for the first time in a dozen years. I took one shelf and my design to a welder friend and asked him to build the smoker to accommodate the shelves. He faithfully executed my instructions and built a smoker that I continue to use, 20-some years later.

The fire pit, built on the ground about 3 feet away from the smoker, is constructed from standard firebrick, a heat-resistant yellowish brick intended for kilns and fireplaces. Red building bricks would not stand up to the high heat generated inside the fire pit. The distance from the firebox to the smoker is not important; it serves only to cool the smoke slightly before it reaches the smoker.

Building Guidelines

Before buying materials or beginning construction, make sure that you can build and operate a smoker in your backyard. The local building department should be able to answer this question, and the fire department may have some good advice as well. I once designed a smoker for a restaurant owner in Manhattan who wanted to operate the smoker on the roof, but the fire department's code would not allow it. Also, it's a good idea to discuss your plans with your neighbors, who might have some legitimate concerns about smoke blowing through their windows.

Once you have taken care of any legal and neighborly hurdles, clear the area of any trees, tree limbs, bushes, leaves, and other flammable materials for 6 to 8 feet from the smoker location. If necessary, level the ground as well

As you begin laying the bricks for the fire pit, leave an opening at the top of one wall just large enough for the stovepipe, the top of which should rest flush with the top of the wall so that the lid will lie flat. If you use stovepipe, you can push it down a bit for a better fit. If you want the pit airtight, plug cracks and gaps with a fireproof caulking compound, found in stores that sell fireplace equipment.

During those early days of firing up smokers, I regularly used 18-inch-long hardwood logs, and so I built the fire pit a spacious 12 inches by 28 inches by 32 inches to provide ample room. Eventually I began using wood chunks, then chips and corncobs, and now I use dried corn kernels. But I still use the same fire pit. This size accommodates 18-inch logs or a propane burner and a smokepan (see *Fig. 11.2*).

While laying bricks for the foundation of the fire pit, you might find it helpful to leave an opening at the bottom, about a half-brick size. This makes for better venting and helps move up the air into the stovepipe. I discovered that by pushing dirt around the opening, I could fine-tune the circulation of air in the fire pit and smoker. If you plan to use propane, you will also need to leave an opening in the side for the hose.

In place of hardwood logs, you may want to use propane (LP) as your fuel source. Propane dealers supply 50-pound tanks, which they will refill on a regular basis. Alternatively, you can use 20-pound tanks like those used with outdoor grills, and refill them yourself.

The first burner that I used in the fire pit was a powerful one, which I already had due to my ex-wife's interest in pottery. I had built several kilns for her in the past and conveniently had one or two burners left over. For a smoker, you do not need the high BTUs that this type of commercial burner can generate. Recently I have found an inexpensive substitute in the form of the burners that are used for turkey cookers, which can be purchased for about $20 from catalogs and large home building stores. Your propane supplier may also be able to order you one, as mine did, along with the proper ⅝-inch hose with fittings.

You can also look for a single or double stovetop grill at a camping supply store. These units have a cast-iron support for pots and pans and are inexpensive and extremely adaptable. Most of them come equipped with a hose, but you might need to add the thicker ⅝-inch hose to meet code.

You will also need a separate regulator on the gas line, between the tank and the burner, an essential safety item, with more ability to fine-tune the flow of gas. If you have any doubts about assembling the unit, have a licensed plumber or the propane supplier do it for you. Keep a fire extinguisher handy at all times.

Two or three dampers installed in the stovepipe help control the draft. By adjusting one or all dampers, along with the vent holes in the top of the smoker's lid and the vent hole in the wall of the fire pit, I can closely control the draft passing through the smoking chambers.

If you want to be able to hang pieces of food in your smoker, include support rods. Weld a piece of angle iron to the tops of the front and back walls and span the angle iron with ¾-inch-diameter rods. Use strings, wires, or hooks to hold the food on the rods.

The fire pan on which I place my corn or wood chunks is simply a 13-inch by 18-inch aluminum baking pan purchased in a kitchenware store. Do not use metal with nonstick coatings, which could emit toxic fumes as the coating burns off. After hard use over a long period the tray will eventually warp and burn through, but it is the most economical choice. You could fabricate a pan from steel or cast iron, but because the pan is constantly being moved around, I like the lightweight aluminum.

For the fire pit cover, I cut a 24-inch by 30-inch piece of 11-gauge (⅛ inch thick) hot rolled steel. I also welded two pieces of ¾-inch bar stock about 12 inches long, bent at an angle, for handles. I then drilled holes in 1-inch dowels, which were sanded and shaped for the hand, and slipped the ends of the bar stock into them. Close-fitting drilled holes should hold the handles, but you could also use glue or epoxy. These wood handles allow me to lift the cover without having to use mitts or gloves. The cover will not get hot enough to burn the wood, but will become hot enough to burn your hands.

You will also need two baffles on the floor of the smoke chamber, also cut from 11-gauge steel, drilled with several dozen quarter-inch holes throughout.

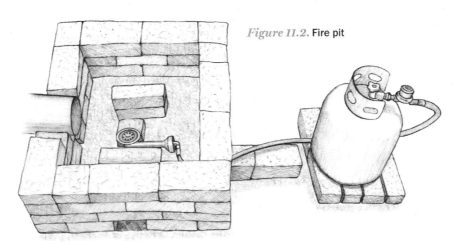

Figure 11.2. **Fire pit**

This aids circulation in the chamber; without a baffle the smoke would enter from the pipe and go straight up, heavily smoking the food directly in its path and missing anything on the perimeter. A baffle cushions smoke, distributing it equally to all areas by encircling the chamber, allowing the food to be completely encapsulated. Baffles also slow the hot air entering the smoker, and can be another tool for controlling the temperature *(Fig 11.3)*.

Cut the baffle about 3 inches shorter on all sides than the total inside dimensions of each chamber. I rest the baffles on stones or bricks to raise them a few inches above the smoke hole. Smoke is then allowed to rise through the drilled holes as well as from around the edges.

All corners and angle iron brackets to support shelves are made from ⅛-inch-thick stock. The doors should be made from heavier, 3-gauge stock, which is about ¼ inch thick, and fashioned with hinges and any kind of clamp that will hold the doors tightly shut. Because the top has to be lifted rather than swung out, I suggest making it with the ⅛-inch-thick steel welded to a frame of angle iron.

The legs supporting the smoker are made with standard concrete blocks, which can be stacked as high as you like. The legs on my smoker are about 24 inches high. With the heavy smoker placed on top, the blocks form a solid foundation. You could mortar them in place, if you like, for additional strength.

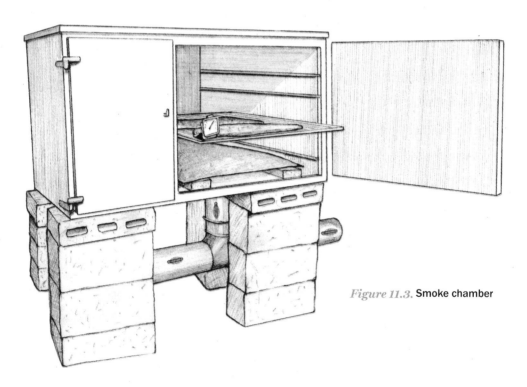

Figure 11.3. **Smoke chamber**

Chapter 12

The Rose Smokehouse

PLANS FOR THE SMOKEHOUSE that follow are from Mason Rose, who seemed to enjoy my smoked foods and paid close attention when I consulted with him on his own smokehouse. Fastidiously, he set about to build this "designer" smokehouse, one I have envied since first watching the foundation go in and the entire structure rise up in grand style, reflective of Mason Rose's typically high standards (see *Fig. 12.1*).

Rose, a self-taught craftsman, proceeded to draw up plans himself and oversee every detail of the construction, contributing his own skills and muscle to the project. His attention to detail resulted in attractive twists on a pragmatic concept, right down to the hand-wrought hinges and the 2-inch-thick handmade oak door, among other things. This is a smoke*house*.

In the plans, there are two fireboxes, one remote and one inside the smokehouse (at the base of the east elevation) but isolated from the rest of the chamber. Mason has said that he uses the internal smoke pan more often than the external because it takes considerably more time and effort to generate enough heat from a distance. This additional time is good for cold smoking but not for hot smoking. Thus, Mason has the best of both worlds with this design.

Detailed instructions for building this smokehouse are not included here because I am assuming that anyone who intends to build this type of project will undoubtedly already possess the knowledge, techniques, and tools to pursue such an avenue (see *Figs. 12.2–8*).

Keeping a smoking log is a good idea; it can be used another time or another year. The notes need only to be scribbled into a notebook. When I started smoking fish, I did not keep a daily record, but later I realized the importance of looking back at weather conditions, time of year, types of woods used, and, most important, length of smoking times. Once you see the value of keeping records, you may want to do the same.

Rose Menu

I would like to include a menu Mason Rose created for one of his more ambitious smokings, after he had worked out the kinks. There were eight of us for dinner, including his wife, Laura Chester, the "shine" at any dinner party at the Roses' home. The rest of us contributed to the meal by supplying fish, game, wine, or work for the festivities, all happy to be sharing the delectable meal.

MENU

Smoked Malpeque Oysters &
Salmon with Toast Points,
Salsa & Lemon

■ ■ ■

Smoked Mozzarella Cheese Ravioli
with Laura's Red Pepper Sauce

■ ■ ■

A Choice of Mixed Smoked Meats,
including Pheasant, Elk Chops,
Venison Steak, and Duck Breast
with Haricots Verts, Celery Root &
Fennel, Toasted Almonds &
Petits Pommes de Terre

■ ■ ■

A Fresh Garden Salad

■ ■ ■

Smoked Cheddar, Apples & Port

Figure 12.1. **Rose smoker with remote firebox**

Figure 12.2. Front of Rose smoker

Figure 12.3. Rear of Rose smoker

Figure 12.4. Side view
showing internal firebox

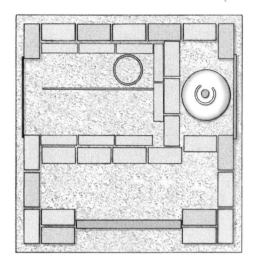

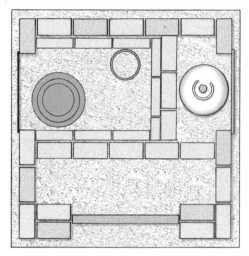

Figure 12.5. Floor plan with propane and wood fire chambers

Figure 12.6. Floor plan with propane fire chambers

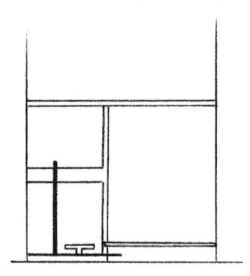

Figure 12.7. Main firebox detail

Figure 12.8. Detached firebox

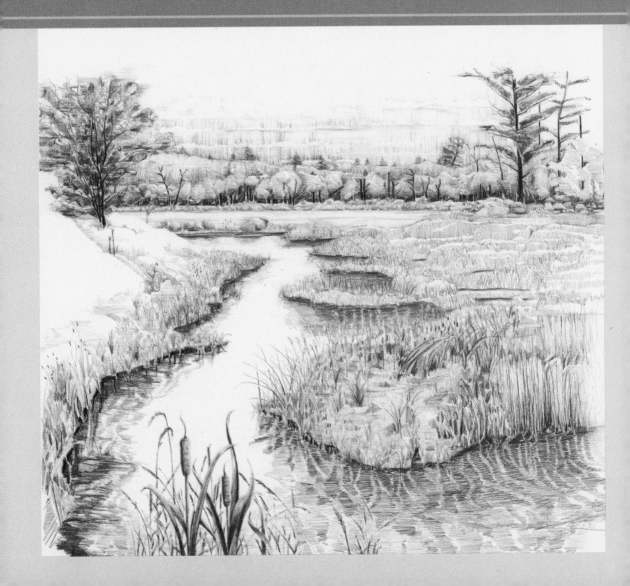

Side Dishes

Smoked Corn on the Cob

Smoke several ears. Eat a few immediately while they are still warm and save the rest to go with Corn-Smoked Lobsters (page 117) or with the Corn-Smoked Lobster Salad (page 169).

Fresh corn on the cob, husked, cleaned, and stripped of silk, one per person
Melted Lemon-Tarragon Butter (see page 226)

1. Preheat a grill for smoke grilling.

2. Brush some of the butter over the corn.

3. Lay the cobs on the grill directly over the smoke pan. Be sure no cob touches another. Close the lid and cook for 6 to 8 minutes. Brush with butter. Cook another 6 to 8 minutes, or until slightly charred for a light smoke flavor, longer for a deeper flavor.

4. Serve immediately with extra butter.

Grilled Red Onions

I love grilled onions and they go with anything off the grill. Slice the onions about ¾ inch thick. By securing the slices with toothpicks inserted horizontally to form a pinwheel, they will hold together while being handled.

1   **large red onion, peeled and thickly sliced**
1   **tablespoon olive oil**
1   **teaspoon dried oregano**
1   **teaspoon cracked black peppercorns**
1   **teaspoon Worcestershire sauce**
¼   **teaspoon salt**
Toothpicks

1. Preheat a grill.

2. Slide three or four toothpicks into each onion slice horizontally.

3. Drizzle each onion with the oil, oregano, peppercorns, Worcestershire sauce, and salt on both sides.

4. Lay on the grill and cook for 6 minutes; turn and cook 6 to 8 minutes longer, or until softened. Serve hot.

SERVES 4

Spaghetti Squash and Fresh Tomato

Spaghetti squash is an edible gourd, delicious and noodlelike in appearance, sweet with maple syrup.

1   **medium to large spaghetti squash**
½   **cup pure maple syrup (or brown sugar)**
1   **tablespoon ground coriander**
1   **tablespoon ground cumin**
½   **teaspoon ground nutmeg**
¼   **teaspoon ground cinnamon**
2   **medium tomatoes, washed and diced**

1. Preheat an oven to 400°F.

2. Cut the spaghetti squash in half lengthwise and scoop out the seeds. Place upside down on a baking sheet and place the sheet on the middle shelf in the oven. Pour a cup or so of hot water into the pan surrounding the squash. Bake for about 1 hour, or until soft.

3. Remove the squash, let cool, and scoop out the inside with a large spoon.

4. Simmer together the squash, maple syrup, coriander, cumin, nutmeg, and cinnamon for 15 minutes in a medium saucepan over medium heat.

5. Add the tomatoes and simmer for 5 minutes longer.

6. Serve immediately.

SERVES 4-6

Ratatouille

This clean-out-the-garden dish goes well with smoked fish but can be served as a side in late summer. It will keep refrigerated for 2 or 3 days.

2　medium tomatoes, cut into ¼-inch-thick slices
2　small zucchini, cut in half
1　green bell pepper, seeded, deveined, and cut in half
1　large eggplant, peeled and cut into ½-inch-thick slices
1　medium Vidalia onion, cut into ¼-inch slices
¼　cup olive oil
Juice of ½ lemon (about 1½ tablespoons)
4–5 garlic cloves, coarsely chopped
½　cup fresh basil leaves, coarsely chopped
Freshly ground black pepper

1. Preheat a grill.

2. Toss together thoroughly the tomato slices, zucchini, bell pepper, eggplant, and onion slices with 2 tablespoons of the oil and the lemon juice in a large mixing bowl. Drain in a colander.

3. Lay the vegetables on the grill with tongs. Grill for 10 to 12 minutes; turn and grill 10 to 12 minutes longer, or until they are softened and slightly charred.

4. Transfer to a cutting board and dice the vegetables. Place in a large mixing bowl. Toss together with the remaining oil, garlic, the basil, and pepper to taste. Set aside, covered, for about 30 minutes before serving.

SERVES 4-6

Smoked Tomato Mousse

Use ripe, medium-sized tomatoes, preferably during the summer and fall harvest, when they are at their prime and perfectly ripe. This recipe may be used as a side dish for dinner or served with a cold fish salad for a leisurely lunch. It will keep in the refrigerator for 2 to 3 days, covered.

6　ripe tomatoes
1　cup heavy cream
3　eggs
2　egg yolks
½　cup fresh basil leaves, loosely packed
½　teaspoon freshly ground black pepper
¼　teaspoon cayenne pepper
⅛　teaspoon salt

1. Preheat a grill for smoke grilling.

2. Bring water to a boil and immerse the tomatoes in it for about 45 seconds. The skin will look loosened and a bit wrinkled.

3. With a sharp knife, remove the tomato skins and discard. Place the tomatoes on the cool side of the smoker on the second shelf. Smoke for 1 hour at 200°F, or until soft but not mushy. Carefully remove with tongs and set aside to cool.

4. Slice the tomatoes in half and remove the seeds and stems. Purée for about 1 minute in a food processor.

5. Preheat an oven to 375°F.

6. Pulse the cream, eggs, egg yolks, basil, pepper, cayenne, and salt with the tomato purée until blended.

7. Pour the mixture into six 3½-inch or twelve 2½-inch nonstick or oiled muffin cups. Place the muffin tin in a larger baking pan. Pour hot water into the outer pan about halfway up the side of the muffin pan.

8. Carefully place in the oven. Bake for 45 to 55 minutes, or until a toothpick inserted in the middle of one comes out clean. The smaller pan will require less time. Remove and let cool for 15 minutes.

9. With a sharp knife, cut around the outside of each mousse. Cover the top of the muffin pan with a cutting board, hold the pan tightly, and flip over quickly. Gently tap the bottom of each mousse. They should fall out onto the board. Serve immediately or refrigerate and reheat later.

MAKES 6 SERVINGS IF USING 3 ½-INCH CUPS OR 12 SERVINGS IF USING 2 ½-INCH CUPS

Grilled Tomatoes Marinated in Balsamic Vinegar

Use ripe tomatoes, preferably fresh from the farm stand or your garden. Cut them thick so they remain stable and don't deteriorate during grilling.

2   large tomatoes, cut into 1-inch slices
2   tablespoons balsamic vinegar
¼   cup basil, finely chopped
¼   fresh thyme, stemmed and finely chopped
Salt and freshly ground black pepper
2   tablespoons good-quality extra-virgin olive oil

1. Spread out the tomato slices in a large container, drizzle the vinegar over the top,

and sprinkle the basil, thyme, and salt and pepper to taste over all. Marinade for 20 to 30 minutes in the refrigerator.

2. Preheat a grill.

3. Oil the grate and grill the tomato slices for 3 to 4 minutes; turn and grill 3 to 4 minutes longer, or until they are charred but still firm.

4. Remove from the heat, drizzle the oil on top, and serve immediately.

SERVES 4–6

Plum Tomato Cups

Plum tomatoes are firm and hold their shape well, which makes them an ideal edible vessel. This is a great finger food.

10 ripe plum tomatoes, halved, seeded, and
     scooped
¾   cup olive oil
¼   cup fresh tarragon, coarsely chopped
Salt and freshly ground black pepper
½   pound goat's-milk cheese, cut into
     ½-inch cubes
¼   cup grated Parmesan

1. Preheat an oven to its lowest possible temperature, 150°F.

2. Thoroughly toss the tomatoes, oil, tarragon, and salt and pepper to taste in a large bowl. Remove the tomatoes, drain, and place on a baking sheet.

3. Place the cheese cubes in each tomato cup and sprinkle liberally with the Parmesan cheese.

4. Bake for 3 to 4 hours, until the tomatoes are cooked through but still firm.

SERVES 4 OR 5

Wild Mushroom Ragu

I used boletes and puffballs — wild mushrooms — for this recipe, but you can use most any combination of mushrooms you find in the supermarket, such as oyster, shiitakes, portobello, and criminis.

½ cup (1 stick) unsalted butter
1 teaspoon olive oil
7 ounces (half a 14-ounce can) low-fat chicken stock
1¾ pounds cleaned, stemmed boletes and puffball mushrooms
½ cup brandy or cognac
Salt and freshly ground black pepper
¼ cup port

1. Melt the butter and oil in a large saucepan or wok over medium-high heat. Add the stock, mushrooms, brandy, and salt and pepper to taste, and lower heat to medium. Stir, then simmer for ½ hour, or until mushrooms are tender and stock is reduced by half.

2. Remove the mixture and pour the port into the hot pan. Stir over high heat for 1 to 2 minutes, scraping up any residue from the bottom of the pan. Pour the glaze over the mushroom mix and serve immediately.

SERVES 6–8

Mixed Wild Mushroom Pasta

Use any mix of wild or cultivated mushrooms you like. This loamy dish goes well with grilled or smoked catfish, walleye, or other freshwater fish.

⅓ pound fresh linguine
3 tablespoons canola oil
3 garlic cloves, finely chopped
3 plum tomatoes, seeded and coarsely chopped
1 cup cleaned and coarsely chopped mushrooms such as morels, boletes, chanterelles, and portobellos
¼ cup fresh basil, finely chopped
1 tablespoon cracked black peppercorns
1 teaspoon salt
Juice of 1 lemon (about 1½ tablespoons)

1. Boil 4 quarts of water in a large pot and cook the linguini for 2 to 3 minutes, or until tender. Drain and toss with 1 tablespoon of the oil. Cover and set aside.

2. Heat the remaining oil in a large saucepan over medium-high heat. Sauté the garlic and tomatoes in the oil for 1 to 2 minutes. Add the mushrooms, basil, pepper, and salt and sauté 3 to 4 minutes longer, or until the vegetables are softened.

3. Toss the linguini and vegetables in a large bowl. Separate onto four warm plates and drizzle the lemon juice over each.

SERVES 2 OR 4 AS AN APPETIZER

Sautéed Morel Mushrooms

This can be a side dish or, if you've had a productive spring morel forage, a main course. You may mix in other fungi if you do not have enough morels.

4 tablespoons unsalted butter
1 tablespoon good-quality olive oil
2½ cups morels, cleaned and thickly sliced
2 tablespoons brandy or rum
1 teaspoon freshly ground black pepper
½ teaspoon salt
1 tablespoon finely chopped parsley

1. Melt the butter in a large skillet or wok over medium-high heat. Add the oil and heat 1 minute.

2. Add the mushrooms, stir, cover partially, and simmer for 8 to 10 minutes.

3. Add the brandy, pepper, and salt and cook for 3 to 4 minutes, or until the liquid is reduced by about one third.

4. Sprinkle in the parsley and serve immediately.

SERVES 4

Purée of Fava Beans

Puréeing is the classic way of serving the *feve* bean; Spanish cuisine features *fabada*, a kind of bean cassoulet. The fava beans need to be shelled; the outer skin is tough and should be discarded.

1   tablespoon canola oil
½   cup sesame seeds, plus more for topping
2   cups fava beans, shelled (about 2 pounds)
¼   cup garlic cloves
4   tablespoons melted butter
Salt and freshly ground black pepper

1. Heat the oil in a large skillet until it smokes. Add the ½ cup of sesame seeds and stir until browned, about 1 minute. Do not leave unattended, or the seeds will burn. Blot on paper towels and set aside.

2. Bring 3 quarts of salted water to a boil. Add the beans; bring water back to a boil and cook for 25 to 30 minutes, or until soft. Drain.

3. Purée the beans with the garlic, butter, salt, and pepper in the bowl of a food processor. Scrape down the sides with a spatula and transfer to a serving bowl. Top with the remaining sesame seeds and serve.

SERVES 4

Tomato-Mint Salad

This refreshing summer salad is delightful by itself, though you might also consider grilling herring, whole fresh sardines, or fresh anchovies (or simply purchase pickled herring, cut into chunks) and mixing with this salad. Guests will never be disappointed.

3–4 large fresh tomatoes, thickly sliced
1   cucumber, peeled and diced
¾   red onion, thinly sliced
½   cup fresh mint, stemmed and finely chopped
Juice of 1½ limes (about 3 tablespoons)
3   tablespoons extra-virgin olive oil
Zest of 1 lime (about 2 teaspoons)
1   tablespoon freshly ground black pepper
1   teaspoon salt (optional)

1. Thoroughly mix the tomatoes, cucumber, onion, mint, lime juice, oil, zest, peppercorns, and salt (if using).

2. Divide equally on four plates and serve immediately.

SERVES 4

Blood Orange Salad

Use this salad as just a side dish, or grill an extra cutthroat trout or two and refrigerate. For lunch the next day, flake pieces of trout on top of this salad for an alfresco summer outing at Two Jake Lake north of Banff, British Columbia, where you can look down to watch bald eagles soar during your lunch.

4–5 blood oranges, peeled and cut into
      ¼-inch-thick slices
3   slices large red onion
¼   cup pecans
2   teaspoons extra-virgin olive oil
1   teaspoon balsamic vinegar
1   teaspoon ground cumin
Salt and freshly ground black pepper

1. Lay the orange slices on four plates.

2. Cover with the onion rounds and pecans.

3. Drizzle with the oil and vinegar.

4. Season with the cumin and salt and pepper to taste.

SERVES 4

Sautéed Cucumbers with Cilantro

This approach to cucumbers makes one of my favorite dishes. Use European cucumbers, which have few or no seeds.

3   tablespoons ghee (or unsalted butter)
1½ cups peeled and sliced European cucumber
½ cup cilantro, coarsely chopped
½ teaspoon sea salt
Freshly ground black pepper

1. Melt the ghee in a medium sauté pan over medium heat. Add the cucumbers and cook, stirring, for 3 to 4 minutes, or until they just become soft.

2. Add the cilantro, salt, and pepper to taste. Stir and serve immediately.

SERVES 4-6

Spaetzle

Spaetzle, spätzle, or spätzl, depending upon which part of the European continent you hail from, is not unlike pasta dough. If the mixture is too wet to pass through a sieve, add more flour; if too dry, more half and half.

2   cups all-purpose flour
⅛   teaspoon salt
2   eggs
1   cup half-and-half

1. In a large bowl or on a cutting board, combine the flour and salt, then add eggs. Slowly drizzle in the half-and-half while beating the mixture with a spoon (or mixing with your hands) until thoroughly combined.

2. Bring a large pot of water to the boil. Using a spaetzle press or hobel, a food mill, or a colander, press dough through the holes, letting it dribble into the water in 1-inch strips. When the noodles float, in about 1 minute, they are done.

3. Remove, drain, and set aside. Use while hot, or refrigerate for later use. Reheat spaetzle by submerging it briefly in hot water.

Grilled Marinated Eggplant

2   large eggplants, cut into ½-inch slices
2   cups Ponzu Sauce (see page 232)
Olive oil

1. In a nonreactive container, cover the eggplant slices with the Ponzu Sauce. Mix gently to be sure eggplant is covered completely. Marinate for 30 minutes.

2. Preheat a grill.

3. Drain eggplant in a colander and brush with the olive oil.

4. Lay the eggplant slices on the grill with tongs. Grill for 5 minutes; turn and grill 5 minutes longer, or until softened and slightly charred.

SERVES 4-6

Condiments and Sauces

Rose Butter

Roses are edible flowers. This puréed butter makes a dazzling display, especially if you mix colors.

Three or four multi-flecked disks look particularly attractive fanned out on a bread plate. Serve two disks on top of grilled salmon or rainbow trout; serve two or three disks on top of a green vegetable.

The butter must be prepared ahead of time to cool, and will keep 3 to 4 weeks refrigerated or 2 to 3 months frozen.

1 cup (2 sticks) unsalted butter, at room temperature
1 cup rose petals

1. Cut the butter into 1-inch cubes.

2. Process the butter in a food processor until smooth, 20 seconds.

3. Add the petals. Pulse 6 to 8 times, not long enough for the butter to become soft and unable to shape.

4. Spread out a piece of plastic wrap, about 12 inches by 20 inches. With a rubber spatula, remove the rose butter from the bowl and spread on the plastic. With your hands, form a smooth, consistent cigar shape. Roll tightly in the plastic wrap and twist the ends, eliminating all air. Refrigerate.

5. Cut off disks as needed.

ABOUT 1 CUP

Lemon-Tarragon Butter

Use this as a dipping sauce with a simple grilled lobster, or with the recipe for Corn-Smoked Lobster (see page 117), or even over popcorn.

Plugra is unsalted "European-style butter" with a wonderful rich flavor. It is more expensive than regular butter, but well worth the price, especially when paired with those all-American icons corn on the cob, lobster, and popcorn.

1 cup (2 sticks) unsalted butter
Juice of 1 lemon (about 3 tablespoons)
¼ cup finely chopped fresh tarragon
1 tablespoon freshly ground pink peppercorns (or substitute black peppercorns)

1. Melt the butter in a medium saucepan over medium heat.

2. Add the lemon juice, tarragon, and peppercorns. Lower the heat and simmer for 1 to 2 minutes, or until thoroughly combined and hot.

3. Reduce heat to low to keep warm until ready to use. Butter keeps in the refrigerator for several weeks, covered.

MAKES ABOUT ⅔ CUP

Dill Butter

Use this flavored butter to top almost any grilled fish, to swab grilled vegetables (such as corn), or simply as a dipping butter.

This recipe can be prepared ahead and refrigerated for several weeks, covered. To reheat, warm in a saucepan over low heat.

1 cup (2 sticks) unsalted butter
½ cup finely chopped fresh dill
Freshly ground pink peppercorns (or
    substitute black)

1. Melt the butter in a medium saucepan over medium-low heat.

2. Add the dill and peppercorns to taste. Stir, remove from the heat, and use immediately, or refrigerate for later use.

MAKES ABOUT ⅔ CUP

Tarragon Butter

This butter is simple, and tasty with grilled salmon, cod, sable, or striped bass.

4 tablespoons unsalted butter
Juice of ⅔ lemon (about 2 tablespoons)
2 tablespoons fresh tarragon, finely chopped
Zest of 1 lemon (about 1 tablespoon)
1 teaspoon freshly ground black pepper
¼ teaspoon salt

1. Whisk together all of the ingredients in a medium saucepan over medium-low heat and simmer for 6 to 8 minutes, or until butter is melted and tarragon is wilted.

2. Transfer to a covered container and refrigerate for up to 2 weeks, reheating as needed.

MAKES ABOUT ¾ CUP

Lemon Beurre Blanc

Use this traditional sauce with most any fish, but I especially like it with grilled salmon or tuna.

1 medium shallot, finely chopped
2 tablespoons apple cider vinegar
Juice of ½ lemon (about 1½ tablespoons)

⅔ cup unsalted butter
½ teaspoon salt
1 teaspoon white or pink peppercorns, finely ground
Zest of 1 lemon (about 1 tablespoon)

1. Combine the shallot, vinegar, and lemon juice in a saucepan over moderate heat. Raise the heat to high and cook until reduced by one quarter, about 2 minutes.

2. Add one quarter of the butter, the salt, and the pepper; whisk together with the shallot mixture and bring to a boil.

3. Immediately remove from the heat and slowly whisk in the remaining butter, a little at a time.

4. Add the zest just before whisking in the last of the butter. The sauce should thicken like mayonnaise.

MAKES ABOUT ¾ CUP

Aïoli

Swirl this garlicky sauce into fish soups, stews, or bouillabaisse just before serving or dab on smoked fish with rye bread as an appetizer.

The aïoli may be kept refrigerated, covered, for up to 2 weeks. For a slight variation, add ¼ cup of dill or tarragon with the dry ingredients.

6–8 garlic cloves
¼ teaspoon cracked black peppercorns
¼ teaspoon sea salt
3 egg yolks
1½ cups olive oil
2 tablespoons lemon juice
Zest of 1 lemon (about 1 tablespoon)

1. Pulse the garlic, peppercorns, and salt in the bowl of a food processor three to four times.

2. Scrape down the sides, then purée for 15 seconds.

3. Add the eggs and purée for 15 seconds.

4. Through the feed tube (with the machine running), slowly drizzle in the oil, a few drops at a time. When just about completed, add the lemon juice and zest along with the remaining oil until the mixture becomes emulsified.

5. Transfer to an airtight container and refrigerate for up to 1 week.

MAKES ABOUT 1 1/2 CUPS

Pink Peppercorn–Chervil Cream

Buy whole pink peppercorns. I have three pepper mills on my table, one with black peppercorns, one mixed (with black, white, pink, and green), and one with only pink peppercorns. I love the delicate bite pink peppercorns add to almost any dish; they are not as potent as black peppercorns.

Crush peppercorns either with a mortar and pestle or by placing between two sheets of wax paper and crushing with the wide blade of a chef's knife (lying on its side, of course), pressing with the palm of your hand.

Serve with grilled pompano or redfish. Peppercorn cream will cut the slightly strong flavor of either fish, enhancing it with the zing of pepper.

2   tablespoons unsalted butter
1½ cups heavy cream
¼ cup pink peppercorns, crushed
1   cup chervil, stemmed and finely chopped

1. Melt the butter over medium-low heat in a medium saucepan.

2. Add the cream and peppercorns and simmer, covered, for 4 to 5 minutes, or until slightly thickened.

3. Add the chervil and simmer 5 minutes longer.

4. Turn off the heat and let the sauce rest 30 minutes to allow the flavors to blend.

5. Strain through a cheesecloth while still warm, then serve.

MAKES ABOUT 1 1/4 CUPS

Yum-Yum Yogurt with Celeriac and Turmeric

This is a good dipping sauce for use with vegetables. You can also serve it chilled on the side of grilled orange roughy. The naturally bright yellow of the turmeric makes this a bright and sunny presentation.

3½ cups peeled and diced celeriac
¾ cup plain yogurt
Juice of ½ lemon (about 1½ tablespoons)
1   tablespoon ground cumin
1   tablespoon ground black peppercorns
1   teaspoon ground turmeric

1. Bring water to a boil in a 4-quart saucepan and add the celeriac. Reduce the heat, cover, and simmer over medium heat for 15 to 20 minutes. Drain.

2. Purée the celeriac in a food processor until smooth, about 1 minute.

3. Add the yogurt, lemon juice, cumin, peppercorns, and turmeric and blend thoroughly, about 1 minute.

4. Transfer the mixture to a covered container and refrigerate for at least 30 minutes or up to 12 hours, and serve cold.

MALES ABOUT 2 CUPS

Shrimp Paste

This sauce makes a tasty hors d'oeuvre, simply spread on toast or on little pumpernickel cocktail breads, found in the deli section of a supermarket in long, slim loaves. It is also a good dip for cut vegetables. Mixing 2 to 3 tablespoons into rice as it cooks enhances the flavor greatly. I like to swirl it in just before serving chowders or fish soups to give them more body and intense flavor. The sauce may be prepared ahead and will keep, refrigerated, for up to 3 days.

To further highlight the flavors, consider using large shrimp, grilling them first, and then following the recipe. Galangal, also called Thai ginger, has a wonderful "zing" to it, a hot quality that does not require the addition of hot peppers. If you cannot find galangal, substitute ginger and add a little chili powder.

2-inch piece galangal, in chunks (or substitute ginger)
¾ cup cooked cocktail shrimp (70–90 count), tailless
1 tablespoon low-sodium soy sauce
¼ cup tangerine juice (or substitute orange juice)

1. Process the galangal in the bowl of a food processor for 1 minute, or until finely processed.

2. Scrape down the sides, add the shrimp, and pulse for about 30 seconds, or until thoroughly combined.

3. Add the soy sauce and juice and purée until smooth.

4. Use immediately or transfer to a covered container and refrigerate.

MAKES 2 CUPS

Shrimp Sauce, 1805

"Take a half pint of shrimps, wash them very clean, put them in a stew-pan with a spoonful of fish-lear, or anchovy-liquor, a pound of butter melted thick, boil it up for five minutes, and squeeze in half a lemon; toss it up, and then put it in your cups or boats."

—*The Art of Cookery Made Plain and Easy; Excelling Any Thing of the Kind Ever Yet Published*, Mrs. Glasse, 1805

Horseradish Sauce

You have to have a horseradish sauce for fish. Use this recipe to brush on fish before grilling, or as a dip with blue tortilla chips. The yogurt makes this sauce somewhat lighter in character than if you used only mayonnaise.

½ cup mayonnaise
½ cup prepared horseradish
½ cup plain yogurt
Juice of 2½ lemons (about ½ cup)
1 teaspoon salt
1 teaspoon freshly ground black pepper

1. Pulse the mayonnaise, horseradish, yogurt, lemon juice, salt, and pepper in a food processor for 30 seconds, or until thoroughly blended.

2. Transfer to a covered container. The sauce will keep refrigerated for several days.

MAKES ABOUT 1½ CUPS

Romesco Sauce

I love the nuttiness of this sauce. Use it on grilled fish or brush on grill-toasted sourdough bread as an appetizer. Toast the almonds ahead of time by placing them on a baking sheet, sprinkling with 1 teaspoon salt, and drizzling with olive oil. Bake at 375°F for 7 to 9 minutes, or until browned.

Finally, use this sauce in the Patagonia Wellington recipe on page 164.

2   scallions, cleaned
1–2 hot chiles, seeded and deveined (jalapeños or poblanos)
1   yellow bell pepper, seeded and chopped
1   cup toasted almonds (see page 168)
4–6 garlic cloves, peeled
½   cup olive oil

1. Purée the scallions, chiles, yellow peppers, almonds, and garlic, in the bowl of a food processor for 30 seconds, or until combined.

2. Add the olive oil and blend for 10 seconds, or until puréed.

3. Scrape down the sides of the bowl with a spatula and transfer to a covered container. This sauce will keep, refrigerated, for 2 weeks or more.

MAKES ABOUT 1¹/₂ CUPS

Coconut-Lime Sauce

This refreshing sauce will accompany a wide range of grilled or smoked fishes. Buying fish sauce (nam pla, nuoc mam, tuk trey — derivate names from various Asian countries) can sometimes be confusing. The bottle in my pantry simply reads FISH SAUCE, but it nearly always adds depth to sauces.

1   tablespoon canola oil
1   medium onion, finely chopped

3–4 garlic cloves, finely chopped
1   jalapeño pepper, seeded, stemmed, and finely chopped
1   tablespoon finely chopped ginger
4   teaspoons curry powder (or to taste)
1   teaspoon fish sauce
1   can (14 ounces) unsweetened coconut milk
1   tablespoon sorghum (or substitute maple syrup or corn syrup)
Juice (about 2 tablespoons) and zest (about 1 teaspoon) of 1 lime

1. Heat the oil in a medium saucepan over medium-high heat.

2. Add the onion, garlic, jalapeño, and ginger. Cook for 3 to 4 minutes.

3. Add the curry powder and fish sauce and cook 1 minute longer.

4. Add the coconut milk and sorghum. Bring the mixture to a boil and simmer for about 30 minutes, or until the sauce is reduced by about half.

5. Stir in the lime juice and zest.

6. Remove from the heat; use immediately.

MAKES ABOUT 1¹/₂ CUPS

Green Sauce

An adaptable sauce, this can be brushed on fish just before grilling, used as a spread on toast, or added to a sandwich.

To roast the pine nuts, you could spread on a baking sheet, drizzle a little olive oil and salt (optional) over the top, and bake at 375°F for 8 to 10 minutes. I find, however, that the stovetop is best for toasting. Cook in a very hot skillet with a little oil for 2 to 3 minutes, with constant stirring and vigilance. Blot on paper towels.

12 medium green olives, pitted
4–6 anchovy fillets
4   cups cleaned and stemmed parsley
¼ cup toasted pine nuts
Juice of ½ lemon (about 1½ tablespoons)
1   tablespoon Dijon mustard
½ cup extra-virgin olive oil

1. Purée the olives, anchovies, parsley, pine nuts, lemon juice, and mustard for about 30 seconds in the bowl of a food processor. Scrape down the sides of the bowl.

2. Add the olive oil and pulse five or six times, or until thoroughly combined.

3. Transfer to a covered container and refrigerate for up to 1 week.

MAKES ABOUT 1¼ CUPS

Dill Mustard Sauce

This sauce goes well with the Gravad and Smoked Salmon with Cilantro-Mint Rub (see page 40) and many other kinds of fresh fish, not just cured salmon. I have used it in place of tartar sauce on fish sandwiches, but I think it is one of the best sauces for smoked salmon.

1¼ cups Dijon mustard
1   cup loosely packed dill, stemmed
¾ cup mayonnaise
⅓ cup corn syrup
Juice of ⅔ lemon (about 2 tablespoons)

1. Purée the mustard, dill, mayonnaise, corn syrup, and lemon juice for 1 minute in the bowl of a food processor.

2. Scrape the purée into a noncorrosive container and refrigerate for up to 2 weeks, covered and refrigerated.

MAKES ABOUT 2½ CUPS

Curry Sauce

Substitute curry powder in place of the cardamom, coriander, and cumin if you'd like (curry is a blend of these and other spices). Use this over most any grilled or smoked fish. Eliminate the cayenne if you prefer a milder sauce.

¼ cup ghee (or unsalted butter)
1   teaspoon peanut oil
1   large baking apple, peeled, cored, and sliced
1   large sweet white onion, finely chopped (about 1½ cups)
1   teaspoon tomato paste
1   tablespoon ground cardamom
1   tablespoon ground coriander
1   tablespoon ground cumin
1   teaspoon cayenne pepper (optional)
½ cup apple cider

1. Melt the ghee in a skillet over medium heat. Add the oil and sauté the apple and onion for 25 to 30 minutes, or until slightly caramelized, stirring occasionally.

2. Add the tomato paste, cardamom, coriander, cumin, and cayenne, if using. Stir for 2 to 3 minutes.

3. Add the cider and simmer for 12 to 15 minutes, or until reduced by about half.

4. Remove from the heat and let cool. Use immediately, or cover and refrigerate for up to 1 week.

MAKES ABOUT 1½ CUPS

Ginger Soy Sauce

Use this sauce as a marinade or as a dip with fresh tuna. Or try it as a salad dressing. Galangal is brightly spicy and adds a pleasant zing to food, especially fish.

2 **tablespoons fresh galangal, chopped (or substitute ginger)**
1 **tablespoon vegetable oil**
1 **teaspoon sesame oil**
1 **tablespoon rice vinegar**
1 **tablespoon low-sodium soy sauce**

1. Pulse the galangal in the bowl of a food processor for about 1 minute, or until finely chopped.

2. Add the oils, vinegar, and soy sauce. Blend thoroughly, 30 to 45 seconds.

3. Refrigerate in a glass or noncorrosive container for up to several weeks.

MAKES ABOUT ¼ CUP

Ponzu Sauce

This sauce will keep for several weeks, refrigerated. It makes a good dipping sauce for raw scallops, a dressing over mizuna and mustard greens, or a marinade for tuna and shrimp. You can find bonito flakes in Asian markets and some supermarkets.

4 **cups dried bonito flakes**
1½ **cups dark soy sauce**
¼ **cup low-sodium soy sauce**
⅓ **cup mirin**
Juice of 8 lemons (about 1½ cups)

1. Mix all of the ingredients in a large mixing bowl. Cover and refrigerate for 2 days.

2. Strain through cheesecloth into a glass container and refrigerate for up to 1 month.

MAKES ABOUT 4 CUPS

Papa's Papaya Chutney

Papayas vary greatly in size. I found one in the market that weighed more than 6 pounds. Make sure the ones you use for this recipe are fully ripe.

You will need to make the pickled lemons several weeks ahead, but you may substitute fresh lemon; just increase the sweeteners if you do.

Serve at room temperature with smoked fish or a salad.

2 **cups seeded and cubed papaya**
1½ **cups water**
1 **cup fresh plums, seeded and cut in half**
1 **small white onion, diced**
1 **pickled lemon or lime (see page 155), seeded and cut into cubes (or substitute fresh)**
½ **cup sorghum (or substitute honey)**
½ **cup brown sugar**
½ **cup apple cider vinegar**
2 **cinnamon sticks**
2 **tablespoons curry powder**
1 **tablespoon ground cumin**
1 **teaspoon cayenne pepper**

1. Bring all the ingredients to a boil in a stockpot or 4-quart saucepan over high heat.

2. Reduce the heat to low and simmer for 15 to 20 minutes.

3. Remove from the heat and let cool for about 1 hour. Transfer to covered containers and refrigerate for up to 1 month.

MAKES ABOUT 4 CUPS

Basic Salsa

If you have the time, grill the scallions, tomato, and onion for 5 to 6 minutes to give the salsa a deeper, grilled flavor.

Mexican oregano is available from Atlantic Spice Company. The salsa will keep for several days in the refrigerator.

3–4 scallions, sliced (use all but 1-inch of green parts)
1 large ripe tomato, cubed
1 medium sweet white onion, coarsely chopped
1–2 jalapeño peppers, seeded, deveined, and finely chopped
4–5 garlic cloves, finely chopped
½ cup coarsely chopped cilantro
Juice of 1 lime (about 2 tablespoons)
1 teaspoon olive oil
Zest of 1 lime (about 2 teaspoons)
½ teaspoon dried Mexican oregano

1. Stir together all of the ingredients.

2. Cover and refrigerate for 1 to 2 hours, until thoroughly chilled, before serving.

MAKES ABOUT 2¾ CUPS

Lemony Corn Salsa

This sauce may be used as a dip but goes well over grilled haddock or croaker.

2 tablespoons unsalted butter
1 small leek, finely chopped (or substitute 4 scallions)
½ cup finely chopped celery
2 ears of corn, cleaned and stripped (about 2 cups)
1 medium tomato, seeded and finely chopped
2 tablespoons lemon juice
Salt and freshly ground black pepper

1. Melt the butter in a medium saucepan.

2. Add the leek and celery; cook over medium-low heat for 3 to 4 minutes.

3. Add the corn and tomatoes and cook for 3 to 4 minutes longer.

4. Add the lemon juice and salt and pepper to taste; simmer 1 minute longer.

5. Remove and use immediately or refrigerate for up to 1 week.

MAKES 2¼ CUPS

Mango-Cucumber Salsa

It seems like an odd combination, but it works. You may use English cucumbers, which have few seeds. Serve with cold fish, with a fish salad, or with the Smoked Salmon Frittata with Fiddleheads and Morels, on page 110.

The salsa will keep for 3 to 4 days, refrigerated.

1 medium mango
1 cherry pepper, seeded, deveined, and finely chopped
½ cucumber, peeled, seeded, and cut into ¼-inch slices
¼ cup orange juice
2 tablespoons olive oil
1 tablespoon lime juice
½ teaspoon cayenne

1. Peel and remove the mango fruit from its seed. Cut into ½-inch slices and place them in a large mixing bowl.

2. Add the cherry pepper, cucumber slices, orange juice, oil, lime juice, and cayenne. Mix together, cover with plastic wrap, and refrigerate for about 1 hour, until chilled.

MAKES 2½ CUPS

To Drink

FISH ALONE IS SIMPLE to match with a beverage, but add seasonings such as oregano, sage, turmeric, curries, and coriander, or confuse it further with an acidic lemon juice, fresh mint, or balsamic vinegar, and, well . . . what drinks complement all of that?

I'm a believer that one should drink whatever one prefers. When a palate is splashed with intermingled tastes, however, choosing the right wine, microbrewed beer, or dessert wine becomes slightly more challenging.

I'll try and keep this simple. First of all, you don't have to subscribe to the old canard: "white wine with fish." My favorite, red wine, may work with some fish.

It does for my palate, but perhaps may not for yours. Just remember that most, and I say here most, bold reds — a California cabernet sauvignon with its big tannins, for example — tend to fight, rather than complement, the subtlety of the delicate white meat of flounder or freshwater perch.

To accompany a sizzling panfried meal of walleyed pike that you will enjoy in the fall at lakeside, try a light Beaujolais-Villages, from France, young and bright, neither too tannic nor too heavy.

What to do with a glistening fillet of smoked arctic char? Serve it with a Pinot Gris from Oregon or Alsace. It might not interfere with the dill or fresh oregano you used as a dry cure. Pinot Gris has its own inherent flowery spice.

A young Muscadet from the Loire Valley might comfortably highlight that mess of sunfish served with a fiddlehead salad, the dry Muscadet's own tartness filling in for an absence of lemon.

Like pike? Burgundy wines do well with the bony horrors from northern latitudes. Dry whites don't interfere as much with the unobtrusive taste of freshwater white meat as do those with a low alcohol content. Pinot Noir, a light red wine often intertwined with some berry and smokiness, also works well.

Strong fish don't always go well with red wines of high tannin. Avoid, say, a blazing saddle red, such as a California Zinfandel or Cabernet Sauvignon, with peppered mackerel or sardines sprinkled with Old Bay seasoning!

That is not to say reds can't work with fish; ask help from a trusted, knowledgeable wine merchant to select a young, fruity red with good acid and soft tannins. French rosés fit in here, such as from those from Tavel.

Matching flavors, a case in point: A friend and I had a wonderful dinner at an Indian restaurant: shrimp in hugely flavored sauces composed of fragrant garam masala, yogurt with lemony cucumbers, and chiles galore — powerful, delightful blasts on the palate. While I stuck to Kaliber, a flavorful nonalcoholic beer made by Guinness that I've come to enjoy, my friend chose an Italian Pinot Grigio. Dry, dry, dry.

Halfway through the meal, as I ordered another beer, she pushed away her wineglass and remarked: "Ugh, this isn't what you should drink with this food." I agreed; she should have ordered something fruity, not so acidic, not as dry.

Hoppy beers or full-bodied brews such as stouts, porters, and bock complement Indian foods quite well. In other words, don't be shy. Thai-flavored fish need similar pairing: Dark, malty lagers and ales often show better up against spice.

What to do about salads? Do you refuse wine during the salad course? You don't have to. But it can pose problems: Lemon juice and vinegar don't mix with wine. Solution? Simply decrease the amount of vinegar and acidic juice, and add more in the way of lightly smoked and flaked fish, olives, avocado, and other vegetables as well as roasted nuts and freshly cut herbs to the salad. In other words, increase the flavors so you will need less in the way of a dressing and your guests might not even notice. You can still serve a wine, white or red, but with a high acid content with some fruitiness to it. A sparkling Vouvray might blend nicely with a salad as might a semidry Riesling from the Mosel or Rhine region of Germany. Or try an Italian Soave for a pleasant change.

Another possibility with salads is,

again, beer. For example, a German wheat beer may have a smoky character to it; however, it is also fruity and light enough not to battle acidic lemon juice or vinegars. Or try golden or blond ales and pilsners.

Smoky wines with smoked foods? Some wines, both red and white, offer a hint of smoke, from charred barrels usually, but often smoked foods are powerful enough in themselves and can negate any subtle smoky flavors of a wine. I prefer to contrast, rather than match, the flavors in this case. Something fruity and flowery, such as a Riesling or a Pinot Noir rather than a Pouilly-Fumé or a big Barolo, will match up better with smoke.

When it comes to brews and smoked food, full-bodied stouts, bocks, and dark lager just may be the exception to matching heavy with heavy. Try it. If you don't agree, try something else until you find your perfect match.

What about lemonade? There's nothing quite like a tall glass of freshly squeezed lemonade laced with a bouquet of fresh mint leaves (and possibly a *little* dash of tequila gold) to accompany freshly grilled salmon alongside the Matane River in Quebec after a hard day's battle on the water.

Dessert wines? You bet. Match grilled pineapple or mango with . . . what? If you've never had a late-harvest Muscat, you're in for a treat. Try an orange Muscat. Always make sure that the wine is sweeter than your dessert, and you can't go wrong. Sauternes? Of course, any time — but try a heavenly Tokay. My all-time favorite drink experience: the year I made my own mead, with my own honey and just-picked strawberries. Ah, mead, the nectar of the gods. Makes for a great ending to any meal.

Lemonade

On a summer afternoon, ice-cold lemonade is just the thing.

½ water, plus 4 cups ice water
1 cup sugar
Zest of 1 lemon
Juice of 4 lemons (about 1 cup)
Sprigs of fresh mint to garnish

1. Bring the ½ cup of water and sugar to a boil in a medium saucepan. Cook for 5 minutes, until the sugar is dissolved. Add the zest. Remove from heat and allow to cool.

2. Combine with the lemon juice and ice water in a tall pitcher. Stir well. Serve garnished with the mint.

SERVES 6

Lime Margaritas

These will take you away to a sunny clime.

1½ cups tequila gold
¾ cup Triple Sec
Juice of 3 limes (about ¾ cup)
2 tablespoons sugar
8 cups crushed ice
2 tablespoons kosher salt
6 lime wedges

1. Combine the tequila, Triple Sec, lime juice, and sugar in a large pitcher; stir to dissolve the sugar. Add crushed ice.

2. Put the salt into a shallow bowl. Moisten rim of six margarita glasses with a lime wedge. Holding each glass upside down, dip the rim into the salt. Pour the margarita into the glasses. Garnish with lime wedges.

SERVES 6

Mango Liquadas

This is a refreshing summer drink, something I drank nearly every day while living in Guatemala.

Pulp and juice of 1 mango
2 bananas, peeled
¾ cup whole milk
½ cup orange juice

1. Pulse the mango pulp and juice and the bananas in the bowl of a food processor five or six times, scraping down the sides.

2. Add the milk and orange juice and purée for 30 seconds.

3. Serve chilled.

MAKES ABOUT 3½ CUPS

Gin Rickey

This is best served outside on a beautiful evening.

½ lime
1½ ounces gin
Ice cube
Chilled club soda

1. Squeeze the lime into an 8-ounce highball glass and add the rind.

2. Drop in the ice cube; add the gin and top off with the club soda.

SERVES 1

Desserts

Bananas Foster

Traditionally, Bananas Foster hails from New Orleans. It makes for a wonderful summer dessert after a light meal.

4 ripe bananas, peeled and sliced lengthwise
4 tablespoons unsalted butter
½ cup brown sugar
1 teaspoon cinnamon
½ cup banana liqueur
½ cup rum
Vanilla ice cream
Caramel sauce
Zest of 1 orange (1 to 2 tablespoons)

1. Preheat a grill.

2. Lay the bananas on an oiled grate. Cook for 2 minutes; turn and cook for 1½ minutes longer, or until softened. Remove from the heat and set aside.

3. Melt the butter in a large skillet over medium-high heat. Add the brown sugar and cinnamon and cook 2 to 3 minutes, or until the mixture caramelizes to a dark brown.

4. Whisk in the banana liqueur and rum and stir constantly for 1 to 2 minutes, until the liquor burns off. Stand clear of the flame when it ignites.

5. Add the grilled bananas to the pan. Stir until they are coated, then remove them.

6. Layer two slices of the banana over the ice cream in four dessert dishes or large brandy snifters. Drizzle the caramel sauce on top and sprinkle with the orange zest.

SERVES 4

Grilled Fruit with Orange Flower Water Syrup

Make sure the peaches and plums are ripe. If you use dried cherries, soak them for about 30 minutes in the simple syrup to reconstitute them.

To conserve time, you could grill the fruit along with the main course, combine all of the ingredients, and let the fruit sit in the syrup through dinner.

1 cup water
½ cup sugar
¼ cup orange flower water
1 medium orange, washed, seeded, and cut into eight pieces
1 large peach, pitted and sliced
1 plum, pitted and sliced
½ cup fresh blueberries
½ cup cherries, pitted and halved (or substitute dried)
Crème fraîche or whipped cream
½ teaspoon ground cinnamon

1. Bring the water to a boil in a 4-quart saucepan. Add the sugar, reduce the heat to low, and simmer until the sugar is dissolved, 2 to 3 minutes. Remove from the heat and let cool.

2. Add the orange flower water and refrigerate for at least 1 hour, until thoroughly chilled.

3. Preheat a grill.

4. Grill the orange slices, peach, and plum for 3 minutes; turn and grill 2 minutes longer, or until fruit is softened and slightly charred. Place fruit in a bowl.

5. Add the blueberries and cherries to the bowl, stir in the simple syrup, and let sit for 30 minutes to absorb the flavors.

6. Serve with the crème fraîche with cinnamon sprinkled on top.

SERVES 4

Grilled Marinated Pineapple and Mango

Try this alone or over ice cream. If you can find Goslings Rum, the dessert will benefit from the addition of the dark Caribbean liquor. You will also have discovered a delightful new mix for those cooling summer rum and tonics.

3   cups fresh pineapple, peeled and sliced
1   medium mango, peeled, pitted, and sliced
½ cup dark rum
1   tablespoon pure maple syrup or honey
1   teaspoon ground cinnamon
1   vanilla bean, broken into ½-inch pieces
Vanilla ice cream (optional)
Fresh mint leaves for garnish

1. Combine the pineapple, mango, rum, maple syrup, cinnamon, and vanilla bean in a large bowl. Soak for 30 minutes.

2. With tongs or a slotted spoon, transfer the pineapple and mango slices to a plate and set aside the marinade.

3. Preheat a grill and oil the grate.

4. Lay the fruit slices on the grill and sear for about 3 minutes. Turn with tongs or a fork and sear 2 minutes longer. Set aside and keep warm.

5. Cook the marinade in a medium saucepan over medium heat for 5 to 6 minutes, or until reduced by about one third.

6. Scoop one serving of ice cream, if using, into four separate bowls, divide the warm fruit, and spoon over the ice cream. Ladle sauce over each. Garnish with sprigs of mint and serve immediately.

SERVES 4

Nectarine, Plum, and Cherry Wellington

This mixed-fruit dessert Wellington seems made for the grill. Be very watchful that the dough does not burn. Lift up the edge after a few minutes to see how it is browning.

If you do not have fresh cherries, substitute dried cherries and reconstitute them in rum for several minutes before using.

Dough for four 10-inch pizzas (see page 39)
    increasing the amount of sugar to 2
    tablespoons
1   cup sugar
¾ cup almonds
2   egg whites
1½ cups pitted and thinly sliced nectarines
1   cup pitted and quartered plums
¾ cup pitted and halved fresh cherries
2   tablespoons unsalted butter, cut into
    small pieces
1   tablespoon flour
1   teaspoon ground cinnamon
1   teaspoon freshly grated nutmeg
Zest of 1 lemon (about 3 tablespoons)
Handful of flour and cornmeal mixture (about
    ¼ cup each)
Ginger ice cream
Pure maple syrup

1. Pulse the ¾ cup of the sugar, the almonds, and egg whites in the bowl of a food processor for about 30 seconds, or until thoroughly blended. Set aside.

2. Toss together the nectarines, plums, cherries, the remaining sugar, and the butter, flour, cinnamon, nutmeg, and zest in a large bowl. Set aside.

3. Preheat a grill.

4. Sprinkle a pastry or cutting board with the flour and cornmeal mixture. Roll out four circles of the dough. Make them about ⅛ inch thick and 10 inches in circumference.

5. Draw an imaginary line across the center of each dough circle. Spread the egg mixture over the side closest to you, keeping it 1 inch from the edge. Spread the fruit mixture on top of the egg mixture.

6. Carefully lift and fold the untopped dough over the ingredients, pinch the edges tight all around, and trim with a knife. Brush top and bottom with oil and gently place inside an oiled grill basket.

7. Lay the pocket on a gas grill, reduce the heat to medium, and close the cover. Cook 8 to 10 minutes. Turn and cook 8 to 10 minutes longer, or until lightly browned. If using charcoal, move most of the off to the sides and place the grill basket in the center. With charcoal, cook for 6 to 8 minutes on each side.

8. Remove the Wellingtons from the grill basket and serve immediately with the ice cream and the maple syrup.

SERVES 4

The River Spey

I WAS ONLY A BIT SURPRISED when Alasdair Little opened the door wearing a kilt. Well, we were in Scotland. He was dressed appropriately in his clan's colors. He was the owner and host of the Culdearn House, a B&B where we were about to stay in Grantown-on-Spey.

Alasdair wandered about the dining room that first evening, delivering guests their choice of some 45 local single-malt scotches and eventually dinner. The inn offered some of the best meals we enjoyed in a country that is centuries old and in some parts still dining in the shadow of those food concepts.

I was here to fish, though . . . on one of the most famous salmon rivers in the world, the river Spey. But no guidebook fully prepares one for salmon fishing in Scotland.

"First you need a permit," a local guide informed me. "The association might have a beat available. This is the slow season, not many fishermen around."

The Strathspey Angling Association booked from Mortimer's Outfitters and Fly Shop in town. It was a convenient location from which to book fishing permits, at $150 per beat.

My minuscule 7-food 6-inch Orvis trout rod must have appeared as a child's toy to the locals, compared to the 20-foot Spey rods traditionally used on these waters. I eventually rented a rod, waders, and everything else I needed to command the challenging Spey.

That evening, casting with what felt like a telephone pole out across the river, I looked up to the snowcapped Cairngorm Mountains. The Spey flowed swiftly past my waders, holding treacherously deep pools that I avoided. My arms quickly tired from the unfamiliar casting technique and I soon felt the strain in my shoulders from wielding such a hefty rod. Scottish author and ghillie Crawford Little (no relation to Alasdair) warns in his fishing guidebook: "The Spey should not be seen as a river for the inexperienced, elderly or infirm." I wasn't inexperienced, elderly, or infirm and I didn't care if my arms fell off. I was finally fishing the river Spey.

The next morning a heavy mist parted, the mountains emerged, and I was off once again, after Isobel Little's breakfast, fit for a Loch Ness monster's appetite.

Donning my waxed waterproof jacket — looking the part, I hoped — casting my Spey rod and carrying a brilliant array of Jungle Cock Shrimp, Munro Killers, Stoats Tails, and purple Haywood flies, I somehow felt accomplished. Perhaps not as a fisherman (I did not catch any fish), but for having tried. I had come all this way and certainly could not go home without having at least tried.

"Did you enjoy your time on the Spey?" Carole inquired as we drove back on the wrong side of the road to the B&B.

"Yes, I did."

"Even though you didn't catch anything?"

"Sure. It doesn't matter if a fisherman catches anything," I explained. "People fish for relaxation, too. To unwind, enjoy the great outdoors, the scenery, and the wildlife. The mountains back there were spectacular. There is more to fishing than catching fish. Fishing is an excuse to enter nature's window, ponder the ecological importance of our role in the scheme of things, to see, close up, the insect world, and harmonize with the plant and aquatic life. It enables one to philosophize about life's balances and imbalances, consider man's obligation and contribution to the planet, and consider what we need to give back." I babbled on. "I didn't come here just for the fishing. There is more to life, you know."

Back at the Culdearn House, Isobel Little considerately served a freshly poached salmon for dinner. Out of sympathy, I guessed.

Acknowledgments

Many thanks for all the help that went into this publication: Andrea Dodge, my quick-as-a-whip, always cheerful editor; Kent Lew, for his masterful artist's outlook; Jennifer Jepson Smith, creative graphic designer, and all the terrific, forward-thinking staff at Storey Publishing on MASS MoCA Way; Mason Rose, for allowing us to publish blueprints for his "designer" smokehouse; Mike White, for his well of construction advice; Lawrence Bach, meteorologist at the U.S. National Weather Service in Albany, New York, for checking my weather-related facts; Larry Burke, for his fresh publicity photos; Felicia Sprott, from Guido's Marketplace, for modeling her dexterous hands; Louis Blanchett, for modeling his hands in a chilly Quebec outpost; and all those people who tasted test recipes, whether they liked them or not.

Eternal gratitude to an altruistic group of people without whose combined as well as individual efforts I would never have been motivated enough to get up, move on, and, ultimately, make this book—their heartfelt encouragement came in all the right doses at all the right times: Carole Clark, Laurie Norton Moffat, Craig Moffat, Liz Foley, Jim Williamson, Peter Bergman, Deb Tibenski, Jeff Rigby, Lou Blanchett, Sandy Rup, Laura Chester, Carol Gullickson, Marc Manikowske, John Leibowitz, Marianne Swan, Jon Swan, Jane Burke, Don Goudey, Carolyn Bell, and all the caring people on the outside looking in.

And a warm thanks to my fellow editors in the rural suite of the *New Marlborough 5 Village News* for keeping my name on the masthead; and finally, to the loyal members of my Tuesday Writer's Group, Peter Bergman, Peg Dietemann, Virginia Finn, Paul Marino, Virginia Rowe, and Rosemary Starace, all of whom stayed with me during the critical time of my . . . sabbatical. Thanks for being there.

Bibliography

Brillat-Savarin, Jean Anthelme. *Physiologie du gout* (Flammarion, Paris, 1982).

Claiborne, Craig. *The New York Times Cookbook* (Harper & Row, 1961).

Davidson, Alan. *The Penguin Companion to Food* (Penguin, 2002).

Fisher, M. F. K. *The Art of Eating* (Macmillan, 1937).

Kurlansky, Mark. *Salt* (Penguin, 2003).

Lang, Jenifer Harvey, editor. *Larousse Gastronomique* (Crown, 1988).

McGee, Harold. *On Food and Cooking: The Science and Lore of the Kitchen* (Scribners, 1984).

Toussaint-Samat, Maguelonne. *History of Food* (Blackwell, 1992).

The list of the following out-of-print cookbook sources is courtesy of James T. Ehler, webmaster, cook, chef, writer, of Key West, Florida. His Web sites are listed under Resources.

Eliza Acton. *Modern Cookery for Private Families* (1845).

Catherine E. Beecher. *Miss Beecher's Domestic Receipt-Book* (1846).

Fannie Merritt Farmer. *The Boston Cooking-School Cook Book* (Boston, 1896).

Charles Elme Francatelli. *A Plain Cookery Book For The Working Classes* (London, 1861).

Mrs. Glasse. *The Art of Cookery Made Plain and Easy; Excelling Any Thing of the Kind Ever Yet Published.* (1747).

Lafcadio Hearn. *La Cuisine Creole* (1885).

Eliza Leslie. *Miss Leslie's Directions for Cookery* (1851).

Mrs. D. A. Lincoln. *Mrs. Lincoln's Boston Cook Book* (1884).

Resources

www.johnmanikowski.com Here you'll find quotes about the outdoors and more of my artwork, essays, and recipes.

Outdoor grills and smokers, home products, and commercial equipment

www.bbqwoods.com Makes a solid, larger-than-average smoke pan. (509) 961-3420

www.biggreenegg.com Largest manufacturer of Kamado-style smoker/grills. The functional design is sleek and loved by many. (404) 321-4658

www.broilmaster.com Makes grills and accompanying equipment.

www.cabelas.com Manufacturers of quality gear and equipment for outdoors enthusiasts and culinary-minded campers. Grills, water smokers, and outdoor gear. Often priced lower than competitors, with tolerant warrantees. (800) 237-4444

www.charbroil.com Char-Broil Co. Sells combo gas/charcoal grills.

www.coleman.com Manufacturers of outdoor camping and cooking equipment. Maker of the enameled smoke pan that I recommend for smoke grilling. (800) 835-3278

www.cookshack.com Sells a line of commercial smokers plus seasonings and other products. (800) 423-0698

www.corngrill.com Makes corn stoves for home heating and corn-fueled grills. (828) 684-4444

www.dcsappliances.com The DCS company offers durable, professional cooking equipment. Has built-in infrared heaters in back of many models. (800) 433-8466

www.ducane.com A builder of quality outdoor cooking equipment.

www.jennair.com This company developed an exhaust system for in-kitchen grilling that works.

www.kamado.com Japanese design of highly effective smoker and grill. Can reach high temperatures for grilling using charcoal or electric elements.

www.mortonsalt.com The maker of household salt also makes a meat pump for injecting brine.

www.oxo.com Maker of OXO Good Grips tools. (800) 545-4411

www.sears.com Durable, reliable grills for any budget. Sears's warranties are usually worth the extra expense.

www.thebrinkmanncorp.com A reliable company that produces upright, torpedo-shaped smokers and more. (800) 468-5252

www.vikingrange.com Viking has made professional-level grills, stoves, and ovens for decades. Now it has expanded into the outdoor realm. (888) 845-4641

www.weber.com A manufacturer of grills and smokers, this is a reliable company with quality products. (800) 446-1071

Wood chunks, chips, and related products for use in a smoker

www.bbcharcoal.com A Texas firm offering lump charcoal as well as wood.

www.bbqrsdelight.com An Arkansas company selling a good variety of chips and chunks for smoking.

www.naturesownonline.com Good source for a variety of woods. Affordable and reliable. Makes its own "charwood" charcoal, which is petroleum-free. (800) 729-5800

www.peopleswoods.com Offers a vast array of sizes of wood from "mini" to giant "chunks" for restaurant use. A wide variety of woods, including hard-to-find sassafras. (800) 729-5800

Fish and food concerns

seafood.ucdavis.edu/home.htm University of California, Davis, has much legal and technical information concerning fresh and smoked fish: guidelines and recommendations for safe handling, cooking, and smoking.

www.cfast.vt.edu Commercial Fish & Shellfish Technologies Program at Virginia Tech. Lots of results of studies, marine biology reports, and so on.

www.fda.gov Food and Drug Administration. It is the one government agency responsible for "regulating the treatment of fish from its journey from the catch to the table." Check out the Fish Encyclopedia, everything you've ever wanted to know about more than 150 species, and much more.

www.foodreference.com Good source for food-related information of all kinds, including historical recipes.

www.nmfs.noaa.gov National Marine Fisheries. Good information on endangered species.

www.uaf.edu/coop-ext University of Alaska Fairbanks Cooperative Extension Service.

Fish and spices

Hatch's Fish and Produce Market An institution in Wellfleet, Massachusetts (508) 349-2810

www.atlanticspice.com A good source for Mexican oregano and other herbs and spices (800) 316-7565

Index

Page numbers in *italic* indicate illustrations.